THE SMALL INVESTOR

A Beginner's Guide to Stocks, Bonds, and Mutual Funds

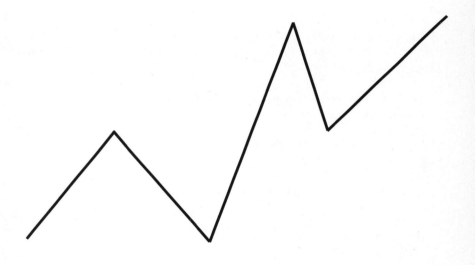

JIM GARD

Ten Speed Press
Berkeley, California

🔟

Ten Speed Press
P.O. Box 7123
Berkeley, California 94707

Distributed in Australia by E. J. Dwyer Pty. Ltd., in Canada by Publishers Group West, in New Zealand by Tandem Press, in South Africa by Real Books, and in the United Kingdom and Europe by Airlift Books.

Cover design and interior illustrations by Gerry O'Neill
Interior design by Toni Tajima

Library of Congress Cataloging-in-Publication Data

Gard, Jim
    The small investor: a beginner's guide to stocks, bonds, and mutual funds / Jim Gard.
        p.   cm.
    Includes bibliographic references and index.
    ISBN 0-89815-825-7
    1. Portfolio management. 2. Investment analysis. 3. Stock exchanges. 4. Mutual funds. I. Title.
HG4529.5.G369 1996   96-1031
332.6'78—dc20   CIP

First printing, 1996
Printed in Canada

        3 4 5 6 7 8 9 10 — 00 99 98 97

This is for Lynn, and Laura, and Matt, who sustain me.

CONTENTS

Acknowledgments   vi

Introduction   1

Chapter 1: The Small Investor   5

Chapter 2: It's Not a Game   23

Chapter 3: A Personal Investment Strategy   41

Chapter 4: Professional Help   68

Chapter 5: If You Snooze, You Lose   88

Chapter 6: Bonds and Bond Markets:
The Standards of Comparison and Value   105

Chapter 7: Investing in Stocks   132

Chapter 8: More on Stocks:
Selling, and Losing, and Taking Profits   166

Chapter 9: Mutual Funds   187

Chapter 10: Selecting Mutual Funds   215

Chapter 11: Investing or Gambling—
What's the Difference?   249

Glossary   265

Index   278

ACKNOWLEDGMENTS

WHEN I WAS A FRESHMAN at Georgia Tech, we were all required to take a year of composition and rhetoric. That probably did more to make me a successful person than all of the math, physics, chemistry, and engineering I studied over the next ten years. The English department at Georgia Tech doesn't get a whole lot of recognition and thanks. They should—particularly if they are still teaching the freshman to write simple, direct sentences. So herewith I acknowledge my debt to the English department.

A number of people have been of more recent support. In working on this book, I always felt confident that I could get my facts straight; the problem has been whether it could be made readable. Particular thanks go to my sister, Susan Kolesar, and my sister-in-law, Carol Sunderman, who read several chapters and helped me understand what would appear more direct and effective for my audience. Their contributions have made me much more confident of the final product. One other person had a major influence on the tone and style of the finished text. Jeff McGraw, owner of a bookstore in Roxboro, North Carolina, was a zealot for simplicity and efficiency in the text. He read many chapters and unfailingly dragged me back to the reader's needs and point of view. Jeff was your champion before you knew that you needed a champion. You'll never know what a debt you owe him unless you get some copies of early versions. Of course the errors that remain are there because I was too stubborn to listen to good advice, or had too high an opinion of the immortality of my prose, but without the help from my friends it only would have been still more breathless.

And finally, I would of course be nowhere without the support and the confidence of my publisher, Ten Speed Press, and my editor, Mariah Bear.

INTRODUCTION

WHO IS THE SMALL INVESTOR? Well, since you are reading this, maybe you are. After all, there are millions of folks, like myself, who could easily be described as small investors.

Introducing the Small Investor

The small investor has a little money that can be spared and risked for investment purposes. That idea of "a little" is up to each individual's point of view. It could be $5,000, or $50,000, or $2 million. It is little enough that you will not want to hire a full-time professional money manager to work just for you. This is not simply a matter of being rich or poor, but of viewpoint. Approximately 2,000 years ago, the Roman senator, Marcus Licinius Crassus, explained to his colleagues what "rich" meant to him. According to Crassus, no man should consider himself to be rich unless he could afford to raise, equip, and maintain a private army. In 1996, that would require disposable income of perhaps $250 million a year for, say, 1,000 soldiers. In other words, defining "small" is pretty arbitrary—rich, not rich, a little money, a lot of money; you pay your money and you take your choice.

The small investor has little experience or knowledge of the financial world. Once again, you'll have to define for yourself what "a little knowledge" means to you, but actually, if the truth were known, everyone has a little knowledge of investing—it's just that some have a little more than others. And, as in any field (whether it's law, medicine, botany, or investments), anyone who claims to know it all should not be trusted.

Finally, and perhaps most characteristically, the small investor harbors some fear, or at least suspicion, about the whole business of investing. If you don't have the fear and suspicion, then this book is not for you—go instead to "How to Turn $100 into a Fortune in the Coming Bull Market" (or Bear Market, if you prefer), or other such fairy tales.

The small investor typically would be worried about losing one fourth of his original capital, and seriously hurt by losing half of it. If you can't afford to lose any of it, then this business is not for you; go back to your bank and buy U.S. savings bonds. If you can afford to lose half of your investment without wincing, then you may find my ideas a bit too conservative. Some of them carry a message for the high roller too, but the overriding philosophy is tuned to the small investor's needs, as I've defined them.

You may be wondering at this point whether I'm really a small investor. The answer is yes, by my own definition, but don't worry. I do have some special credentials as well.

For starters, I manage a modest nest egg in some Individual Retirement Accounts (IRAs) that are important building blocks for my and Mrs. Investor's retirement plans. While I've made some money management mistakes over the years (and learned from them so you won't make them same ones), and while I'm a wild-eyed competitor in a $10

The Small Investor Is Wary and Suspicious

poker game, I'm absolutely resolute that my IRA management is neither a gamble nor a game.

You may ask, "So how does that qualify you to write a book?" I'm glad you asked. It just so happens I have a Ph.D. in mathematics and considerable graduate-level education in finance, accounting, and economics. I've been a regular book reviewer specializing in matters of history, money, and public policy for a major newspaper (the *Tampa Tribune*) and am a registered investment advisor and an arbitrator for the American Arbitration Association in the area of securities disputes.

A few years ago, I found myself with too much time and a little money on my hands. Since my previous financial plan (hoping for the best and expecting something to turn up shortly), hadn't been going too well, I decided to make a major effort towards taking charge of my family's financial management, with particular attention to managing investments for our IRAs. I decided that the first step was education. Approximately six months was devoted to serious financial research before investing the first nickel. During and since that time I read a great many books, including almost everything that was then available in bookstores and libraries. I have studied the *Wall Street Journal* and

Barron's intensely and regularly, reviewed investment newsletters, read a pile of stock and mutual fund evaluations, talked to dozens of professionals in the business, met with an amateur discussion group, and gotten down to the serious business.

The results have been satisfying. I've greatly increased knowledge and confidence, learned that many people share my needs and interests, and achieved a reasonable measure of financial success.

One discovery in particular was interesting: there was no book available that satisfied me with a brief, elementary, and straightforward introduction to investing in stocks, bonds and mutual funds. With all I'd learned, I was in the perfect position to write the book I'd wanted. And so, here we are.

You may ask, "What's in it for me?" Good question—I like your direct approach. *The Small Investor* provides the ABCs of getting started investing in stocks, bonds, or mutual funds—or a combination of the three. It does not cover—except marginally—real estate, insurance, or taxes. And it cannot help you to get a job or get rich quick. See your local yellow pages to satisfy those other needs.

The book is an introduction to a world of hard work, some pleasure, and some reward. As in any field of study, you can extend the research as far as you wish. Once you finish this book, you should know whether you'll want to continue the job. If you do want to continue, you will find specific things spelled out for you to do, and a lot of other material that I suggest you study.

In the end, I hope that you will gain a better understanding of your options for investing, and also feel that you can do some things effectively without taking huge risks or disturbing your lifestyle. You will learn about the amount of work required for various choices and how to tailor your investment strategy to make the work suit you. You will certainly understand that

THERE IS ALWAYS A REAL AND PRESENT RISK OF LOSS, but an astute and industrious small investor can manage the risk to an acceptable level.

GOOD HUNTING.

GOOD HARVESTING.

CHAPTER 1

The Small Investor

Small Investors need to know:

- Is this book for me?
- Is investing for me?
- How much trouble am I getting into?
- How much risk am I inviting?
- How much time and work do I have to put into it?
- Do the big investors have all the advantages?
- Is there anything that works in favor of the small investor?
- Can I control the risk?
- Is there any such thing as safe investing?
- Are there any short and simple rules for guidance?

Is This Book for You?

It is not too late to ask this question. Your time is important, and it's worthwhile to ask yourself if it's worth it to, for instance, make the effort to really dig into studying the financial data for Ford Motor Company, or do the research to select a mutual fund from among the thousands of funds available. By the time you finish this book, you could have an answer to the last question, and by the time you finish this chapter, you will have an answer to the first. If you continue to the end, you will find answers to a lot of questions. There are no bad questions except those that are never asked. For small investors like us, the consequences of not asking the right questions can be devastating. So this book will help you find some of the questions that can, in turn, help you avoid problems. I'll answer some of them, and point you towards finding your own answers to others.

Should I Invest in My Library ?

Neither this book nor any other will give you *all* of the answers. Many of the questions and answers depend on your experience, education, and lifestyle. For example, I can't tell you what stocks to buy; that depends on your personal financial situation and the level of risk you are willing to accept. Similarly, no book can tell you whether or not to buy junk bonds; you have to decide for yourself. What this book attempts to do is prepare you to make those decisions.

If you decide to do any kind of investing, it will affect other parts of your life. It will affect other things you might be considering buying, and your peace of mind when you are watching the evening news. You may choose to say, "No, thanks. I don't need the headaches." That is a reasonable decision for some people. If you stick with me to the end of the book, I think you will be able to make a comfortable and rational judgment. It is not my intent to persuade you to start investing, or to quit, or to change your current investing practices, if any. I just want to help you judge the consequences—in terms of work, risk, time, your comfort level about your finances, and other things you might be doing with the money.

Financial Markets Are Not Like Secure Savings

A bank savings account is one way to invest. You give up some money to the bank as a deposit, and expect that after a while you will get the money back plus some interest earned on the deposit. All investing has this in common: we give up control of our money to another party and we expect to get it back later with a profit. But with stocks, bonds, and mutual funds, we are getting into a different league. A savings account requires little work, and has strong assurance of return. The financial markets that we are looking at may offer greater returns than savings accounts, but also involve much more time and work and risk of loss.

What Are the Risks and Rewards?

What if you buy the stock of a publicly traded corporation? For example, say some outfit called Mogul Corporation needed money to start operations. To raise money they could sell shares of ownership in Mogul. They might split the ownership into 1,000,000 shares (the common stock), and sell them for $20 apiece. If you buy 200 shares, then you own 0.02% of Mogul. You would expect to make money in two ways: first, if the company was profitable, they would pay you some part of their earnings, called a *dividend*; and second, if other investors approved of Mogul's operations, they might want to buy your stock. If enough newcomers wanted Mogul stock, and not many of the owners cared to sell, then the newcomers would offer more than the $20 for each share of stock. You might have a chance to sell your stock for a profit, maybe $27 per share. If you actually sold the stock and took the profit at this point, that would generate what's called a *capital gain*. If you kept the stock and merely acknowledged the potential profit, then it would be called a *paper profit*. I suggest that you keep the view that you don't have a real profit until you sell, because paper profits have a way of disappearing. Likewise, if stock prices go down, you may have a paper loss in the value of your stock. If you choose to sell at that point, then the paper loss becomes a *realized loss*.

Along with the great expectations, there are two very real risks: first, Mogul might not be profitable in some years, and might not pay a dividend; second, other investors might not like Mogul, so that one day when you need your money back, no one wants to buy it (and you realize a capital loss). If you buy shares of well-established corporations, sold on a well-established stock exchange, there will usually be someone around willing to buy the shares, but the price might be lower than what you paid.

An intelligent investor needs to consider different possibilities for what might happen after he or she buys the stock. A lot of different situations may arise; here are some examples of what can happen:

Example 1: This is the situation that we all like to see. The business is good and stock prices go up. In late 1990, the Standard Commercial Corporation, a worldwide tobacco- and wool-processing company, was earning about 62 cents per share of common stock for the calendar quarter. Their sales in 1990 had been 50 percent higher than the total market value of the company, which is good (*market value* means the amount it would take to buy all of the common stock). The stock price was then $10 per share, and for 1990 they had paid 52 cents in dividends for each share (a 5.2 percent yield). The prevailing market view was that this was good business operations and a good stock market opportunity. By the end of 1991 the stock price was pushed up close to $28 per share. Some lucky people bought Standard Commercial for $10 in late 1990 and sold it for $28 around the end of 1991. That's a good score in any league!

Example 2: On the other hand, even if business is good, stock prices can fall. This may seem strange—why should the stock value fall if the company is making good profits? Well, the market has a mind of its own and its logic is not always clear. Stock prices for any given firm are largely governed by the prevailing view of what profits will look like a year or two down the road, and people's expectations about the future in general. You see, everyone else is doing what we are doing: they are trying to evaluate current and future business prospects, but also trying to evaluate the broad market opinion of what's happening.

For many years, the General Electric Corporation (GE) has been one of the most successful and profitable companies in the world. In 1990, their revenues, profits, and dividends were all going up. Standard & Poor's ranked GE as one of the safest stock investments available. In the middle of 1990, some conservative investors bought the stock for $75. Within three months, the price dropped as low as $50, even though sales, earnings, and dividend payout were still increasing. Like I said, the stock market has a mind of its own. Those unfortunate investors were injured by the market psychology, which for some reason decided for a few months that GE was no longer attractive. Within another six months the values had recovered, so the patient long-term investors were not hurt, but some people probably panicked and sold at $50. It is tough to make that judgment call when you watch your investment wasting away for a few months. But, by 1996 those same shares were worth $150, after a two-for-one split. (A *two-for-one split* occurs when a company exchanges new shares at the rate of two new for each one of the old. So, if the price of one share of the old stock was $10, the new will be issued at $5.)

Example 3: Sometimes stock prices may even go up when business operations are poor. Why should the stock value go up if the company is not profitable? The answer is in market expectations. Many investors plan to hold stock for a year or more. They expect that when they sell, circumstances will have changed. If they foresee that a company is recovering from a time of trouble, they may bid up the price of the stock. The Chrysler Corporation is a perfect example. Throughout the late '80s and into 1991, Chrysler had a terrible string of bad results. The stock fell to a value of $10 per share. Early in 1992, some smart investors saw signs that things were going to change in a big way. And, indeed, if you had bought Chrysler's stock for $10 then, at a time when the company was reporting operating losses, you might have held it into 1994 and watched it reach a value of over $60 per share. In early 1991, Chrysler would have been viewed as a very risky investment by many analysts. However, the reward for those who believed turned out to be great.

Example 4: Business is bad, stock price is down. This one makes sense, right? Well, maybe. It depends on the market view of the company's prospects for the next year or two. For instance, take IBM. There has never been a more widely publicized stock decline than theirs. In mid 1989, the stock price bounced around $110 to $120 per share; in 1990 it was between $90 and $120; in 1991 $85 to $140, and by late in 1993 it fell as low as $41. Some people bought stock in a profitable company, with an A+ rating in 1991, and lost 70 percent of their investment within two years. It goes to show, you never can tell. There were plenty of smart, experienced professional stock analysts who said the stock was a good buy at $100, and again at $85, and again at $60. Some people lost a lot of money.

The purpose here is neither to scare you nor excite you about market investment opportunities. But if you decide to get into this business, then you or someone you hire must look at and evaluate a lot of different factors to make your investments successful. And it's tricky. I bought IBM at $85 and sold it three months later at $93. Pretty clever, right? Then I bought it again a few months later at $67, and sold a year later at a value of $54. Not so clever, right? In playing the financial markets, you have opportunities to win and opportunities to lose. The only guarantee I can give you is that if you are careless, you *will* lose.

Make Money the Old-Fashioned Way—Earn It!

Time, energy, work, nerve, decisiveness. Different kinds of investing require varying levels of those assets to reach success. One of the most famous and successful investors of the past twenty years is Peter Lynch. He was manager of the most profitable mutual fund of all, the Magellan Fund. Lynch is an indisputable market genius who says that the small investor can do all right in the stock market. He even implies that it's not terribly difficult, saying, "Everybody has the brains for investing in stocks; the question is whether you have the stomach."

I think by "stomach" he means the will to put in the time and work, as well as the nerve and decisiveness to do something smart, and take the risks.

Those four examples that we looked at show that when you buy a stock you are really dependent on two things. First is the fundamental business condition of the firm, or a judgment of what that may be in a year or two. That is something you can rationally analyze and try to predict. Second is market psychology. No one can consistently predict that. Market psychology can often be a ticking bomb. Listen to Tom Jackson, manager of the Prudential Equity Mutual Fund. He successfully manages over $3 billion of other people's money, and has the experience and credentials you expect in a market guru. Jackson says, "Nobody can forecast the stock market." Who are we to argue?

So before you put up your money, try to judge the amount and kind of work, try to judge the potential for profit or loss, try to judge how much professional help you want, try to judge where you can get information if you choose to go it alone. If you do choose to read the whole book, I think you will be ready to make those judgment calls.

Is There a Chance for Safety in the Stock Market?

Among some midwestern agricultural circles you may hear a saying: "Even a blind pig will find the slop once in a while." Similarly, some people think that even a blind pig could have made money in the stock market during December through January of 1991–92. That's true; however, the blind pig could have lost money, too. A case in point is Schering-Plough (SGP on the New York Stock Exchange).

Plough is one of the larger and more successful drug companies. They had a great long-term record of steadily increasing sales, profits, dividends, and stock price. The company is financially secure, and many people have considered the drug industry as one of the best areas for investment. It appeared to be a safe investment. But if you had bought SGP in early January 1992, you might have paid $66 or $67 per share. Surprise, surprise! Eleven weeks later it was selling for around $56. If you had bought 100 shares at $66, then got cold feet and sold at $56, after paying perhaps 1–2 percent for both the purchase and sale brokerage fees, you would have about an $1100 loss (as of March 1997, after a two for one split, it was selling for $79; SGP was a good long-term investment.

So where does that leave us in the search for safe and sound investing? In the financial markets, safety means a reasonable balance of chances for losses or profits. You don't get guarantees, and you don't get perfect information. Instead, you get a reasonable balance of risk and reward opportunities. One of the small investor's special advantages is

The Small Investor Goes Blind on Wall Street

the freedom to go for modest, safe gains. As another example, to make it more concrete, let's look at the General Telephone Company (GTE). This will illustrate what the small investor can do when safety is a prime concern.

Is GTE safe and predictable? Well, yeah, relatively safe and predictable. To show what that means, we are going to look at three scenarios: a worst case (meaning a worst *realistic* situation—not nuclear war, or the violent overthrow of the government), a kind of average conservative case, and a slightly more optimistic case. Remember there is always some risk, but GTE is about as safe as it gets.

Let's analyze GTE a little. Is their market secure? GTE is the largest of the non-Bell telephone companies and is the second largest provider of cellular service in the U.S. That is a secure market. Is their record secure? Their dividend has been raised *every year* for twenty years until in 1994, when it held steady. Are they strong? The Standard & Poor's rating of their past performance and current position of their common stock is 'A' (second highest out of eight possible grades). The Value Line rating of the company's financial strength is 'A'; the Value Line rating of the common stock safety is '1', their highest grade.

The price per share and dividend for four years are given in the following table. High means the highest price during the year, and Low is the lowest price. Div is the total dividend amount paid during the year. (This table has some rounding.)

	1991	1992	1993	1994	1995
High	$34.50	36.00	40.00	35.00	43.00
Low	$27.50	29.00	34.00	29.50	30.00
Div	$1.70	1.82	1.88	1.88	1.88

Now, let's look at our three scenarios. Suppose that you buy 200 shares for $33 per share, and that all dividends are converted to new stock at the end-of-year price.[2] Say that the broker's fee to buy the 200 shares is $90 and the fee to sell in three years is $100. The initial cost of the investment is $6,690 (200 × $33 + $90). The final return is the number of shares times the last price, minus the $100 sales fee.

Suppose, as a worst-case scenario, that the stock price declines to its lowest value in the past six years, about $25, and the dividend stays fixed at $1.88 per share. Then at the end of three years, you could have 244.4 shares,[3] worth $25 each. They would sell for $6,110, leaving $6,010 after fees. That looks like a loss of $680.

In a normal, stable environment you might project that the stock price grows to $34, $36, and $38 at the end of the three years, respectively, and the dividend stays fixed at $1.88. The investment would grow into 233 shares worth $8,854. After the sales charge this leaves a profit of $2,064.

In a more optimistic view, what if the stock price grows by $3 each year, and the dividend grows too? Suppose it pays $1.88 per share, then $1.96, and $2.05 over the course of three years. The investment would grow to 221.8 shares worth $9,316, yielding a profit, after charges, of $2,526.

---

[2] That is a *dividend reinvestment plan*, or DRIP. Many companies offer such a plan to help you reinvest the dividends you earn.

[3] Calculations assume that the dividend is realized as new shares at the end of each year, at the then-current price. In the worst case, we assume that the price drops to $30, then $27, then $25 at the end of the first, second, and third years, respectively.

So what "safe" means here is that where you started out investing $6,690, the worst realistic case is a loss of $680; a realistic normal case looks like gain of $2,064; and a best case shows a gain of $2,526. Of course, there are no guarantees, but this is one way you might analyze a very conservative stock for possible profit or loss.[4]

As a basis of comparison, we can also look at bank deposits, or U.S. savings bonds. When looking for a safe investment, you should compare the choices among other safe investments. Don't compare GTE with a gold-mining company. They are in different worlds as far as risk and reward standards.

From 1995 to 1998, it is fair to expect that a bank certificate of deposit might pay about 7 percent annual return. U.S. savings bonds would pay 5.5 percent, if you were holding them to maturity in five years.

Is GTE anything to get excited about? I think it is, for the small investor. This is low-risk, relatively predictable behavior, with expectations to do better than bank returns for the next few years. This is probably not a stock that will, as they say, hit a home run in a year or two, but it's not going to kill you either. If you are an investor who likes the idea of earning something like 6–10 percent a year and can live with the possibility of losing a little if things go sour, then this is arguably a safe investment in the stock market.

Estimated Safe Investment Outcomes over Three Years
$6,690 invested for three years

Investment	3-year result	Annualized return
GTE: worst case	$680 loss	-3.5%
middle case	$2,064 gain	+10.9%
best case	$2,526 gain	+11.3%
Bank CD	$1,505 gain	+7.%
U.S. savings bonds	$1,166 gain*	+5.5%

*subject to penalty if held less than five years, but also partially tax exempt

---

[4] The price of GTE has since risen to $43 in late 1995, and the dividend has held at $1.88.

How Big Do You Have to Be?

There is a competitive nature to many things we do in life, whether it's work, love, physical fitness, or investing. It is only natural for many small investors to worry that they can't win because they can't compete with the professionals and the big boys on Wall Street.

KEEPING UP WITH GABELLI

Mario Gabelli is a famous and successful mutual fund manager. He and the people who invested in his Gabelli Equity Fund from 1987 to 1992 doubled their money—that's about 14 percent compound annual growth, which is great work. But what does the small investor care if some high-tech company has its stock double in price over six months? Well, we care to the extent that we would like to find some such opportunities, but we don't need to worry about competing with them. Investing does not have to be a contest. Whenever I get too proud, or too discouraged, about my recent investment results, I just look in *Barron's Mutual Funds Quarterly*. Every time, I can find hundreds of mutual funds that have done better than I for the past quarter, or year,[5] as well as hundreds that have done worse. In either case, that knowledge doesn't put any money in my pocket. Don't worry about what Gabelli is doing, just concentrate on how you are doing. That's enough to keep you occupied. Of course, if you really want to ride with Gabelli, then do it! Buy his mutual funds. Hire him to work for you.

ADVANTAGES OF PROFESSIONAL MONEY MANAGERS

A professional money manager may have $500 million to work with, and produce $10 million of income for an investment company. With this $10 million, the company can hire sharp folks, and buy computers and research resources, and keep most of those resources busy 60–80 hours a week looking for opportunity or trouble on the horizon. Certainly in their business, just as in yours, experience counts. They have quicker access to critical financial news

---

[5] In the interest of honesty and full disclosure, I must confess that in the fall of 1995, I can find very few that have done better than I.

because people are on duty twenty-four hours a day looking for it. The investment company analysts should be able to come up with some good ideas because they eat, breathe, and sleep investing every day.

THE SMALL INVESTOR IN THE MARKET

You are not going to take the money out of the professionals' hands just because you are a nice guy and need a comfortable retirement. But remember that all of that skill and experience is out there. It could be hired to manage your money for you, by investing in mutual funds. But you don't have to compete with these people; you don't have to beat them at their own game. They don't want to kill you, and in fact they don't even care whether you are in the markets. If you don't have a noticeable success record with at least $10 million in the market, then none of the professional investors will ever know or care what you are doing.

The Small Investor Is Not in This Fight

But, in fact, we have some advantages over the big guys. For while they are not competing with you and me, they are competing with each other. And they are fighting every day to keep their jobs and professional reputations. A mutual fund manager who fails to lead the pack one quarter may lose a lot of customers and their money pretty fast. You and I don't have that handicap. If I only make a 1 percent gain on my IRA account one quarter, I might be annoyed, but I don't have to worry about getting fired. (Of course, if you find that your performance is consistently bad, you might want to fire yourself, as it were, and hire a professional.)

We can set our own standards of performance and risk tolerance, as part of setting our investment strategies. You have a real edge because no one else is evaluating you, and your decisions aren't made by committee. Thus, you can set your own standards for the effort and scope of your research. If you decide to buy two stocks, you may want to spend two months studying twenty companies, but you never need to be an expert on the entire market.

Finally, small investors get some advantages just because of the smaller amounts of money involved: flexibility and liquidity. On any given day, either you or Mario Gabelli may decide to buy or sell a position in stocks. You and I can complete the deal in five minutes, and be very confident of the price we will get. Mario can not. The person or investment company working on a $10 million stock position needs days or weeks to finish it, and prices can change over that period of time. An investment manager may lose value just because the word gets out that he is selling a lot of one particular stock. We don't have to worry about that.

Common Errors or Traps for Small Investors

If you do choose to get involved with investing, there are a few basic pitfalls to watch out for.

First, don't buy things you don't understand. Whether it's a stock, or a bond, or a mutual fund, it takes work to evaluate the risks and rewards. In some cases it will be too much work, or too difficult for you to handle alone. While I was going through the process of evaluating brokers, I met a nice guy in Raleigh, North Carolina, who took me out to lunch and asked me about my objectives and interests. He seemed to be intelligent and well qualified to evaluate investments. A few days later, he called me with a hot item. It seems some people were forming an investment trust to put money into a clever scheme, really clever. The plan was to take advantage of the depressed real estate markets in major cities by buying empty land and using it for parking lots. They could then realize the profits from the parking lots, or perhaps tax losses from the investment, and just sit back and wait for the inevitable recovery in real estate prices. Then it would be easy to convert the land to more profitable uses. Good idea, right? I passed. There is some logic in the scheme, and a chance that somebody would make money at it, but I felt that there was no way for me to evaluate the potential risks or rewards. Furthermore, I couldn't make any kind of judgment on what would happen if I needed to get my money back one day. One of the objectives of this book is to help you become confident in making that kind of decision.

Another caution is to avoid buying or selling based on someone else's idea unless you have done your homework. This can be modified after you have worked with an advisor or broker for a year and grown into a trusting relationship, but it's your money and it should be your decision. Your investment results will depend on your decisions, and your decisions depend directly on your sources of information. We'll talk a lot throughout this book about where to look for reliable information. There are countless investment publications. Part of your job is to review some of them and select two or three that you have time to read that clearly address your needs.

Some investors I know seem to think that when they buy something, they have a moral obligation to get all of their friends in, too. When someone comes to you pushing their latest hot investment, you don't have to present a counterargument to knock them down; it's good enough to tell them, "No, thanks. I wish you luck, but it's not for me." What is good for someone else may not be good for you. If your coworker has a very conservative stock portfolio and has $10,000 available to take a high-risk plunge, then the company she's looking at might be fine for her, but not for you.

Finally, if you do any investing at all, be aware that someday when you least expect it, someone is going to call you to tell about a new or unknown stock that is certain to double in price over the next year. If an investment sounds too good to be true, that simply means that the true risks are not clear. No investment offers uncommonly high rewards without carrying commensurate risks. Or at least not to us; remember, there are 50,000 professional market analysts and money managers out there. Who do you think is going to hear about the real gold mines first? If the professionals passed on a great deal, they had their reasons. If the deal sounds too good to be true, that just means that we don't understand the risks and reasons why they passed on it. *The risks are always there.* Anytime you hand over your money to someone else, there is a chance you may never see it again.

Risk, Reward, and Work

Except for a few odd cases like me who find the whole process entertaining, what you are getting into is risk, reward, and work. And don't believe the old adage that risk and reward always go hand in hand. It isn't so. Every time you buy a stock, bond, or fund, you get the risk. It is right up front, immediately, as soon as you let go of your money. The reward, on the other hand, is not going to be apparent immediately. In fact, you may or may not ever see any reward.

However, you should be able to keep the distress involved in such uncertainty at an acceptable level, if you are willing to do some work. Your first task is to get a handle on what kinds of risks you are willing to face. A seventy-year-old retired couple who rent a home and have a retirement income of $25,000 a year plus another $20,000 saved for emergencies would be devastated by losing half of their savings. They would only consider the very safest investments, perhaps tax-exempt municipal bonds for income purposes, or very-low-risk mutual funds. On the other hand, a thirty-eight-year-old executive with excellent career prospects, her own home, and debts that can be managed out of current income might be willing to take half of her savings and put it into some more speculative action, such as growth stocks or growth stock funds (or parking lots!). Whatever money went into those investments, she'd better be able to face the prospect of losing half of it in one year without going out of her mind.

We never think that we are going to lose when we make an investment. We would rather talk about a 50 percent gain. But you need to be aware of the possibilities. A lot of people had a major portion of their retirement plans in IBM stock in 1992, and may have been hurt beyond any rational expectations. You don't have to look very far to find mutual funds that have lost 20 percent of their value in a given year. For example, 20th Century Industries, Morrison Knudsen Corporation, and Hovnanian Enterprises all suffered stock price drops of greater than 50 percent during 1994. In the mutual funds arena, the American Heritage Fund and the Steadman American Industry Fund both lost more than 30 percent. In 1994, while bond interest rates were rising, a number of bond mutual funds lost 20 percent or more of their value.

Your job, if you want it, is to decide what parameters of risk and reward you want to work with, and then find the mixture of investments that fit. For example, when I was looking for something safe to start with, I did the analysis for GTE and decided that I had a very good shot at 10 percent annual return, with very low chances of losing any more than 10 percent over a couple of years. Of course, when I bought IBM, the second time, at $67, I thought that the dividend was secure at about 7 percent (wrong!), and the lower limit on the stock was maybe $60 (wrong!). My point being, as I keep repeating, that the risk is always there.

After you decide on some kind of risk-and-reward guidelines that you can live with, it is almost assured that there are some investment opportunities out there that fit your needs. You just have to go find them.

That can be quite a job, however. Which leads us to our other major concern: time. Your investment research and analysis should not come to dominate your life. So how much work should you plan to do? Good question. If you are going to buy individual stocks, then you may end up seriously studying ten or twenty for every one that you buy. You need to read this book and some others. You need to read some of the financial magazines regularly, and the *Wall Street Journal*, or the *New York Times* business section twice a week. Plan to spend some time in the library with *The Value Line* and other relevant periodicals. A continuing theme of this book will be how much work you have to do to be fairly safe.

The trading floor at the stock exchange is not open to the public. You have to, at some point, get a connection with a brokerage firm or investment company. That search for the right professional contact is perhaps the most critical thing you will do. You should only have to do it once, if you get it right, but plan on spending a month studying the choices and visiting people. I did it wrong the first time. I just walked into a convenient local office of Paine-Webber and took the first broker who was available to talk to me. More fool I! We will get into all of this in more detail in later chapters, but the point for now is that it requires work, and time, and planning. Figure out how that is going to fit into your life, and how much time you want to devote to it.

Reading this book is your starting point. Next, sit down—perhaps with your significant other or a friend—and make some notes. You need a good picture of your current and future financial prospects. Make sure you know what your assets and current risks are. Then you can reasonably decide on how much of your money, your time, and your energy you want to put into risk-oriented investing. And keep in mind that one of your options is to "Just say no." Many readers may quite validly end up deciding that they just don't want to step into these waters.

Recommended Further Reading

Throughout this book, at the end of each chapter, I'll be recommending books that elaborate, comment on, or help out with ideas raised in the chapter. A few of them are out of print, unfortunately, but can be readily found in used bookstores and libraries—and they're worth the effort. One such out-of-print book is *Once in Golconda*, a wonderful account of the 1929 crash—its causes and consequences.

Brooks, John. *Once in Golconda*. New York: Harper & Row, 1969 (out of print).

Chilton, David. *The Wealthy Barber: The Common Sense Guide to Becoming Financially Independent.* Rocklin, CA: Prima Publishing Co., 1991.

Lerner, Joel. *Financial Planning for the Utterly Confused.* New York: McGraw-Hill, 1994.

Some Rules to Remember

In hopes of bringing some discipline to my own investments management, I have been developing a list of helpful rules as I go along. If you don't want to read the book, that's all right, I don't mind. However, buy the book anyway; tear out this page and carry it in your wallet all the time. If that's too much dead weight, just snip out Rule #1, and carry it with you.

RULE #1:

If you don't understand it, don't buy it.

RULE #2:

Don't expect to find perfect information.
This is a counterpoint to Rule #1.

RULE #3:

Risk and reward do not always go hand in hand.

RULE #4:

Investing is not a contest. Don't worry about how someone else is doing—just pay attention to how you are doing.

RULE #5:

You can't convince the market that you are right and it is wrong (the market is always right).

RULE #6:

You never have a real profit until you sell.

RULE #7:

Buying is easy. Selling takes character and discipline.

CHAPTER 2

It's Not a Game

Small Investors need to know:
- Is everybody getting rich?
- Do the high and mighty sometimes get hurt?
- Do the meek and lowly sometimes get hurt?
- What is compound growth all about?
- Who are the bulls and the bears?
- Does inside information guarantee safety?
- Can I count on my broker for protection?
- Can a market crash happen again?

Happy Talk

Too many people see Wall Street as a street paved with gold. I don't know how skeptical you are by nature, but as long as you think about buying stocks, bonds, or mutual funds, be *very* skeptical. Your stockbroker, the mutual fund industry, and your friends are usually all too eager to bring you the good news. Your broker wants to talk about how much money you would have if you had invested $100 a month in stocks for the past ten years. The mutual fund companies want to advertise how well they have done for the past year, or five years, depending on which is advantageous to their cause. And your friends who bought biotechnology stocks in the fall of 1990 want to brag about how much they made in the next eighteen months (if they had the good sense to sell in the spring of 1992).

Sure, a lot of smart, happy people bought into the Magellan Fund in 1982, and have profited greatly thereby. And some brave pioneers bought stock in Microsoft in 1982, and now they pave their driveways with gold. But we are not going to look at the markets through rose-colored glasses.

Who do you think advertises the most? The mutual funds that made gorgeous profits last year or the ones that lost money? Who do you think wants to talk the most about investing? The guy who bought IBM at 85 and sold it at 100 in 1992, or the gal who bought it from him at 100 and watched it slide to 46? A lot of people want to bring out the good news, but the sadder stories get buried and forgotten.

Even the Mighty Can Fall

Have you heard about Richard Whitney? There was a man who had it all. From one of the most famous and respected old Boston families, he eventually became the president of the New York Stock Exchange. His brother was a partner in J. P. Morgan & Co., the leading investment banking firm of the day. In 1912, he bought a seat on the New York Stock Exchange and later founded his own brokerage firm. This guy started out with good money, all the family ties, all the professional and "old school" connections, and all the training and experience that Wall Street could provide. A lot of people in the business wanted him to succeed. But where was he in 1938? Playing first base for the Sing-Sing Prison baseball team, and bankrupt.

It is not for us to judge Richard Whitney, but there ought to be a lesson in here somewhere. He wanted to succeed, perhaps more so than you and I. He thought he had good information. He should have had the experience and good judgment to buy and sell at the right times, probably more so than we. But Whitney wasted a fortune. He bought things he didn't understand, and failed to take profits when he might have. Finally, driven to desperate measures by the pressures of his failures, he embezzled money from his customers and lost that, too.

In fairness, Whitney was caught up in a maelstrom of markets gone mad, but he above all should have recognized the risks and known how to work around them. If the president of the New York Stock Exchange, with all his connections, experience, and resources, can find his way to ruin, then it could happen to any of us. Don't ever think that you, or your broker, or your friends are too clever to get hurt—really and truly hurt.

The Small Investor Can Get Hurt, Too

Games People Play

In 1992 Cigna Corporation was ordered to pay $5.3 million to a retired investor for selling him unsuitable limited partnerships. Cigna was found to have sold twelve risky limited partnerships to a retired GTE executive who had $2 million to fund his retirement. Those investments lost 90 percent of their value, leaving him with less than $200,000 of his original $2 million. Cigna was also found to have misrepresented the progress of those investments, and charged their client $22,000 in fees for handling the investments.

Who is going to protect you? An arbitration panel ruled that the Advest Group, Inc. was *not required* to refuse to execute orders that implemented a foolish strategy. Other findings on securities disputes have ruled differently as to the broker's responsibility to save a client from his own errors. If you do have an account with a broker, and you lose a lot of money through carelessness or poor decisions, you can take a complaint into courts or arbitration, but it is never clear which way the decision might fall.

Raymond James and Associates is a successful and respected brokerage firm in St. Petersburg, Florida. They make a lot of money for themselves, and make a lot of customers happy. They also make an occasional mistake. In September of 1991, a panel of arbitrators ruled that Raymond James should pay over $400,000 to one of their clients who had lost nearly $100,000 in an account with them due to a broker "churning" her account. *Churning* is the industry term used when a broker uses a client's account to make a large number of trades and produce large amounts of commissions for the broker. Raymond James claims that the broker was a bad apple among a bunch of conscientious professionals—probably true—but this is little relief to the customer. We can only speculate that the problem was due to carelessness, poor training, inadequate supervision, or a foolish client, etc. Name your own poison. The point is that the poor lady lost a lot of money, and the same thing could happen to us.

Inside Information

In 1983, I was working for Florida Federal Savings and Loan in St. Petersburg, Florida, when they offered some twelve-year, 12 percent bonds. I was pretty sure the company was financially sound and growing (it was, then). I thought I knew the management and the business, so I felt very confident in buying a bunch of those bonds and let them sit around and roughly quadruple my money in twelve years.[6] I walked into the nearest brokerage store from my office, opened two IRA accounts, and put up $4,000 for some of those bonds. And I essentially forgot about them. Every once in a while, Paine-Webber would send me a statement showing the values rolling right along, which I didn't study very closely.

One sunny day in 1991, I wanted to get that money back and put it into a new IRA account, so I called my broker and said, "Sell 'em!" The good news was that they still had some records of the account. The bad

---

[6] An investment that earns compound interest of 12 percent will just about double in six years.

news was that the little devils had not been just growing right along at 12 percent, and were worth far less than I expected. After I left Florida Federal, the place went belly-up and the feds took over. The Resolution Trust Corporation seized all the assets and took over the liabilities, including my bonds. But the taxpayers didn't want to pay me 12 percent. They offered to pay somewhat less until such a time as some solvent bank might be found to manage that money. So here is how I stood on my bonds:

- there was no market for the bonds, which I could not cash in,
- their current value could only be guessed at,
- and their fair value was certainly less than the 12 percent compound interest had predicted.

In brief, I had purchased an investment that I had good reason to be confident in. I knew the company was sound. I had fairly decent inside information about the finances in 1983. But I failed to keep close watch on the bonds, and my broker never offered any advice on the situation. Eventually, another bank took over those bonds and paid enough to make the nine-year compound rate work out to a little over 8 percent, so I wasn't hurt too badly. The point is that even the cautious small investor, who is pretty confident of having good information up front, can get tripped.

Markets

There are several kinds of financial markets that we will look at throughout the book, but for this chapter, focusing on risk, it is enough to just talk about stock markets. A stock market is set up to provide several services: it provides the location and mechanisms for people to buy and sell stocks, and it collects and reports information about price changes and sales amounts for every individual stock that is traded each day. The most famous of these is the New York Stock Exchange, with its headquarters on Wall Street. At the end of 1995, the New York Stock Exchange (NYSE) provided those services for the stocks of 2,600 companies, traded through the brokerage services of over 300 member firms. The total market value of all the companies listed on the NYSE was approximately $6.5 trillion.

The NYSE is a business, not a charity. Trading at the exchange is limited to member firms, who pay a high price for holding a seat on the exchange. You and I can place orders through one of these member firms, paying them a brokerage fee each time we buy or sell stocks. We will talk about finding a broker to work with in a later chapter.

There are other stock exchanges around the world. Some other American exchanges include the American Stock Exchange (AMEX), the Pacific Stock Exchange, and the Philadelphia Stock Exchange. Every economically important nation has its own exchange, or *bourse,* as they are often called. There are bourses in Brussels, Paris, London, Tokyo, and Stockholm, to name just a few. We will usually stick with the American markets. A small investor who wants to get into global markets should do it by buying a mutual fund that goes into the foreign markets, as it is much more difficult to get reliable information about foreign business activity.

Market Averages

The mechanism for tracking sales and prices on a minute-to-minute basis is essential to an orderly market. The results are available to the public in the widely reported market averages. No one person can keep track of every daily price on every stock available. Instead, we often use broad indicators that tell us something about the trends of a group of stocks. Such an indicator will not exactly show the price of any one stock. These indicators of stock prices include the Standard & Poor's 500 Stock Average, the Value Line Arithmetic Average, and several others. They are all computed differently, using different groups of stocks and different calculations. The most famous and most watched of them all is the Dow-Jones Industrial Average, or DJIA. The DJIA is widely reported every day to indicate the changes in stock prices of large industrial firms. It is not a true average of stock prices, but is computed by applying a special formula to the prices of thirty individual stocks.[7]

---

[7] The stocks included in the DJIA calculation include IBM, General Motors, Coca-Cola, Merck, AT&T, Sears, Texaco, Westinghouse, and other such. They do not include any utilities or transportation companies, which are averaged and reported separately.

It does not exactly show price changes for any one of the group, nor for the mathematical average of the group. It is, however, a rough indicator of general price trends for those thirty and other similar companies that may include the largest American industrial firms. Since those firms constitute a large part of the total value of the New York Stock Exchange (NYSE), you can think of the DJIA as reflecting the total wealth invested in NYSE stocks. Investors look on the Dow Jones Industrial Average as a general indication of trends in stock prices for major corporations. If the DJIA goes up 1 percent one day, you might take that as indicating an approximate average 1 percent gain for investors in large, well-established American businesses. Or, if you mainly buy stocks of large American industrial firms, then the DJIA is a barometer of your portfolio value. Since it is the most widely known and most widely reported of all the stock averages, the DJIA also has an inordinate influence on market psychology.

Bulls, Bears, and Greater Fools

If stock prices stay flat, or nearly constant for a long time, then investors only make money from dividend or interest payments. Most investors and market analysts devote more attention to price variations than to dividend or interest changes. For example, I held Nationsbank stock over a recent fifteen-month period. The dividends paid a very good $188, but the capital gain was $1600. On the other hand, I recently held IBM for three months and earned $121 in dividends, but the falling stock price produced a loss of about $1700. You can see why many people devote more time and attention to prices than to dividends.

During a time of generally rising prices, the market is called a "bull market." For example, the New York Stock Exchange has been in a bull market for most of the past fourteen years (1982–1995), notwithstanding the temporary setbacks in 1987, 1994, and a few other times. Investors who predict rising prices and invest accordingly are called *bulls*, and they generally want to buy more than they sell.

The major industrial stocks were in a pretty strong bull market from 1942 until 1973. Anyone who had followed a plan of investing

$1,000 each year, buying the DJIA stocks at their average values,[8] would have realized tremendous gains. For those thirty-two years, one could have seen results about like these:

Invest $1,000 per year	→	$32,000 total investment
If she spent the dividends	→	final account value of $92,000 and already received and spent $54,000
If she reinvested all of the dividends	→	final stock holdings worth $227,000

That is the kind of growth and profit that characterizes a powerful bull market.

A declining market is called a *bear market*. People who predict declining prices and act accordingly are called *bears.* They generally want to sell more than they buy. The greatest (worst) of all the bear markets was the stock market of 1929 to 1933.

ELEVATORS

Sometimes We Ride with the Bulls, and Sometimes with the Bears

---

[8] This is just by way of illustration. It would be a rare investor indeed who could manage a plan to buy just the thirty DOW Industrials at the average price of the DJIA for two or three years, let alone thirty-two.

A *market sector* is a group of related companies such as drug companies or automobile manufacturers. You will also hear about bulls or bears for individual market sectors, and advisors who change from bullish to bearish sentiment at different times. For example, a money manager could easily be bullish on automobile stocks, bearish on oil companies, and neutral on banks—all at the same time. He would be buying General Motors or Ford, and selling Exxon or Texaco.

The bulls and the bears also have a couple of friends, who don't get so much publicity. We'll refer to them as "Someone" and "The Greater Fool." If you plan to either buy or sell stocks or bonds, then you need to deal with Someone on the other side of the transaction. That Someone probably has a different opinion of the current market and price levels than you.

I bought stock in National Presto Corporation after they had been through a good strong run-up. Whoever was on the other side of that deal probably was taking a good profit, and didn't see much room for more advancement. I bought the stock at $61½ from Someone who wanted to sell (she may have thought I was The Greater Fool). People kept on buying at successfully higher prices, assuming that more Someones would keep buying. Over the next few months it got up as high as $83—a level that was probably not justified by their business earnings. At that point, if the price kept on going up, it was because some buyers thought there was a Greater Fool around who would pay higher yet. I sold as the price fell through $76, for a good profit.

The Greater Fool is the buyer who comes in at the end of the price run-up and doesn't do his homework on the underlying value of the firm. That process can go on for a while, as long as more Someones and more Greater Fools keep on putting in their buy orders. But eventually a day comes, or a price is reached, when no one, not even The Greater Fool, is willing to buy any more. When buyers disappear, there will always be people who want to sell, and start offering their shares at lower prices. Then the bullish Someones, and Greater Fools who bought near the top are stuck. They can sell immediately and take their losses, or hold the stock and watch the value of their investment fall every day as prices go lower and lower. Then one stock or the entire stock market may go through a bear market with prices falling ever lower, until a point is reached where all of the bears have sold, and a few people start looking at the stock as a bargain. A few bold new bulls start to pick up the stock again and the whole cycle repeats.

A trend of falling prices can be established on any kind of evidence, and it will continue until the sellers are worn out. Sometimes these turning points are precipitated by news about the company or its industry. At the end of 1992, with the presidential election nearing, there was a lot of talk that a Democrat would win and that he would then roll back prices on drugs. That was apparently enough to stop a bull market in major drug companies. The threat scared away the prospective new bulls and Greater Fools from buying at the current prices. Anything that scares away a lot of new bulls can turn the trend the other way.

Liquidity

Besides the lesson that even good advance information doesn't provide safety forever, my Florida Federal bonds deal also points out the need for liquidity. Liquidity means the ability to get back to cash quickly. Any investment gains in value if it has better liquidity, and loses value conversely. Liquidity of anything you own will vary with the price. You may own 100 shares of stock that can be sold instantly at $48.25, but has no buyers at $50. If you hold a stock or a bond, you always hope, and assume that Someone is there to provide liquidity. You won't know on any given day if your Someone is going to be a bull or a bear. If he is a bull, he may offer a higher price just as you offer to sell. If he is a bear, he may wait and not offer to buy until you have lowered your price enough to satisfy his bearish tendencies. He may even be selling the same stock or bond at lower prices than you want to accept. When IBM fell from 100 to 46 in a few months, that was not likely to have been based solely on a rational reevaluation of the company's finances. It was also a reflection of the fact that Someone was not there to buy; in fact, she was an active seller. The stock lost value because shareholders could sense that the buyers were running for the exits. When the price was 70, the company didn't just suddenly lose its assets or accounts receivable, but the stock lost its liquidity in the market at that value.

On different days, the market may swing through bull or bear moods. In 1989–91, investors were excited about biotechnology companies that were working on new drug development. Some of those companies had never sold a product nor made a profit, nor paid any dividends to stockholders. But their prices went up. Biogen Inc. went from a price of $8 in January 1989, to $16 in January of 1990, to $32 in January of 1991. The story on Wall Street was that they had great expectations, and The Greater Fool was coming in. The buyer was going to make a profit too because the new bulls had brought their foolish friends. That process can go on for an indefinite period, until The Greater Fool (T.G.F.) fails to show up for work one day. And woe to the market if word gets out that T.G.F. is taking a vacation.

Bear Markets, Panics, and Crashes

Through most of the years from 1983 through 1987, the stock market was enjoying a spectacular run, going from Dow-Jones Average of 1000 to over 2700. Now, if market prices nearly triple in five years, that's a good deal for most investors, but it should not be expected that it can continue forever. One day in October 1987 (as he had done before a few times), T.G.F. failed to show up for work. Taking notice of that (and the related fact that bond yields were getting a bit high), the stock market promptly took a dive. Stock prices, as indicated by the Dow-Jones Industrial Average, lost 20 percent of their value in one day. Translated into English, that means you could have seen your savings, invested in stocks, fall from $50,000 to $40,000 in one day.

Wall Street was seized by a panic on October 19, 1987. There were probably any number of good reasons to think that prices were too high, but the reaction was out of proportion to existing business conditions. The DJIA was on a roller coaster as different market forces came into dominance, but in the end, pandemonium reigned. Even seasoned and wise investors started selling everything at whatever price they could get because the market ran away from any rational analysis. Within a few days, after people had time to digest what had happened, buyers were back in picking up loose bargains in everything from H&R Block to Honda Motors, both of which very quickly recovered the lost ground and went on to higher values.

The Small Investor as the Greater Fool

In 1987, the pain was over pretty fast. Within a few weeks the market was advancing again. In 1929 something worse happened: The Mother of all Bear Markets, in fact. When the Bear seizes investors' minds, they become willing to sacrifice more and more of their value for liquidity. They may watch helplessly as their investment values fall lower and lower day after day with no end in sight. In October 1929, after two years of strong price increases on the New York Stock Exchange, Someone, in his role as T.G.F., failed to report for work. Well, prices fell a good bit, and in fact, by the end of the year, were down roughly 50 percent, but it didn't end there. In 1930, prices fell another 20 percent, and in 1931, another 50 percent. A retired couple who had their entire savings of $5,000 in the market in 1929 would have been down to about $1,000 by the end of 1931 (if they had held onto their stocks). It got worse in 1932, and only slightly recovered in '33 and '34. In fact from the market crash in 1929, it took almost 25 years for the Dow-Jones Industrial Average to recover its previous value. (That's right, I said *twenty-five years!*) And of course, almost all of the people who had been buying stocks in the years leading up to the crash were dead or otherwise out of the market long before that full recovery. There have been other significant bear markets in 1940–42, 1969–70, and 1977–78. Each time, stockholders were faced with the difficult choice of whether to sell at a loss and just get out of the market, or hold on and wait to see how long it would take for recovery. Each time, they were in the position of not knowing if the bear market was to run for six months or six years. However, the brave individuals who started buying a few stocks every month, beginning in 1942, rode a thirty-two-year bull market to a comfortable retirement.

What about those bear markets in 1969 and 1970, you ask? Well, most people who were holding stocks or trading them *did* show a loss in those years. But the *overall* trend between 1942 and 1973 was up. The DJIA went from an average value of about 107 in 1942 to an average of 920 in 1973. Every bull market and every bear market has days, weeks, or even months of corrections, or reversing action. So, for example, at the beginning of 1942 and the end of 1957 and the first half of 1962, prices generally fell. But if one had been consistently putting money into stocks every year from 1942 to 1973, there would have been a large profit for the entire period.

On February 3, 1993, the Dow-Jones Industrial Average went up about 45 points. That was approximately a 1½ percent gain in one day with an unusually large number of trades. Pretty hot stuff. Some commentators spoke of it as a buying panic. Apparently a lot of people, predominately professional money managers, got scared. They weren't scared of a crash; they were scared of missing the boat. Remember those guys' jobs and customer loyalty depend on what they have done lately. A lot of people must have feared that the market was running away from them, and they felt like they just *had* to spend that money. Does that sound like a healthy investing environment to *you*? In a market where prices suddenly run away, with little apparent relationship to the underlying business realities, that action is usually called a mania or a bubble. In 1928 and '29 the mania lasted for most of two years, and led to a crash. You never know how long the next one will last.

History indicates that prices will eventually return to a level that is supported by business conditions. If that happens over a decent time period, and settles into a reasonable value level, it is called a *correction*. In 1984, during a long-running bull market, the DJIA fell from 1287 to

1027, about a 20 percent decline, over about six months. That was uncomfortable for many folks, but it probably qualifies as a respectable correction. It recorrected over the next six months, and got back close to the previous high. If that same (first) correction had occurred in a week, it would be called a panic, or a crash, depending on your point of view. Probably a panic in this case because market values stayed in the ballpark range of reasonable value. The really wild times come when a panic becomes excessive. Fear, of course, breeds more fear and confusion. That applies to professional money managers, just it does to us.

The nightmare of all investors is a genuine crash. It can begin whenever a bull market becomes overeager and prices reach their tops. The early stages of the dying bull can be unpredictable, because, as the old Wall Street saying goes, "Every bull market climbs a wall of worry." That means that the experienced investors are aware of risks and uncertainty all along the way. How nervous is the mob at the top? Several things can happen. Maybe nothing happens for a while. Prices may stay in a trading range, perhaps up and down 5 percent for a few months, or longer, as in 1992. The important question is whether one day a crowd of sellers will show up with no new bulls in sight. How many sellers will cut their asking prices, and how far, in order to unload stocks?

The delicate balancing point hangs on the market's consensus perception of selling pressures. As long as most investors feel that the selling is orderly, and that the market is just a little overvalued, then there can be a managed retreat to a reasonable level of prices. But if the balance of investor confidence tips to the side of fear of big losses, then a panic may start. If the panic runs its course in a day or two, then many cool-headed professional investors will come back in to pick up some bargains. This is called bottom fishing. But if the panic really picks up a head of steam, it can turn into a horrible crash, such as the one that occurred in 1929.

TELL ME IT CAN'T HAPPEN AGAIN

But, you may say, this is the 1990s, and we are all much smarter than folks were back then. That kind of insanity couldn't get a hold of us, or our fellow investors, could it? Well folks, you place your money, and you make your bets. You can read any kinds of opinions you want, from knowledgeable, experienced investors. My own personal investment philosophy says that a true market crash that makes the whole world sick for years is unlikely, but still possible.

On the one hand, investors today have far better, easier access to good information about individual stocks and the entire economy. Everyone has access to a television and a public library. That means that every small investor can be better informed today than any of the wizards of Wall Street were in 1929. That should help to maintain a rational and balanced market. However, on the other hand, much more money is in the hands of professional money managers. Along with their superior analysis and information, they have superior discipline. The result is they don't sit around and watch values erode. The professional money manager is much quicker than you and I to cut his losses by quick selling, which can contribute to panic in the markets. You will have to figure out your own approach to the questions about possible crashes; don't just put your head in the sand. Too many nice people have gotten hurt that way. As we read along, there will be a few suggestions about how to deal with the mania, panic, and crash scenarios. But just remember, when/if it happens, I'll be taking care of my money, not yours. And so will your broker.

Compound Growth

When you see a series of annual gains or losses for an investment, it is usually not helpful to simply average the yearly percentages to get an overall figure for the duration of the investment. We need to stay in tune with the way almost everyone talks about investment returns, and that is by looking at *equivalent compound annual rate of return.*

The rate of return of an investment for one year is the change in the investment divided by the original value.

Examples (all for one-year investments)

Investment	Final value	Change	Rate of return
$100	$120	$20	20 ÷ 100 = 20%
$100	$85	-$15	-15 ÷ 100 = -15%
$8,000	$12,500	$4,500	4500 ÷ 8000 = 56.25%

The *equivalent compound rate of return* (or equivalent annual rate), for a period of more than one year, is the one rate that would have produced the same final value, if applied throughout the period, with all gains reinvested.

We have to introduce a little math lesson here. It helps to produce an efficient view of market gains and also will help you read other sources. Everybody talks about or writes about compound growth, so we should also.

Here's the deal: you invest $1,000 for five years and gain 8 percent return each year. That's fine work.

If you take the profit ($80) each year and spend it on caviar, then the value of your account goes like this at the end of each year: $1,000...$1,000...$1,000...$1,000...$1,000.

If you reinvest the profit each year, then the value of your investment grows like this: $1,080...$1,166.40...$1,259.71...$1,360.49...$1,469.32; after five years that is a $469.32 profit, which is 47 percent on your investment. That looks a whole lot better than five times 8 percent doesn't it? That is compounding the earnings.

If you take out the earnings, then after five years you profited by 40 percent (five times 8 percent). If you left the profits in to earn more, than after five years you get more than five times 8 percent.

When you talk about investing, or read other books or magazines, you must deal with profits in terms of compound earnings. You do not have to do the math, but you do have to deal with the idea. Here are some more examples to illustrate the issues:

> **Example 1:** The Elrods invested $25,000 and left it for six years. They also told their broker to reinvest all of the dividends or capital gains. After the six years they had an account value of $52,000. Their profit was $27,000, which is 108 percent of the original $25,000. That looks like an average annual gain of $27,000 ÷ 6 = $4,500. Since $4,500 is 18 percent of $25,000, or because 108 percent ÷ 6 = 18 percent, then it may appear that their gain was 18 percent per year. In fact, though, the important value to consider here is the equivalent compound rate of return. For a return of 108 percent in six years, the equivalent compound rate is 12.98 percent. If the Elrods had invested their $25,000 for six years, and reinvested the dividends, at a fixed rate of return of 12.98 percent, then after six years they would have made the same profit.

In investing, *compounding* means to reinvest all dividends, yield, capital gains, or whatever flows from the investment. If an investment returns a profit each year, and if you compound the investment every year, then the compound rate of return is not the same as the average of the six years' returns. The compound rate will be smaller than the average.

> **Example 2:** Major Jones had an investment that returned profits of 2 percent, 8 percent, 9 percent, and, finally, 6 percent over four years. The total return over the four years was 25 percent if he did not compound the gains, and 27.3 percent if he did. The average annual return for the four years was 6.25 percent, but the equivalent compound rate of return was 5.74 percent. If he had invested the same amount, and compounded the profits, at a fixed rate of return of 5.74 percent, he would have made the same final return.

> **Example 3:** Eleanor Marbake had some money in the stock market for three years. Her stocks did not pay any dividend, so there was nothing to compound. In 1994, she was down 25 percent, in 1995 up 50 percent, and in 1996 down 25 percent again. The average of the yearly rates of profit was zero (the average of -25, +50, -25). But the average compound rate of return was -6.5 percent. How so? Well, if she started with $1,000 she would have seen:

> first year, lose 25 percent to leave $750
> second year, gain 50 percent to reach $1,125
> third year, lose 25 percent down to $844.

> If she had simply invested $1,000 at a fixed yearly rate of -6.5 percent (a loss) per year, that would have produced the same result after three years. So the equivalent annual rate of return is -6.5 percent.

You do not have to do the math, and I don't want to spend a whole chapter on it, so let's just let it go. The critical points to understand are these:

1. The average of the yearly returns is not the same as the equivalent compound rate of return.
2. The average generally overstates the compound rate.
3. Most people who analyze or write about investments prefer to use the equivalent annualized compound rate of return, so we should, too.

Recommended Further Reading

John Rothchild's book is a little autobiographical sketch of his own investing adventures over a couple of years. It is particularly worthwhile as instruction for us. He was a small investor who tried everything to turn a fast profit. The book describes how he jumped from stocks to options to futures to commodity trading with his eyes always on the prize. He tended to ignore risk. It is well written and entertaining, and has some serious lessons between the lines.

Chase, David. *Mugged on Wall Street*. New York: Simon & Schuster, 1987 (out of print).

Elias, Christopher. *Fleecing the Lambs*. Washington, DC: Henry Regnery Co., 1971 (out of print).

Rothchild, John. *A Fool and His Money: The Odyssey of an Average Investor*. New York: Viking Penguin, 1989.

CHAPTER 3

A Personal Investment Strategy

Small Investors need to know:
- Is there an easy way to success?
- What kind of planning do I have to do?
- What is asset allocation?
- Where is the risk?
- Where is the work?

Talk Is Cheap—Get to Work

Talk, talk, talk. Enough talk already. Talk is cheap. Sooner or later we have to cease the idle talk and do something. The preceding chapters were filled with ideas about the nature of investing, but they didn't say much about making any specific decisions. In this chapter we will get into a plan to do something. Actually, not a single plan, but more like many possible plans, with as many variations as you could ever want.

We all know the old saw about explaining things: first, describe what you are going to do; then do it; and finally, explain what you have done. Well, I believe it's useful, even though it requires repetition. Similarly, this chapter may require more than one reading. You may want to go through the separate sections several times to get a grip on how the ideas discussed all interrelate. And you *do* need to understand those interrelations, because they will help you start making some real decisions about how, or if, you will begin investing. This is not a simple process. Some other investment books represent aspects of investing as simple ideas, when in fact they require a lot of work or expertise. For example, some authors recommend that the investor evaluate the strength and experience of a company's management. That's a fine idea, but difficult for a part-time investor who has no experience in that industry. We need to be realistic and practical about what we can do. I won't present the ideas as if there were one simple process to guarantee success. If you are going to be an investor, then you will have too much at stake to treat it as a simple process.

Your Personal Investment Strategy

If you planned to drive from Kansas City to New York and visit the New York Stock Exchange, you would plan ahead, right? You would need a map, and hotel reservations, and some idea of how you could get into the Stock Exchange, and some estimate of the costs and time required for the trip. Well, if you are not going in person but just sending your money, you better have a plan, too. I call that plan a *personal investment strategy*. The plan can be as detailed and complicated as you like, or it can be much looser and general, but one way or another, you need to have some kind of a plan. Here are a few of the questions that the plan should address:

- How much money do I want to put into risk-oriented investing?
- How should I divide that between stocks, bonds, and mutual funds?[9]
- How much work and research will I do myself?
- How much could I lose, without destroying the fabric of my life?
- Do I want to find a full-service broker to advise me, and how much will I rely on him or her?
- What types of diversification methods will I use?
- What is my target for annual gain?
- What discipline will I use to control losses?

---

[9] Real estate, annuities, and rare coins may also have a place in your investment strategy, but fall beyond the scope of this book.

You will certainly think of more questions as we go along. Remember, the aim of the book is not to answer all your questions, but to help you have the confidence to find good information and determine your own answers.

Now, the best-laid plans of mice and little squirrels oft go astray. You know that. You know that every major corporation and every military leader, and every lover, have seen their plans disintegrate in the face of changing events. You know that we are not likely to think of everything, and even if we did think of everything, circumstances would change by the end of next month. The planning process may be difficult and possibly discouraging because you see the complexity ahead of time. But don't give up. Get a plan. What would you think about a captain who led his battalion into battle without a plan?

The military analogy is appropriate here. A smart and responsible military leader has to be both organized and flexible. As does the small investor. An officer leading a unit has to have a clear objective that he understands. We do, too. He has to have an idea about the cost and risks of going after that objective. He has to have the discipline to stick to the plan in the face of difficulty and resistance, but he also must keep his eyes open and his head clear. A battlefield leader should be constantly collecting and analyzing new information about his situation, and should be prepared to make changes in the plan when that is necessary. We must, too. Both we and the battlefield leader should respect our plans and stick to them with discipline, but we do not stick to them with blind obsession. In other words, a plan is better than no plan, but you can't expect the plan to be perfect.

We start out with a plan, because that provides a better start. We stick with the plan because that will make us more effective in achieving our goals. We can change our plans when it is necessary to change, but only you can make that choice for your personal investment strategy.

As an aspiring small investor, you must keep the following in mind. You will need:

- a plan: some kind of a personal strategy
- discipline: stick to your plan and work at it
- effort: work at judging the situation and getting new information

• flexibility: don't be afraid to modify the plan, or too proud to recognize your mistakes

A Smorgasbord of Investment Options

The Small Investor Has a Smorgasbord of Investment Options

At first glance, the number of choices seems simple enough. As the introduction explained, this book is concerned only with stocks, bonds, and mutual funds. That looks like three choices, right? Wrong! That looks like thousands of choices, or if you want to get technical about it, trillions of choices!

Now we are getting into the process of establishing a personal investment strategy. Part of the plan is to make this a realistic and workable process for you. Even though there are many ways to set up your investments, we don't have to study them all. We don't have to be knowledgeable about every one of 8,000 mutual funds, or every one of 7,000 publicly traded stocks. You just have to find a plan and a mixture of investments that works for you. So let's explore this gray area between the many, many choices available, and the practical matter of selecting something that works for you.

MANY INVESTMENT MIXTURES

What follows are some of the options. Pretty soon you will see the ideas developing, and you will think of many more options for your money. Then you will be able to focus on the areas that seem appealing to you, and explore in depth perhaps ten or twenty possibilities that might fit your investment strategy.

FOUR WAYS TO ALLOCATE YOUR MONEY

The simplest view of where to put the money can be described in four choices: buy individual stocks, buy bonds, buy mutual funds (which may be funds that invest in stocks or bonds), or don't buy any of those. The last option we will call the bank option. The bank option assumes you don't keep your money at home, but rather in a savings account, CD, or money market account. The bank option should fit into your personal investment strategy, because it takes care of your reserve funds. When you sell an investment or collect interest and dividends, you might not want to reinvest that money immediately. So, it could go into your reserve funds. There may also be times during which you feel the markets are *all* too risky, and decide to keep all of your investment money in the reserve funds. Before you make any decisions about stocks, bonds, funds, keeping your money in the bank, you should read the chapters dedicated to each of these investment choices. They are designed to help you understand the trade-offs between risk, reward, time, and work for each option.

MANY WAYS TO ALLOCATE YOUR MONEY

To reiterate, you might decide to divide your money between these four options, or some combination thereof. These combinations yield at least fifteen choices. Here are a few of those choices; you can figure out the others.

1. buy stocks *and* bonds
2. buy stocks *and* bonds *and* mutual funds

3. buy mutual funds *and* keep money in the bank
4. buy bonds *and* keep money in the bank (or in your broker's money market fund)

Well, you get the idea. Let's look more closely at a few possible choices. Let's say you have $20,000 to invest. Here are some possible allocations:

	stocks	bonds	mutual funds	bank
option 1	4,000	8,000	0	8,000
option 2	10,000	0	10,000	0
option 3	0	5,000	10,000	5,000

Of course, there are many, many more ways to divide the money. And, in addition to choosing how you're going to allocate the money, you also have to make choices within each option. If you want to put $5,000 into individual stocks, for instance, you would need to choose some stocks to buy from among the thousands available. If you put $7,000 into mutual funds, you might want to pick two or three from among the thousands of funds. In this way we can imagine a vast number of possibilities for how you might invest your money. One of the most challenging tasks that you have is to figure some allocation that works right for you. That will be affected by the variations in risk and work for each option. We will get into this in a lot more detail later, but for starters, look at the first four primary choices according to some relative risk, work, and reward estimates.

	risk level	work level
choosing and buying individual stocks	highest	highest
choosing and buying individual bonds	variable[10]	medium
buying mutual funds	low to medium	medium
banking the money	very low	none

The possible reward levels are roughly commensurate with the risks, except that mutual funds may be extremely rewarding if you pick the right ones. Note that there is no *guaranteed* reward level, only a *possible* reward level.

---

[10] If you buy junk bonds, the risk could be very high.

And in the final analysis, you always have the choice to simply walk away from it all. I hope that the final decision on that will be an intelligent and informed decision for you.

More about Risks

Risk again! The guy never gets off of it! Will he never relax on the subject of risk? Not in this lifetime. And not in these markets that we are studying. If you ever, for one little second, lose sight of the risks in investing, please don't tell anyone that you read my book.

We need to make rational judgment calls on how to minimize the risks. In order to figure things out, we need to look at different kinds of risks that occur in different markets, or at different times. My philosophy says that I have three main ways to avoid or minimize risk. I can work hard at my research, diversify my investments, and keep money in the bank. Each of those ideas will help, some more and some less in different situations. There is not one single magic key to the kingdom of low risk, but we can try several things.

On every investment, the small investor should try to achieve three things: protect the principal, increase the principal, and earn some dividends or yield. With different investments, you emphasize one or another of those. The bank option is almost entirely focused on protecting the principal, but some high-risk stock investments are almost entirely focused on increasing the principal. All three concerns should be important. You will balance them out in deciding which mixture of investments to use.

That leads us to three corresponding views of risk:

- the risk of loss of principal (may, for example, occur if you buy junk bonds),
- the risk of no growth in principal (say, if you keep all of your money in the bank), and
- the risk of low yield (as with a stock that pays no dividend).

If you think that the second one is a red herring, that it is not really a risk, then you haven't heard about inflation. The family that put $30,000 in a shoe box in 1953 could have bought a lot of stuff with the money. If they opened the shoe box today, they could not buy so much. The original economics lesson is this: wealth is not measured by dollars, but by the amount of goods and services you can purchase. For a fifty-year-old couple who are planning their retirement today, the risk of no growth in principal is a very serious risk.

Different Kinds of Risk

To explore all the risks would require the life's work of ten thousand economics professors. Our eyes glaze over. In addition, the very term "risk" has extremely technical and specific meanings to economists, and they might well quibble with how I use the word. Well, that's fine for them, but I when I say "risk," I mean it in the plain ol' English-language sense of the word: a danger, a potential hazard, the possibility for a loss. Indeed, I intend to widen your vision to see risk all around. If we teach a man to fish, then we don't have to show him every fish in the pond.

To see risk all around, no matter when or how silently it approaches, we should become familiar with some of its usual faces. The next few paragraphs point out some of the ways that risk creeps in. You should be able to think of others.

In late 1992, a broker in Knoxville, Tennessee, was fined $200,000 and barred by the National Association of Securities Dealers for converting customers' accounts to his own use. The most obvious, but probably least common, risk is simply that a broker is either crooked or stupid. You give him $20,000 to buy Chrysler Corporation stock and he uses the money to buy his girlfriend a new Mazda. That's misappropriation of funds. The initial buy or sell order is the first or last step in the sequence of events that get the money out of your hands and around the market and back to you eventually. If the buy or sell order is never followed, or if someone else grabs your money, then it doesn't matter how sharp your planning and analysis were. We should not blindly trust just anyone who calls him- or herself a securities dealer. There are a lot of things you can do to get a relationship with one who is smart, honest, and productive. So the very first risk is that the person or firm with whom you do business is not good enough. The next chapter focuses on this problem.

We know and accept the fact that every purchase of a stock, bond, or mutual fund involves some risk. Those risks show up in different forms, the likelihood of each type may change from day to day, and our ability to predict and manage each kind is different.

RISK OF POOR DECISION MAKING

There is a risk of poor decision making. This is probably the most common risk of all. Furthermore, it is a risk that you will have to learn to live with. If you do any investing of any type, you will have to make some decisions, and sometimes, your decisions will not work out for the best.

THE RISK THAT YOU'RE NOT AS SMART AS YOU THINK YOU ARE

In the case of the Florida Federal bonds, I was confident that I knew the business, the competitive environment, and the management. I knew for sure that the company was financially healthy and making good profits. But I made two misjudgments: first, I was wrong about the management (I didn't dream that they would find a way to ruin the company in a few years after I left), and second, I thought that I didn't have to keep a close eye on that investment. There is a lesson, or two or three, in this: even the wise guys with inside information, guys who are trying to be careful, will make some mistakes. It has happened before, and it will happen again. Do your research. Try to manage your money carefully. But don't give up the first time you make a mistake. Remember that mistakes are good teachers.

THE RISK THAT GOOD JUDGMENT CAN STILL FAIL

Errors can also show up as selling the wrong thing at the wrong time. Let's look at the case of Hewlett-Packard Company. A great organization, their revenues, earnings, and dividends have climbed steadily for quite some time. Their stock has been fairly consistent, if not spectacular. In early 1992, the stock share price reached about $83, and promptly went into a swoon. Over a few weeks it fell to $65. Sales had even climbed strongly during the recession years of 1991 and '92. So I bought Hewlett-Packard (HWP) at $61¼. Back then, I was very nervous about the stock market—the economy was so weak, and consumer confidence so wan, that I thought caution was required. So I watched HWP closely, along with everything else. I put in a stop-loss order to sell the stock if the price fell as low as $54. About 30 seconds later, it hit 54, and my efficient broker sold it all. It turns out that 54 was the rock-bottom low; the stock immediately turned around and started back up, and never quit until it hit 100. So what should have been a $35 per share opportunity turned into a $7 per share loss, because I sold one day before it started back up.

Obviously I remember that mistake. I am writing about it today. But I have never regretted it. I had made a plan to protect my capital, and was following through on it. I didn't want to sit idly by and watch the stock fall to who-knows-where. Even though everything about the business looked solid, it was necessary to remember that the market has a mind of its own. It will go where it will go, and we must either follow or get out of the way (we don't have the option to lead, you have to have ten billion dollars to do that). Sometimes it will work out that you may do the smart thing, and the market makes it into a mistake.

THE RISK THAT GOOD RESEARCH ISN'T GOOD ENOUGH

In 1992, I was looking for a good safe stock. I went through a risk analysis on Potomac Electric Company, much like the one illustrated in chapter 1 for GTE. I also talked to several experienced professional money managers and looked at the current portfolios of several good, conservative mutual funds. Many of them held Potomac Electric (POM). I knew something about how POM does business, as well as the Washington economy in general, because I had personal experience living in their service area. I studied their annual report and their report to the Securities Exchange Commission (called the 10 K report), and bought some at 23⅜. I feel that it was, and is, a good, safe investment for me. But I know that bad things can always happen, in any market. Late in 1992, the share price of POM had risen as high as $28, and I was feeling pretty good about it. Suddenly and unexpectedly, over a few weeks, the price dropped to about $23. I had lost about 18 percent of the share value for no reason that I could understand. Well, I learned later that Potomac Electric had a little side business going, which I had never heard of. (I didn't read the reports closely enough.) They also owned and leased out some airplanes. Their customers' business went sour and the planes were returned. So POM had a few hundred million dollars worth of assets sitting around with no income being produced. They also sold another 6 million shares of the common stock, which diluted the value of other holdings. That apparently spooked enough investors so that their 1993 profit projections went down the drain. Since then, the stock price climbed back to $28. Even your best-reasoned, most conservative investments will hiccup once in a while. Can you sit calmly and wait for the business to correct itself?

THE RISK THAT THERE AIN'T NO JUSTICE

Sometimes you just can't make a buck. Hewlett-Packard fell to a bargain price level, and I bought some. It kept on falling and I sold. Wrong! IBM fell to a bargain price level, and I bought some. It kept on falling and I held it. Wrong again! Can you stand the aggravation? Remember what Peter Lynch said about having the stomach for investing!

THE RISKS IN THE BUSINESSES YOU INVEST IN

If you buy stock in Ford Motor Company, it stands to reason that you want Ford to build good cars and sell a bunch of them. The stock price and the dividends will not give you much reward unless Ford's auto workers and dealers are doing their jobs. There are two parts in this problem: first, you have to do good analysis to try and predict the success of the company, and second, their management has to make the profits come through. You can't control their management or the actions of their competitors, so you are left with trying to predict their chances of success. That is extremely tricky business. The people who successfully predicted in 1991 the turnarounds of Chrysler Corporation and Unisys have been greatly rewarded. Investors who predicted a resurrection of computer maker Wang Labs might have bought the stock at a "bargain price" of four to five dollars a share in 1991. Wang closed 1992 in bankruptcy with the stock worth less than 50 cents per share.

So it is difficult. In later chapters we will get into more ideas about finding good information and trying to forecast things. But for now, let's look at the most immediate and obvious problem: can you forecast future earnings? No. One of the very best sources of data, opinions, and analysis for stock research by individual investors is the publication called *The Value Line*. You can subscribe to it or read it in your library. Let's watch them forecast earnings for some of the companies in the Dow-Jones Industrial Average. Very large, successful, and well-known companies. That should give us a best shot at forecasting. After all, it's easier to predict where a fifty-year-old oak tree is likely to be next year than to make the same prediction for a potted plant.

I picked eleven companies from the thirty industrials in the DJIA. Here are the forecasts for 1992 earnings (*The Value Line* is careful to identify these as *estimates*), with the dates of those predictions, and the actual results:

Company	Date of forecast	Forecast 1992 earnings ($ per share)	Actual 1992 earnings ($ per share)
AT&T	10/18/91	3.00	2.59
Alcoa	11/18/91	4.40	0.43 loss
Caterpillar	11/15/91	3.25	4.76 loss
Eastman Kodak	9/20/91	4.10	0.91
General Motors	9/20/91	2.75	6.26 loss
IBM	11/1/91	8.75	5.00 loss
McDonalds	9/27/91	2.65	2.53
Philip Morris	9/27/91	5.85	4.95
Sears	8/30/91	4.06	1.02
Westinghouse	11/1/91	2.35	1.13
Woolworth	8/30/91	3.08	0.10 loss

(earnings per share equals total company earnings divided by the number of shares of stock)

This is not a terrible record (as I said *Value Line* is one of the very best sources for an investor)—note that some of the estimates *were* fairly close. It *is* backup for my contention that forecasting earnings is really tough. Some of the more dramatic discrepancies between forecast and actual earnings occurred as a result of the Financial Accounting Standards Board's new ruling on how to report future liabilities to pension and retirement benefits. But so what? That's life. Stuff happens.

---

[11] Source: *Barron's*, February 8, 1993

THE RISKS OF BEING IN THE MARKET

Some folks argue that you don't have any choice as to whether you take risks or not. They say that whether you invest in anything or not, inflation, the economy, and taxation will affect you one way or the other. Some argue that not investing is simply a bet that the pieces of paper called cash are better than the pieces of paper called stocks and bonds. We cannot resolve those arguments. But there is risk.

On February 16, 1993 the American stock markets all took a dive. All of the major averages used to report stock prices showed large losses. The Dow-Jones Industrial Average dropped about 2½ percent. Some people thought this was in reaction to President Clinton's public statements on economic policy. Some people thought it was the beginning of a great bear market. Some people predicted a real slam-bang crash. Whatever the true causes, it is obvious that the businesses whose stocks were watched didn't just all collapse overnight, nor lose 2 percent of their sales, nor their customers. This was a case of market psychology taking control of events. The bears who thought we were in for a long-overdue decline, along with the bears who thought Clinton's policies were wrong, managed to induce a panic that lasted about seven hours. And because a huge number of shares were traded, we can be sure that it was not just a panic of small investors. Oh no, this was a panic of the best and the brightest, and their friends and their bosses.

We have to keep in mind that market psychology sometimes overwhelms business reality. It may produce a great boom or a great bust. But when it happens, we can't change the tide of events.

THE RISKS FROM OUTSIDE FORCES

The value of a bond you buy is affected by nationwide and worldwide economic forces. We will get into this in greater detail in chapter 6, which is devoted to investing in bonds, but for now it is enough to know that when overall interest rates go up, the resale value of a bond goes down, and conversely. If you buy a high-grade $1,000 bond and hold it to maturity, you can expect to get the $1,000 back. If, however, you want to sell it before it matures, the value will be affected by interest rate changes since you bought it. The actual dollar value of interest to be paid should be fixed and predictable, but the resale value will vary depending on how early you're selling it, among other things. If you want to predict the value of a bond investment, or an investment in a mutual fund that buys bonds, you are in the business of predicting interest rates. If anyone could consistently forecast interest rates, they would be richer than Midas. The value and expected profits from your bond investments are subject to the winds of worldwide economic forces. Even though some types of bonds are among the safest investments, it is still worthwhile to balance them with other investments that may behave differently relative to interest rates.

So too, for stocks. Part of my strategy in 1991 was to invest in companies that had strong marketing and sales outlets in Europe. European economies were not healthy, but I expected to see improvement in the near future, and consequently figured that the companies with good markets over there would be strong. Some of the candidates that I liked were Ford, General Motors, IBM, General Electric, and Wolverine World Wide (shoes).

Well, that ship has not come in. I made good profits on Ford and GM because they were way down when I bought, and I am looking at some profit on GE, although I expect to hold it a long time. IBM has been a good-news/bad-news story for me (more on this later). The European countries generally went from bad to worse, and there didn't seem to be a whole lot I could do about it. Then, after I sold Wolverine, it tripled! In short, then, my European strategy has never paid off. I'm still not sure that I exercised bad judgment—it may yet prove to be a winning strategy by next year—but this does illustrate the problem of investing in the face of economic forces that dwarf one's power to predict.

We can't really run away from that. Even if you confine your attention and your money to Georgia chicken ranches, there will be outside factors that you cannot always predict or control. Fortunately, I had my stock portfolio balanced with some stocks that were doing well in the 1992 economic environment—for example, my electric utilities and Nationsbank. The small investor hopes for the best while preparing for the worst. We also plan an investment strategy to try to avoid the worst. Work hard and diversify!

Risk and Volatility

The meaning of *volatile* in financial terms is that a security is subject to rapid changes in value. This should be understood relative to what is expected, or normal, for the markets at that time. There is no single best agreed-upon formula or method for judging risk, so many people substitute their view of volatility in place of risk. I think that is a mistake. It does not necessarily follow that a stock is risky just because it is volatile, but it is worthwhile for us to be in tune with the normal language and usage of the markets, so we will look at volatility.

In the first graph, ABC and XYZ are two stocks that start at $20, and after nine months, both end at $23. XYZ is more volatile, and presumably would be regarded by many investors as more risky.

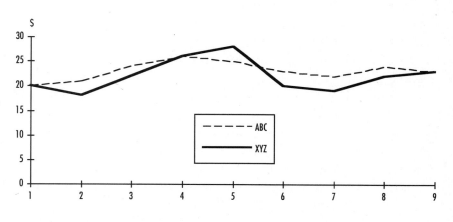

End-of-Month Prices for Nine Months

In the second graph, RST and PDQ are two stocks that have good growth during the nine-month period. RST climbs steadily from $18 to $23, while PDQ climbs, not so steadily, from $15 to $27. PDQ is more volatile, and by a certain point of view, more risky, but it is clearly a superior investment over that time frame.

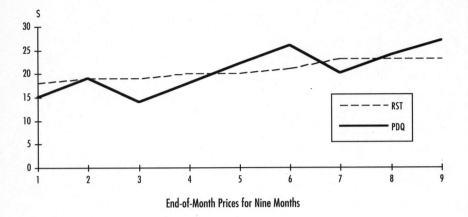

End-of-Month Prices for Nine Months

If you had held PDQ during that time frame, you would have had more headaches and nervousness over it. You even might have been scared into selling during one of the dips. There were also some opportunities for people to buy PDQ and sell it at a loss, whereas RST was profitable no matter when you bought and sold within this period.

Volatility should be interpreted as indicating chances for loss, and more chances for worrying, but it does not necessarily indicate a bad investment. There is no exact, clear,easy way to measure risk—but we *can* measure the volatility relative to some agreed standard. For instance, we might show that stock XYX was 30 percent more volatile than the Dow-Jones Industrial Average over some set time period. This is done by calculating a value called *beta,* which we will discuss in greater depth later on.

What Is Diversification?

There are a million flavors of diversification. There are many ways to do it right, and a few ways to do it wrong. Let's start out by looking at some examples of how it works. Suppose you and I and Jack have a chance to invest in three ways: bond A, stock WXZ, or stock OUC. We each put up $1,000. Jack buys the bond, I buy WXZ, and you buy OUC. In five years we each evaluate our holdings and find:

	Cost	Return in 5 years
Bond A (Jack)	$1,000	$1,400
Stock WXZ (me)	$1,000	$2,200
Stock OUC (you)	$1,000	$ 600

You are not happy. But suppose we pooled our money and shared the risk and reward of all three options. Then after five years we would be splitting $4,200 among us, for a total of $1,400 each. Having each bought an interest in the three investments, and thereby passing up the best and worst results, we achieved a good average result. We have all diversified our risk and reward expectations. (We actually formed a tiny investment club.)

But you wish we had all bought stock WXZ and made a killing. A delightful wish, but not practical, for we could not have predicted the outcome of each investment with any certainty. The good news and bad news of diversification are that we avoid both the best and the worst, in search of an agreeable middle ground. Diversification does not guarantee safety—it seeks safety.

The real value and science of diversification come into play when you foresee some risk and reward possibilities for each investment, and try to balance them for protection. To illustrate what an individual investor can do, and how to do it, let's look at another, slightly more complicated example.

Let's imagine three investments. Call them Mighty Motors (MM), Good Food (GF), and U.S. bonds. Let us also imagine only three future economic scenes for the next three years: recession, slow growth, and strong growth. Let us further say that we can make some decent guesses at the value of each investment, in each economic scenario, three years down the road.

The Value of a $1,000 Investment after Three Years

Investments	Recession scenario	Slow-growth scenario	Strong-growth scenario
U.S. bonds	$1,225	$1,225	$1,225
Mighty Motors	700	1,300	2,200
Good Food	1,100	1,400	1,700

So, for example, in a recession we would expect the bonds would grow in value to $1,225; in a case of slow growth, we guess the MM stock would grow in value to $1,300, and so on.

Suppose you have $6,000 to invest. Obviously, if you care to gamble on the strong-growth result, then you put all your money into MM, and hope to turn $6,000 into $13,200. But you face the prospects of losing in a recessionary economy, and then only having $4,200 to support your retirement.

The conservative investor will avoid the worst risk by diversifying the money among two or three investment choices. Here are three such plans:

plan 1: Broad, even diversification. Put $2,000 into each investment.

plan 2: Buy $3,000 of MM, $1,000 of GF, and $2,000 of U.S. bonds.

plan 3: Buy $3,000 of GF and $3,000 of U.S. bonds.

After three years, here's what you might have left, given each of our three economic situations:

Result of Investing $6,000 for Three Years

Investments	Recession scenario	Slow-growth scenario	Strong-growth scenario
plan 1	$6,050	$7,850	$10,250
plan 2	5,650	7,750	10,750
plan 3	6,975	7,875	8,775

Plan 1 offers low risk and possible high gain. Plan 2 offers more risk and possible higher gain. Plan 3 offers the lowest risk, and good but not great possible gain.

Is plan 3 a risk-free investment? No—as I keep reiterating, there are no risk-free investments. These calculations are subject to the estimates we started with, which are no better than our sources of information and our analysis. For example, MM might have a strike, or the stock markets might crash.

The table above depends on how much money you started with. In case you wonder about the results in terms of percentage growth of investments, the table below shows each choice in terms of the annualized compound rate of return on the investments.

Annualized Return after Investing for Three Years

Investments	Recession scenario	Slow-growth scenario	Strong-growth scenario
plan 1	+ 0.3%	+ 9.4%	+ 19.5%
plan 2	− 2.0%	+ 8.9%	+ 21.4%
plan 3	+ 5.1%	+ 9.5%	+ 13.5%

You pay your money, and you take your choice. Different people will have all kinds of different feelings as to which of those choices is more or less attractive. It requires a **personal investment strategy**. No one method can possibly suit everyone. And you could choose among a lot of other ways to invest your money, or even bank part of it, if you wanted other options.

DIVERSIFICATION IN PRACTICE

Now how do we put this theory to use? We just looked at three choices: an automobile company, a grocery store chain, and a very high-grade bond. You would normally expect that each of the three would react differently to different conditions in the economy. That is what you want. When looking at the wealth of investment options available, you want to choose a range of investments so that they won't all sour together. If interest rates go down, you would like to have at least one investment that does well. If the government imposes higher taxes, you would like to have at least one investment that does well (good luck on that). If the price of oil falls to the lowest level in twenty years, you would like to have an investment that does well, perhaps a trucking company. If your judgment just turns out to be bad, you would like to have an investment that does well.

Forty Billion Different Ways to Diversify

In the rest of this chapter, I want to explore some of the different ways that you might diversify your investments. As we saw at the beginning of the chapter, there are unlimited ways to diversify. I am going to present some of the ideas that I have used, and trust that you will think up a hundred others.

DIVERSIFY ACROSS MARKETS

First, don't put all your money into individual stocks that you pick, or into individual bonds. The stock market is mean country. It is tough on everyone who comes in, and requires constant monitoring. It is certainly the highest-risk direction you could go (with the possible exception of junk bonds), although it might offer very high reward. In chapters 7 and 8 we will explore what you can try in the stock markets, and offer some support to ease the risk and the work, but it is at all times the high-risk option.

Furthermore, depending on your background and education, it is entirely possible that you might start picking stocks and do everything wrong. If you want to work that side of the street, then ease over to it. Test yourself and see how you are doing before you make any huge commitment. What I have done is buy both mutual funds and individual stocks. I slowly worked up to a position where I have eleven stocks now. That has varied from one to fifteen at a time, and I took a long time to get more than four. I also own seven different mutual funds, and my plan is to watch things for two or three years. If I find that my own stock picks are doing either much better or much worse than the mutual funds, I will make some adjustments. It is possible that I might even forego buying individual stocks.

Some of the same ideas apply to the bond market, although it might not be quite so dangerous. Of special concern is the so-called junk-bond market. Those are bonds that offer unusually high yields. Remember that higher return implies there are higher risks.

DON'T PUT ALL YOUR EGGS IN ANY OTHER BASKET, EITHER

Diversify by choosing more than one investment. Some of the people who bought nothing in 1992 *but* IBM stock, or Wang Labs bonds, or the Lexington Strategic Gold Fund, have been hurt badly. Some others who balanced those investments among five or six others were not hurt so bad. If you have discretionary, risk-oriented capital of perhaps $10,000 or more, then you, or a good advisor, should be able to identify four or five decent investments you can use. That could provide a reasonable balance of risk and return in different situations. If you have no more than $4,000 or $5,000, use a mutual fund, so that they will plan and provide the diversification for you. Or use two or three mutual funds with differing investment strategies. If you buy a mutual fund that specializes in small companies, you might balance that with another fund that specializes in large, well-established ones. If you choose to buy stock in several oil companies, you might balance that with a trucking company stock, on the theory that they will do better when gasoline prices are down. This kind of diversification is complex, and may be the area where you have to do the most homework, or seek some outside help (perhaps from an investment club).

It would not be great diversification strategy to put all of your money into five different savings and loan companies, or to buy four automobile companies, or five gold-mining outfits. The problem is that if you own stocks in companies that all share the same markets and products, they might all go bad at once. There is usually a presumption that when you buy a mutual fund, you get automatic diversification, but that can fail in some ways. If the fund only buys oil-company stocks, or biotechnology companies, or candy companies, then there is not much diversification in that. The advantage in using Mighty Motors, Good Foods, and U.S. bonds in the example was that they could be expected to behave differently in different economic conditions.

DIVERSIFY OVER TIME

When you first start out, you should plan on keeping a lot of money in cash or money markets funds. No matter what your investment plan is, it would probably be a mistake to invest all the money at once. There is no great hurry, and haste can cost more than it rewards. Take time to buy one stock or one mutual fund. Then take time to think about how you are doing before you pick something else—perhaps a bond, or a fund of bond investments. For most small investors who might end up buying five to ten investments, it would be reasonable to take six months to get 75 percent of your money invested. I took over a year, of which the first six months was dedicated to research. But the initial investments should be made with a view of what your final mixture of stocks, bonds, and funds could be. That means you should be following a plan.

Practice Time/Game Time

RESULTS FOLLOW THE PREPARATION

If you have found a very reliable broker or financial advisor, it might seem reasonable to throw in all the money at once. She could probably make up a good plan in a few days. The catch is, how do you know she is smart and experienced and reliable until you see some of how she works for you? Remember that any recommendations or results you hear initially are from a biased sample. Your friends' recommendations may be valuable, but their financial plans are different from yours. When will you know how this broker will work for you? Only after you have tested her.

DIVERSIFY ACROSS COMPANY SIZE

For much of the past ten years, small company stocks have, on balance, done better than big company stocks. That may continue; it may not. The small company stocks are interesting because they offer the greatest chances for strong growth. If GE does great work, revenues might increase by 10 percent next year, but if Fred's Fertilizer in Nashville does great work, they could have a 10,000 percent increase, with profits going through the roof. Of course, there is also a greater risk of Fred going bankrupt.

Another fact of life for the small companies is that it may be more difficult to get good, up-to-date news. Every day, the *Wall Street Journal* is going to tell me all the news on GE, but they may not ever report about Fred's new fleet of trucks. Or his high debt from buying them.

With a multibillion dollar corporation there is a legitimate presumption that they know something and have some markets. With the small and new companies, we might have to search for months to find two of them that look promising. If you decide to try the small-company market, it might be best to buy a mutual fund that has a good record on specializing in that group. Another way is to study small publicly traded companies in your own town or state. You should have a better chance of getting good information about them.

DIVERSIFY YOUR SOURCES OF INFORMATION

Remember that we can't be too confident of our own infallible judgment. Pretty soon, we will explore the ways to find good information, but whichever way you decide to use, be receptive to varying sources. I read some local papers for local and North Carolina business information. That's part of my investment strategy. I study (not browse, but *study*) the *Wall Street Journal* and *Barron's* for the national business scene and hard data on my investments. I have selected two particular investment advisors that seem to make sense for me (*The Value Line* and Martin Zweig). All that takes a good bit of time and energy, but I still keep an eye open and an ear alert for ideas or news or recommendations from other directions. I reject about 98 percent of that as extra noise, but I don't totally ignore it. You never can tell.

THE EXPENSES THAT ATTEND DIVERSIFICATION

If the small investor does her own stock picking, then typically she might own between five and ten stocks. That number is restricted by the amount of money available, the amount of time for research, and the investor's knowledge. If the fees for each purchase and sale average out to 2–3 percent of the amount invested, then that is a lot of money going into the broker's hands. The total fees can be reduced by buying bigger blocks of stock. You can buy 200 shares of one stock a lot cheaper than 50 shares each of four stocks. For example, if you had $6,500 to put into stocks, with one well-known discount broker, you might buy:

50 shares at $30	and pay a fee of $55
50 shares at $20	and pay a fee of $47
50 shares at $10	and pay a fee of $39
50 shares at $70	and pay a fee of $55

For a total investment of $6,500, your total fees would be $196, or 3 percent of your investment. On the other hand, for 200 shares at $32.50, you would only pay $98.10 in fees.

So the investor has some choices between reducing fees and getting adequate diversification. Some experts say that a decently diversified stock portfolio should have at least ten stocks. That becomes a significant problem for the investor with less than $20,000. If you were making the same stock purchases at a full-service broker such as Merrill-Lynch, the fees would be higher. Of course, they also offer research and advice which might be worthwhile. That is an individual judgment call and should be part of your personal investment strategy.

Tax Considerations

I am not a tax specialist, and don't wish to advise anyone on tax matters. However, that said, a few things are pretty obvious. If you can invest in a tax-sheltered plan, such as an IRA or a 401(k) plan, that is better[12] than paying taxes on all of your dividends and capital gains each year. There are two possible reservations: first, the money in tax-sheltered plans is generally not readily available whenever you want to use it. Second, some employer-sponsored 401(k) plans don't offer a whole lot of good investment options, or much diversification. (And some of them *do* offer good choices.) If you have a chance to invest through an IRA or 401(k) plan, then certainly look at it very closely. You might even want to have some money in tax-sheltered plans and also have another side account for ready access to the money. One important advantage of an employer-sponsored 401(k) plan is that you

[12] Better for most investors, who can expect their tax rate after retirement to be lower than before.

can probably put more money into it than an IRA, and your employer may contribute to it, too.

If you have money in a tax-sheltered account, it might be one where you can choose any investments you want, for example, a self-directed IRA. In that case, do not use tax-exempt investments within a tax-sheltered account. The tax-exempt bonds, for example municipal bonds, pay less than other bonds. A municipal bond paying 6 percent is better than a corporate bond paying 8 percent if you are paying 30 percent taxes on the dividends, but if the income is already tax-sheltered, then the higher yield is better. Even that idea depends on some assumptions about your tax rates after retirement. Also, don't buy zero-coupon bonds (see Chaper Six) until you understand the tax requirements. There are a lot of different angles to figuring tax advantages. The planning has to be tailored to the needs of each individual or family.

The Small Investor Looks for a Safe Path

If you are in a high-income situation where the tax costs become serious, then by all means include tax planning in your personal investment strategy. Talk to a professional who can help you see the costs and benefits of different options.

A Review of Personal Investment Strategic Planning

Let's review and summarize some key ideas.

1. You must have a plan, otherwise you're just playing games with your money.
2. Your entire personal finance situation and expectations should be reviewed as part of your planning process. How much money can you risk?
3. The stock market, bond market, and mutual funds involve more risk and more work than just keeping your money in the bank.
4. How much work and research do you want to do? Picking stocks requires lots of work; bonds may take somewhat less (arguable point); and mutual funds require much less.
5. How much background and experience in business and finance do you have? Picking stocks requires some knowledge and experience, bonds perhaps less, and mutual funds still less.
6. How much do you want to rely on a paid professional, or a team of professionals to help you? You can pay higher fees for a full-service brokerage firm, or rely completely on one or more mutual funds.
7. How do you want to diversify? Again, there is the question of whether you want to manage that yourself or pay someone else to plan it.
8. What kinds of risk and reward guidelines will you try to meet? If your investments do very well or very poorly, how will you decide when to sell?
9. Do you have the stomach for it?
10. How will this affect the rest of your lifestyle, and is it worthwhile?

Recommended Further Reading

I particularly recommend *The Money Game*. Never mind that it's over twenty years old—some of the basic facts of life just don't change that much. *A Guide to the Financial Markets* and *Invest Your Way to Wealth* are both very good for beginners.

Bernstein, Jacob. *Investor's Quotient: The Psychology of Successfully Investing in Commodities and Stocks.* New York: John Wiley & Sons, 1993.

Geisst, Charles R. *A Guide to the Financial Markets.* New York: St. Martin's Press, 1989.

Miller, Theodore. *Kiplinger's Invest Your Way to Wealth.* : Kiplinger Books, 1995.

Smith, Adam. *The Money Game.* New York: Random House, 1976.

Smith, Adam. *Supermoney.* New York: Random House, 1972 (out of print).

CHAPTER 4

Professional Help

Small Investors need to know:

- Do I have to buy a seat on the stock exchange?

- What kinds of help can I get, for what kinds of prices?

- How does the professional person fit into my personal investment strategy?

- What process will help me choose a good broker, or other professional?

- How can I control the costs in working with a professional?

- Where should I look for more information?

The Small Investor Hires a Gun

An investment strategy has to recognize and manage risks. That's kind of tough if you haven't seen enough of the history or learned enough about other people's losses. It might be wise to ask someone who has been around longer, or has an education in finance, or access to a lot of research material. You might think, for instance, that there is no risk in buying long-term United States Treasury bonds—guess again! Ask a pro, he or she will tell you about the very real risks. Your investment strategy should guide your money into places where the balance of risk and rewards fits your personal situation. An important part of that strategy might be finding professional help.

You understand about dentists, plumbers, and lawyers. There are some necessary jobs or services in life that we just don't tackle alone. That also applies to getting in and out of financial markets. There are many different types of investment services available, and this chapter is going to help you decide how many and which of those professional services you want to hire.

The starting point is this: no matter how smart and independent you may be, if you decide to invest in the financial markets, at some time you have to actually buy a security, or a fund. Later on, you may want to sell it. When you buy, you need the services of some sort of investment professional, and again when you sell.

Here again we are going to look at lots of choices. You don't need to become an expert in all of the varieties and flavors; you just need to decide on one or two that will help you be a successful investor.

Mutual Funds: Looking for the Easy Way

In chapters 9 and 10, we are going to take a long look at the opportunities and risk (that word again) in mutual funds. I agree with those who say that mutual funds offer an excellent way for the small investor to have a chance at reasonable returns with moderate risk. For many individual investors, mutual funds offer the only reasonable avenue to get into the markets. For example, if you absolutely detest reading financial statements, or working any calculations with percentages, or if you simply refuse to do any more than the minimum required amount of work, then mutual funds may be right for you. Or you might be better off simply staying away from financial markets.

The full discussion of mutual funds starts in chapter 9, but briefly, a mutual fund is a business managed by an investment company that will sell you shares, and promise to buy them back from you at the current fair price on any given day. They will use your money to invest in stocks and bonds.

There are many potential advantages to using mutual funds. For the small investor who might want to risk $100 each month, it would be impractical to buy individual stocks or bonds. The transaction fees from a broker would be greater than the profits. Some mutual funds will let you buy in at that rate, or perhaps $300 each quarter. That is particularly appropriate if you are working on a retirement account. Some mutual funds require an initial investment of $3,000 or more, but waive the minimum, or greatly reduce it for an Individual Retirement Account. Even if you have built up a pile of savings to start with, if it is less than $20,000, you should use mutual funds. You probably could not get decent diversification investing on your own in individual securities.

The three main promises of mutual funds are *less work*, *better diversification*, and *better management* than most of us could provide on our own. In fact those three promises still make sense for those of us who might hire a broker or a professional money manager.

Not Enough Good Professionals to Go Around

The paragraph above described the best-case scenario for mutual funds. In reality it is not so simple. There are now more than 8,000 mutual funds holding roughly $1 trillion in stocks and much more in bonds. Suppose that each fund has at least one dedicated primary manager and on average one analyst for every $50 million dollars of assets. This adds up to over 25,000 people who share the responsibility for managing the funds. Do you believe that those 25,000 people are all experienced, intelligent, well trained, and ethical? Do you believe that most of them are more capable than most of us? I do not believe it. In fact, you would do well to ask some questions in that direction. The results achieved by mutual funds over the past quarter, or year, or five or ten years show that there are always some losers. And there are consistent losers. In 1994, the CGM Capital Development Fund lost 23

percent and the Steadman Technology and Growth Fund lost 37 percent. In the five-year period ending with 1994, the latter lost 61 percent.
Once each quarter, *Barron's* runs a full section of mutual-fund results.
They show recent dividend yields and total return over the preceding
quarter, year, or five years, compiled by Lipper Analytical Service. That
is one of the places to look for help when you start studying mutual
funds. That list will always include a bunch of funds that you will be
glad to not have owned.

Chapter 10 is devoted to the question of picking a mutual fund, or
two or three, that might be good for you. That is a critical question that
deserves your time and attention. After all, you understand there is no
free lunch. If the only work and the only decision that you will handle
on your own are to pick a mutual fund, you better get it right.

Choosing an Investment Company

Mutual funds are managed by investment companies. If you are planning to buy mutual funds, you might buy only from one company that
has several funds, or from several companies. If you choose to use several companies, you will obviously have more choices of funds to buy,
but staying with one company will be simpler. Of course, simplicity
and convenience are among the main reasons why anyone chooses
mutual funds for their investments. How should you go about selecting a company? Some of them offer dozens or even hundreds of funds.

If an investment company has an office close to your home, that
might be of value to you. Some folks just feel better if they have the
chance to sit down face-to-face and get to know a real live person who
represents the firm. All of your mutual-fund business could be handled over the telephone and by mail, but it might be easier or more
satisfactory to get questions answered if there is a representative near.
What are you going to do if they send you a monthly statement that
you can't understand? It is easier to arrive at clear explanations if you
can sit down next to a representative who will go over the statement
with you.

What about your bank? They probably advertise their investment
services, and you may well feel that it would be nice to keep your financial business with the bank you know and have been dealing with for

ten years. I'm afraid the news is not very comforting on that. I contacted four large banks in my area that currently advertise investment services, including my own bank, with whom I have been doing business for fifteen years.

Those banks did not have much to offer. I have never yet, after repeated tries, been able to find a service representative on duty in any office who had any knowledge of the investment services other than indicating another office that I could call. The fact is that, for legal reasons, those banks do not offer investment service through their branches. Instead, they have purchased or set up subsidiary businesses for brokerage service. They want you to contact and deal with a brokerage firm with whom the bank has an arrangement to share fees or profits.

Your bank may have ten to one hundred offices in your area. Ask them if the brokerage subsidiary has any. Ask them if they can consolidate your financial statements to show your loans, savings, checking, credit cards, and investments in one useful monthly statement. Ask them if they can arrange to have funds automatically transferred in or out of your money market account when you buy or sell mutual funds or stocks. Find out if your personal bank service representative has any knowledge of investing or is willing to counsel you. Find out if the bank has anything to offer besides giving you a name and telephone number of a broker. If they do, that may be of value to you. My experience has been that they do not.

On the other hand, the larger investment companies do offer many services similar or identical to those found in banks, and will offer to integrate those services with your investment needs. It might make more sense to take your banking business to an investment company rather than vice versa. You should carefully evaluate both convenience and breadth of services before deciding whether to consolidate the two areas.

If you do decide to handle your investments through your bank, there is one thing that it's essential for you to learn, and that's how many mutual funds they can sell, and what kinds of variety and fee structure they offer. Do not let your bank push you into the arms of a broker that only sells funds with sales commissions attached (front-end loads, see chapter 9).

Stockbrokers

The following is a critical exercise. Keep your money carefully locked away until you are confident that you can pass this test.

Repeat in a firm, loud, and clear voice:

No, thank you.
No! I am not interested in that investment.
No, I do not want to hear any more about it!
No. Thank you, and good-bye

Repeat that out loud, several times, until you feel comfortable and confident in saying it. If you cannot get comfortable in saying it, then do not contact any stockbrokers—leave your money in a bank, or in a mutual fund.

If you cannot do this, and if you nevertheless persist in talking to stockbrokers, then you are (pardon the expression) dead meat.

Practice Saying NO!

One of the large national brokerage firms has been running a series of ads on TV in which they show some people at work being annoyed by their stockbrokers. They then break into the scene and describe how they are so much nicer, how they don't harass clients, how their attitude is a more refined and professional approach of waiting on your pleasure and convenience. Their point is that you should find a sweet broker. The ad misses the mark. The fault is not with the aggressive brokers, but with the passive clients. The clients whom they picture are apparently unable or unwilling to tell their brokers, "Buzz off, Charlie, I'm at work and have business to attend to."

A relationship with a stockbroker is a business relationship, not a social one. Woe to you if you can't remember that! You may find a broker who is competent, friendly, sociable, honest, and successful. But he or she is also a shark. It's a business for sharks. They live on commissions and competition with all of the other brokers. The industry is cutthroat and aggressive. For a stockbroker, no sales means no income.

The *Wall Street Journal* regularly runs full-column stories in small print about disciplinary or legal action against brokers or firms in the business. Do you know why they run them in small print? Because there are too many cases to run all of them in regular, readable type. I think I know some honest, reliable, professional brokers. But there are as many types of broker as of doctor, lawyer, or writer. Be prepared to deal with them.

If you do begin talking to brokers, investment companies, financial advisors, or if you subscribe to certain publications, there is a good chance that your name and telephone number will get spread around. Be prepared to say no. Be ready to call your state securities registration office if anyone harasses you about investing.[13]

But now, given all that negativism, maybe we can find a good broker, with good references and experience. By all means, try. It can be a rewarding experience if you succeed. Here are a few ideas that should help.

Try the following approach and talk to at least a half dozen brokers if you are going to talk to one. Ask your friends. If any of them have a broker they been happy with for five or more years, talk to him or her.

---

[13] Every state has a securities registration office. It is usually part of the Secretary of State's duties.

Seek a broker with several years' experience. I would insist on at least five years. If you merely call or walk into a brokerage office, you may be assigned to the newest green hand in the office who doesn't have much to do. If you don't have a specific reference, ask for their most experienced broker, or one with at least several years with the firm. I know from personal consultation that one of the large and highly regarded brokerage firms with an office nearby has one of the best brokers I have ever spoken to, and one of the dumbest. You don't want to just call that office and settle for anybody who is available.

Be thoroughly honest and direct with the broker, and expect the same in return. If at any point you feel as though she is pressuring you, then say so, or leave. If he says things you just don't understand, then tell him so. If he cannot or will not simplify the discussion to your comfort level, then leave or cross him off the candidates list. Do not try to pretend any greater knowledge than you have—the broker will be able to tell, and may use it to your disadvantage.

Ask the broker about her career, training, and experience. Ask for references. Ask how she would evaluate your investment needs and risk tolerance. Judge whether she is listening to your interests and needs or trying to fit you into her plans. Take notes so you will be able to compare several brokers weeks after the interviews.

FULL-SERVICE OR DISCOUNT BROKER?

The brokerage business is highly competitive. As you might expect, people invent many clever ways to discriminate their services and price structure. One of the most popular methods is called "discount brokerage service." Their fees for handling each individual transaction may commonly be one-third to one-half of a full-service brokerage firm's fees. Discount firms include Olde Discount Brokers, Fidelity, Charles Schwab, and Waterhouse. There are many others. The full-service firms include most of the biggest names in the business: Merrill Lynch, Prudential, Dean Witter, PaineWebber.

Every broker has some special services or convenience that might be attractive to you, but the primary differences between the discounters and the full-service firms are research and price. A full-service broker probably has the benefits of a large research department offering steady new evaluations of the economy, the markets, and individual stocks or bonds. You pay for that. The discount broker will usually just take your order and send a monthly activity statement for your account. How should you decide which type to use?

There is no universal answer, but here are a few guidelines. If you feel that you need the advice of professional analysts before buying or selling, the full-service broker offers exactly that. If you consider yourself knowledgeable and decisive in making investment decisions, a discount broker will be easy to work with. If you are willing to spend some time doing research, and if you feel that you can understand the financial news, a discount broker may be good for you. Certainly if you are in an investment club, and have six or eight friends sharing the thinking, a discount broker can handle all your needs. The brokers at PaineWebber, Dean Witter, and Merrill Lynch might disagree with me on that.

The discount broker is cheaper. The full-service brokerage firm may only handle their own mutual funds, or those that have a load (to pay a sales commission). The discounter may not be any better, or it may handle hundreds of different mutual funds. The full-service broker may be part of a larger financial empire that offers many other useful services. Ask yourself if you need those services.

Just as with any other business, the bottom line is, do they offer the services that you need, and is the cost reasonable? Brokerage fees vary widely, and they change whenever the brokers feel the heat of competition, but here are some representative numbers that were effective in early 1996. The table below shows a range of fees that you might expect to see for various stock transactions.

# of shares	share price	lowest likely fee	highest likely fee
1,000	$25	$125	$400
100	$25	$40	$80
50	$50	$40	$80
100	$10	$40	$50

If you see an ad for free stock transactions, read the fine print. Something is up.

The Problems with Getting Mutual Funds Service Through Your Broker

If you want to buy stocks and bonds, almost any broker can trade almost any stocks or bonds you like. This, however, is not the case with mutual funds. If you select any group of five mutual funds, you will probably have to use several different sources for trading them.

For example, I selected these five mutual funds:

Fund	Type	Load
Century Shares Trust	financial services	0
Evergreen Fund: A	growth	4.75%
Franklin Templeton Japan Fund	Japanese stocks	5.75%
Princor Capital Accumulation	capital appreciation	4.75%
Strong Corporate Bond	income	0

I called five major brokers to see if they would sell those funds. Here are the results:

	Charles Schwab	Merrill Lynch	E. D. Jones	A. G Edwards	Paine Webber
Century	yes	no	no	no	no
Evergreen	yes	no	no	no	yes
Templeton Japan	no	yes	yes	yes	yes
Princor	no	no	no	yes	no
Strong	yes	no	no	no	no

The customer service representatives at the investment firms gave different stories as to why this is. Century Shares does not expect many brokers to handle their funds, due to the lack of sales incentive; no front load means no commission for the sales force. Charles Schwab gets around that, and offers better customer service, by maintaining a single account (an omnibus account) for some no-load funds and then pooling investors' money into that account. Schwab does add on a small fee for the service, but at least their customers don't have to open another account in order to use Century.[14] The broker I spoke to at

---

[14] Schwab has removed the charge for many of their no-load funds.

A.G. Edwards was not even aware that Evergreen Fund: A existed. He thought Evergreen only had a no-load fund that Edwards did not deal with. The fact is that the Evergreen no-load fund has been closed to new investors and they have offered the 4.75 percent load fund in its place. The accounts office at Evergreen said they do have a signed agreement with A.G. Edwards to sell their funds, but the broker said they cannot sell them. The Strong Investment Company, in order to maintain their low selling expenses, has no sales agreements with any brokerage firms. Schwab, again, offers the customer service of maintaining its own omnibus account with Strong and letting customers buy shares through that account. The difference is that when a Schwab customer buys the Strong Investment Fund, the customer does not have a personal account with Strong—only with Schwab.

Does this all sound like too much trouble? It is! The only way to make it easier is to find out which funds a broker will handle before you commit to working with that broker. If a broker says, "All of them," she is almost certainly lying to you—ask about those five listed above or some five funds that are interesting to you. If the broker doesn't know, why would you want to do business there? Ask for a list of all the funds that the broker can sell.

Several brokers or funds managers have suggested to me that I could simply establish another account to accommodate buying a different fund. Then what? Open another account for the next one? And if you want to sell Fund X and buy Fund Z, do you have to go through the exercise for several days of withdrawing money at one brokerage account and taking it to another?

What if you want the money in your IRA? Will you establish multiple IRAs and go through transferring money among them? Do you think that sounds extreme? It is not—several brokers suggested to me that I should do that, although it is a practice the IRS frowns upon. The only time it gets fairly simple is if you decide to use only mutual funds that are managed by a single investment company. For example, Fidelity Investments, Merrill Lynch, or PaineWebber offer fairly diverse groups of funds that would appear to satisfy many investment needs. Of course, there is no guarantee that all of their funds will have relatively high performance or low costs.

Build this factor into your advance planning. Decide ahead of time how important mutual funds will be in your investment strategy. Ask every broker or investment company you talk to to give you a list of all the mutual funds they work with. If they don't have such a list, they don't need your business.

Ask them to give you a written guide as to procedures and expenses if you redeem one fund and use that money to buy into another fund from a different investment company. If you don't get a clear response, then the broker doesn't want your business.

Investment Advisors and Money Managers

As a registered investment advisor, I have to admit I am prejudiced. I will, however, do my best to be fair and evenhanded.

Brokers are mainly salespeople (sniff). What can one expect? On the other hand, there are several types of financial professionals who sell *advice* and *service* for a fee, rather than selling the goods for a commission. They go by the title of registered investment advisor, financial manager, or investment counselors, among others. Some of them specialize in working with retirement planning, overall financial planning, business employee benefit plans, or almost any subset of financial planning.

There is also a group of financial services that are available free. Some companies, including many insurance companies, will offer free financial planning and advice. Truly free! No obligation. Possibly good advice. I would be reluctant to make any generalized evaluation of these folks. I have talked to some who are knowledgeable and helpful. However, be advised: these people do not work for fun only. Someone is paying their salaries while they are helping you. If Prudential is going to pay someone to offer you free financial counseling, then is it not possible that they expect some return on their largess? Is it not possible that the advisor might feel a bias towards insurance or annuities? Maybe. It might still be good advice; you will have to decide for yourself. But whenever you find yourself talking to someone who offers free financial counseling, keep in mind that their employer expects to somehow make a profit on the situation.

The Small Investor Gets Free Advice

INVESTMENT ADVISORS

You gotta love us! For a fee, we will spend some time with you and tell you how to invest. Or, for a fee, we will take your money and invest it for you and keep the records.

The fees may typically run $60 to $120 per hour for advice, or 1 percent to 2 percent of the total amount under management. There can of course be extremes of very low or very high fees in some cases. An advisor with an office in Manhattan will probably be much more expensive than one with an office in Paris, Kentucky.

There is no way to judge the quality and value of the advice unless you know the person's track record or spend some time talking to him. Do not be deceived by his title. In order to be a registered investment advisor, one must pass an exam on investment law, but nobody ever checks up on actual investment skill or judgment. Be just as cautious in selecting an investment advisor as you would be in choosing a broker. Also, check with your state securities registration office. They keep records on all the advisors registered in your state. They can tell you whether any advisor or broker has been the subject of complaints.

You might choose to hire an investment advisor who offers only advice, not brokerage or money management service. That may be worthwhile, but keep in mind that you still have to go to a broker somewhere along the line to actually buy and sell stuff. That will require another fee.

MONEY MANAGERS

People who label themselves money managers typically don't offer much advice. They basically just take the money and manage it. Such managers will usually offer their services for some set annual fee, which may be 1 percent or 2 percent of the amount you have invested through them. Most money managers will have some minimum level account they are willing to handle. The minimum will commonly be perhaps a million dollars or more. The small investor is usually shut out of this service.

Michael Stolper is the president of a company that, among other things, evaluates money managers. He has written a nice guide to selecting a money manager that is available by writing to: Stolper and Company, 525 B Street, Suite 630, San Diego, CA 92101-4409. Generally, we will not be using the same managers that he rates, because they have minimum investment limits that shut us out. However, the book is still very instructive and useful for all investors. My favorite line is his description of computer methods: "Computer prowess is a myth—intellectual and judgmental skills are the only sustainable edge in this, or any other, business."

He also observes that people have been known to manipulate statistics in order to make their own results look good. Of course, every financial services firm does that to some extent (it's called advertising), but there should be some kind of limit. However, Stolper wryly suggests: "Methods of manipulation are only limited by the imaginations of those looking to mislead you."

Is there a lesson here for us? Indeed there is. Be suspicious of all of the statistics and claims you see. Think about whether you actually understand whatever the numbers are supposed to represent. If you do not understand, it is not your fault. It is the fault of the person who prepared the information.

SPECIAL ATTENTION FOR THE ELDERLY

Any financial services professional should be able to help any client. Do the elderly have special needs, and can they get specialized help? They may or may not. It depends on the individual. Certainly their money is just as good as anyone's, and they want to be careful with it.

There are a few financial managers or investment counselors who give more of their time and attention to older people. They might well have greater knowledge of conservative investments, tax advantages, or estate planning. They might be more patient and skillful at simplifying the choices to be made. They might offer help with managing insurance claims or paying routine bills. Some advisors might even help you find other services such as cleaning or transportation. If you or a loved one need this sort of financial help, ask around among friends or senior citizens' organizations. There might be one in your city. Such an advisor probably will not come any cheaper than others, but might be easier to talk to.

Grading the Service You Buy

Any financial professional you deal with needs your fees and commissions. He or she will try to hold on to you and your business. They may even act like you have a lifetime service contract, and have no business thinking about other options. Not so! It's your money and your future, and you bear sole responsibility. I am reluctant to tell you that you *absolutely must* do anything, but just this one time: *You* absolutely must *evaluate the results on a regular basis.*

If the results are not satisfactory, plan on making a change. You may or may not want to discuss it with the current broker/advisor/manager, but you have to make up your mind what to do. Nobody else can make that decision for you. If you don't make the decision, that is equivalent to deciding to put your future in the other person's hands.

How to evaluate? Here are some guidelines.

First of all, be reasonable. If you required your broker to be selling you stocks that always increase 50 percent each year, no broker would ever be good enough. If you required your mutual fund to be in the top 10 percent for gains every week, you would always be changing funds, and always losing money on commissions.

So what is reasonable? That is up to you—it's a judgment call. For me, reasonable means that the investment results consistently avoid major losses, and usually do better than some other safe choices. For example, I could make 5.5 percent on U.S. savings bonds, so I want my investments to do better than that.

For instance, I went into one recent year thinking that the major stock averages might appreciate 8 percent to 10 percent. I set a goal of doing at least that well. I keep one of my accounts in mutual funds and the other in individual stocks. I think that the stock market account carries higher risks, and I know it carries higher expenses, therefore I impose a standard that the stock account must do better than the mutual funds, or I will change the plan.

You might reasonably decide to require that your investments meet the following target goals:

1. Each mutual fund should stay in the top half of its peer class each year; *Barron's* and the *Wall Street Journal* and *Business Week* and numerous other magazines will give you the data to check on this.
2. No investment should ever lose more than 10 percent in a given quarter, but this guideline has to be compared to overall market performance and otherwise tempered with reasonableness.
3. No individual stock should fall more than 10 percent (or maybe 15 percent) below the purchase price.
4. The yearly results should always produce profits at least 5 percent above what you could have had on a five-year CD from your bank.
5. The investments that you regard as being high risk must return proportionately greater profits, or else you should stop using them.

There are other ways to do this, but the point is you should set some goals or standards. Evaluate your results once every six months or so. If the results are not satisfactory, then make a change. That change might mean selling a stock, or changing mutual funds, or firing your broker.

Bad News! Changing Brokers

Sometimes, for any one of a variety of reasons, you may want to change brokers. The change process may be a nuisance, or it may be a disaster.

> **WARNING: Before you buy any product from any broker, find out what you would have to do if you wanted to leave their business and take your assets elsewhere. If you don't get a simple and clear response, then do not walk away, but run like mad for the nearest exit.**

If, at any time, for any reason, you lose confidence in a broker, then drop him or her. Never stay with a financial advisor who is causing you anger or frustration. Don't stay with a financial advisor who has consistently failed to achieve the goals you have set for yourself. Any investor may take the occasional loss, but you must be willing to weed out a regular loser.

The Small Investor Fires His Gun

One problem commonly arises when moving your assets. Let's assume you have made a decision to move the account, and you have successfully completed the process of finding a new broker. If the old account held a mutual fund that was sold only by that brokerage fund, then you would have to sell that fund before transferring the assets. Some financial services firms might allow you to transfer their funds across brokerage accounts, but there is no uniform practice on that yet.

Before moving anything, ask your new broker to review everything in the old account. She should tell you just which part she recommends you should keep or sell, and which can be directly transferred to the new account without going through a sale. The new broker should also be able to take care of the details and paperwork of the asset transfer. Be prepared for this to take a few days. The brokerage firms haven't learned much about data communications yet. If you considered the possibility of a move before you invested at the first broker, then this should be painless. If you did not, then it could get complicated and unpleasant. For example, if you held a mutual fund with a deferred sales charge (back-end load) and wanted to move on after just one year with the old broker, then that back-end load might eat up 3 or 4 percent of the value in the fund.

If you hold stocks that are traded on a major stock exchange, a direct transfer of the stocks will be done through the Automated Customer Account Transfer System. Don't let the old broker persuade you that you have to sell them and transfer the cash; this would just generate unnecessary extra commissions and extra costs for you. If the investments are part of an IRA, you do not want to take any money in hand during the transfer. That might generate some surprise extra taxes.

If at any time, for any reason, you feel as though the broker whom you are dismissing is not helping you make a smooth and orderly transfer, call your state securities registration office. I guarantee you that this will produce immediate full cooperation by all concerned. The brokers are not going to risk their state registration because of your little account. It might also be helpful to contact the stock exchanges, or the NASD (National Association of Securities Dealers), but I would start with the state office.

Guidelines for Finding Help

In summary, here are a few things that you might think about when hiring a broker or any kind of professional financial help:

1. **Professionalism:** Advisors should have their skin in the game, too. Be very cautious about accepting advice from people who are not in the business.
2. **Compensation:** What are the fees? How do they get paid? What are they selling?
3. **Experience:** There is very high turnover and lots of shoddy training going on. Experience and recommendations should be counted heavily.
4. **Convenience:** Even if you do 95 percent of the business by telephone, it might be worthwhile to sit down face to face with the broker sometime.
5. **Sincerity:** A very tough call—the field is wide open to phonies and sharks. Find a person who is a good listener and has time to talk about your personal situation. Ask several candidates to make up a short list of what might be good investments for you, and use the lists to try to evaluate whether the broker was really listening to you and understood your needs.
6. **Recommendations:** They should be willing to provide names of a few of their current clients—or you might inquire around among some friends whose judgment you respect.
7. **Reputation:** Again a tough call; you have to look at both the individual broker and the firm and then sort through tons of good and bad things that people might say about any of them.
8. **Price:** Costs vary dramatically. Insist on getting straight answers on fees. You might not want to go with the lowest costs, but you certainly want to know what the fees will be.
9. **Service:** Will this particular professional person provide all of the services that you want from them? Buying and selling stocks, bonds, funds, annuities; advice and research, checking; credit cards?

Recommended Further Reading

Brimelow, Peter. *The Wall Street Gurus: How You Can Profit from Investment Newsletters*. Alexandria, VA: Minerva Books, 1988.

Marcial, Gene. *Secrets of the Street: The Dark Side of Making Money*. New York: McGraw-Hill, 1995.

Mayer, Martin. *Markets*. New York: W. W. Norton, 1990.

Smith, Charles W. *The Mind of the Market: A Study of Stock Market Philosophies, Their Uses, and Their Implications*. Lanham, MD: Rowman & Littlefield, 1981.

CHAPTER 5

If You Snooze, You Lose

Small Investors need to know:
- How do I begin to plan my personal investment strategy?
- What are my resources as a small inexperienced investor?
- What and where are the good sources of information?

Do It the Old-Fashioned Way

I do not personally know anyone who has gotten rich quickly or easily, and this book is not about the easy way. I don't know about the easy way. Although I once held a stock that went up tenfold, I don't believe that will ever happen to me again. Charles Dow, who had a lot more experience than we do, said that the folks who try to get rich quick usually end up losing, and those who try to gain steady, consistent, reasonable profits sometimes end up getting rich. This chapter is about finding and using information to help you do the essential work and make you a better investor.

One of the best sources of information is at once the easiest and the most difficult: it is what you know about your own situation. It is the easiest because it is always right at hand and you are the expert, but it is difficult because it requires you to take a hard and honest look at your lifestyle and finances. That can be a challenge, but you have to do it. You can begin to do some of your own strategic investment planning. That will include a look at your overall financial situation. Take out a piece of paper. Right! Take out a piece of paper! If you are not going to do a little bit of work, then this business is not for you.

Here is an easy idea for a worksheet to start some investment strategy plans. Follow through the next few paragraphs and keep some notes. This process will help you create a summary sheet, a tool that will help you make some important decisions.

You should produce some lists to help you decide how much money to put at risk, and where it will come from. The following two charts are examples of what you might be working towards as you read through the rest of this section. The numbers and examples are just fictional samples of what someone might do; they are not recommendations for you, just examples. Part 1 is for what you already own, and part 2 is for your continuing income.

Asset Allocation Worksheet
(make a similar chart on a pad of paper)

Part 1

Asset	Value	At risk investing	Loss potential
home equity	$90,000	$10,000	$5,000
sell boat	$20,000	$10,000	$5,000
existing 401K plan at work	$18,000	$18,000	$9,000
existing savings	$14,000	$2,000	$1,000

Part 2

Income source	Amount per month	Current expenses	Savings	At risk investing	Loss potential
salary (take home)	$2500	$1900	$200	$400	$200
alimony	$1000	$400	$200	$400	$200

You are going to put some of your financial assets into the charts. Assets are things of value that belong to you. They include your home, your savings account, your jewelry, and insurance or annuities, plus any investments you might have now. If you own a boat, that is an asset, but not a financial asset. If you sell it to raise investment capital, then the new money becomes a financial asset.

Only put the things in the charts that you think you might want to use for investing purposes, which also means things that you can accept the risk of losing. Everything that you might consider as going into financial markets should go into one of these two lists. The things that you know you would never give up, for example, the insurance policy on the principal breadwinner in your family or the value of personal jewelry, don't have to go in here. For the first part of this exercise, don't fill in the two right-side columns, the at risk and loss columns.

Before you start putting money into equities markets, spend a little time with your spouse, a friend, your children, or somebody else who cares enough to share their thoughts. Construct a set of notes before you get into the charts. Making the notes will help you keep things in perspective. Consider your age, health, and prospective continuing income. How will they affect your ability to accept risk and loss? Talk about your housing assets, mortgage, and vacation or education plans, and how much of your income that will require. Look at your legal commitments such as taxes, loans, or child support. If there is something in there that you might put at risk in financial markets, and if you can accept the possible loss of part of it, then write something on the charts.

The Small Investor Talks It Over

Talk about your savings, retirement accounts, or tax-deferred investment accounts. What assets do you already have that are exposed to market risks or other financial risks? Write those down in part 1. Look at your insurance. Do you need insurance? Do you know what you are insuring? Can you estimate the value of your insurance in terms of future payments or current cash values? Is this a source that you want to use to provide funds for investing? For most folks, the answer is probably no. Most people will want to keep their insurance separate from their investments, but the choice *is* worth considering.

No one else can tell you exactly how those things should be balanced to produce a proper view of risk. What every financial advisor will tell you is that it would be unwise to even look at financial markets unless you have thought about those other factors. This book will help you organize your thoughts about how the markets fit into your overall financial plans. If you have great difficulty or concerns with this part of the planning, that might indicate a good reason for you to talk to a professional financial planner or investment advisor.

In part 1, on the left side, write the names of things you own that might provide value for investing purposes. Would you consider selling your boat to raise investment capital? Do you want to cash in an insurance policy to raise money for investing? If you want to use some of your money for real-estate investing or to start a business, then *do not* put that money in part 1. Those things may be good investments, but they are distinct from the financial market opportunities that we are looking at.

By now you should have considered most of your assets, your current income, projected future income, home, paid-up insurance, or annuities. If you have current investments, those too are assets. The current investments should be included in part 1 to remind you of the full extent of your diversification and your possible losses.

Now we go into the hard part: putting your money at risk. This will use the two right-hand columns in each chart. For each of the items that you identified in either part 1 or part 2, choose a dollar value that represents how much of that item you might put into financial markets. There is no hard and fast rule here; it's your own personal judgment call. Put that number in the at risk investing column.

What are you willing to put into risk-oriented investing? Write down the number that shows how much of each current asset you are willing to put at risk. In part 2, write down how much of current income you are willing to put at risk, and how much you need for current living expenses or for current savings. Current savings includes the money you set aside for unexpected needs such as car repair. You want to have some money set aside for things of this nature. Some advisors say that you need to have six months take-home pay set aside for emergencies.

The at risk list contains something from current assets, savings or investments, current income, and future income. Whatever those "at risk" numbers look like, enter half of that value in the loss column. Think about losing that much. Poof, it's gone. Tough luck.

Now here is a serious question: if you should happen to lose that much within a few weeks, could you pick up your life and go on with the resources you had left?

Or maybe you didn't lose half of it. Maybe you just lost a third. Same question: can you pick up your life and go on, and face your spouse, kids, mortgage company, and neighbors?

Adjust the numbers in the at risk and loss columns until you can answer the last question yes. It may require that some of the at risk numbers go to zero. If that's the case, you've learned something important about your willingness to take risks. Also, in the exercise above, you have to think about what kind of investor you are going to be. How much is really at risk? If you only buy short-term and intermediate-term government bonds, or the Pimco Low Duration[15] Bonds Mutual Fund, the greatest risk of loss might be just 10 percent. On the other hand, if you expect to plunge into buying stock in new, small companies with little or no current profits, then your risk might be 100 percent of the amount invested. You should think about what kind of investor you want to be, and then plan your dollar value of at-risk capital so you can live with the risk of loss, and then manage your investments to maintain that risk level. It would be equally false and self-defeating to plan for low risk and then buy high-risk investments, or to plan for high risk and then buy only low-risk investments such as

---

[15] Duration will be mentioned in the next chapter, on bonds.

U.S. savings bonds. It's a matter of personal choice and personal analysis. You have to do the hard part yourself.

Do not, that is to say, do not get involved with securities markets until you are able to come up with a figure representing the amount of money that you can face the possibility of losing in a hurry.

Now, are you still with us? You may continue reading, but do not spend any money until you have dealt with the preceding difficult questions. You, or you and your family, must accept the personal responsibility for coming to some kind of answers.

The Small Investor and Family Face Loss

Your Investments Are Only as Good as Your Information

Your personal investment strategy is going to be strongly influenced by how much work you leave to a professional and how much you do yourself. Most of this chapter will focus on finding information to make your own investment decisions, but even if you choose to use a hired investment advisor, money manager, or broker, you still have some work to do.

What kinds of decisions? Certainly to buy, or sell, or hold any particular investment. But there are many others, such as whether to use a certain mutual fund company or to change brokers, or simply whether you are satisfied with the results you have had in the past year. The rest of this chapter details the sources of information that can help you make these decisions.

What Kinds of Investment Tools to Use

This section introduces some tools for different jobs. These are only part of the tools of the professional money managers. They have more experience, more resources, and more money to manage than we do, so they use more and fancier tools. These are the tools that we can use. They are effective, generally cheap, and readily available. They can work well if you are willing to apply your own time and decision making.

NEWSPAPERS

Look in your own locality for good investments. Some of the best opportunities may be close at hand and not yet discovered by many professionals. Your local newspaper probably carries news of local business interest. Read it—someday it will tell you about a small local business that is growing rapidly. See whether it is a publicly traded company; if so, you can buy stock in it. If you can get a local business newspaper, that's even better because you get more information focused on your investment needs. The greatest investment success I have had came after reading in my local business news about an initial public stock offering for a new research and development firm in the area.

You should also try to keep current on national and international business activity. That doesn't mean learn everything; remember rule #2, don't try to obtain perfect information, but do try to maintain a sense of the major stories and trends in business. The best way to do that is through the major national newspapers. Make a habit of reading the business sections of newspapers such as the *Washington Post, New York Times, Miami Herald, Los Angeles Times, USA Today*, or comparable major papers that devote significant resources to business coverage every day.

Or else (trumpets and drums), the *Wall Street Journal (WSJ)*. The single most valuable thing that you can do to improve your knowledge, power, and effectiveness as an investor is to read the *Wall Street Journal,* preferably every day, or at least a few times a week. It offers the best combination of business and general news with analysis of the linkage between different trends, and is written in such a way that everyone can follow most of the stories.

Another excellent and widely circulated investment newspaper is the *Investor's Business Daily (IBD)*. It may be a good choice for you, but I don't read it more than a few times a month. Why not, you ask? Well, basically, no one among us can possibly hope to read everything. We can't even read all of the very good stuff. There is just too much of it. *IBD* is certainly a fine paper, and it may turn out to be your favorite, but not for me. The distinction is that *IBD* focuses on markets and market action and stock prices, whereas the *WSJ* offers a broader perspective of business activity and trends. For me, the view and the perspective from *WSJ* are more useful. By all means, try both and see which works best for you.

For a view that is more tightly focused on markets and finance and stock prices, try *Barron's,* a weekly newspaper published by Dow Jones. It should hit the local newsstand on Saturday, or you can subscribe for home delivery. It requires a little more background to read, and it may be only for investors who are fairly serious about doing their own analysis, but for that need, it is excellent. Do know that while *Barron's* does appear on newsstands on Saturdays, the same edition may reach you through the mail anytime from the following Monday through Thursday, which can compromise the value of the news you receive.

Investor's Business Daily will give you a free ten-day subscription. Take them up on it; it's a real bargain. Call them at 800-366-3131 or check their ads in *Barron's* and the *Wall Street Journal* or on CNBC.

MAGAZINES

Almost every general circulation magazine will carry the occasional article on investing: *Time, Ladies Home Journal*—any of them. I can't judge their value; I don't read them. But you should look at the magazines that are focused on business, money, finance, or investing. There are a lot of them, and everyone has their favorites. Among the available choices are *Forbes, Fortune, Smart Money, Worth, BusinessWeek,* and many more. How shall you sort through them to find something worthwhile? Aha! Again that demon, personal choice. Go to the library or bookstore and sample some of them a few times. After a while you will find one or two for which the writing and logic seem to suit your needs and interests. Then think about how much time and energy you will put into financial reading and research. Do you want to give up the time, energy, and money to subscribe to a weekly or monthly business magazine? How many magazines do you have coming in now that go largely unread?

There is a distinction between the value of general reading and doing in-depth research. If you decide to go into a certain area of business in greater detail, then there are specialized magazines that focus on almost any business you can imagine. I use to subscribe to the *Oil and Gas Journal* because I was making an effort to be up-to-date on those kinds of investments. Many people would find it a bit tedious. There are special journals for tire and rubber, restaurant, food processing, hog raising, whatever you want. If you have good experience in some business and consider making investments in that area, it might be worthwhile to subscribe to their trade journal. Your library or a local business could help you identify it.

Suppose, for example, that you have some knowledge about the automobile business. You might decide to make that an area of investing specialization where you choose and buy individual stocks. Then you should go to some nearby automobile dealers and ask to talk to the owner or general manager. Ask them which trade magazines they read regularly. Ask for some old copies, or just get the subscription information. While you're there, look at the cars, or trucks and vans. Your firsthand opinion of their products may be worth more than all the print in the world. That kind of source could be a research tool for you, if you wanted to work in that area and wanted to do your own research.

INVESTMENT NEWSLETTERS

Investment newsletters are usually small monthly publications that focus on news and opinions of current financial markets. They frequently present little else besides the authors' opinions and analysis. A small sample includes *Investor's Digest, Dow Theory Forecasts, The Zweig Fore-cast, The McClellan Market Report,* and *Grant's Interest Rate Observer.* There are a lot of others. The cost of a year's subscription may commonly be $100 to $500. So what do you do? These folks offer a lot of advice, which is certainly not cheap. Some of them offer good writing and excellent market analysis. It may or may not be worth the cost and your time.

How to decide? Well, your library probably carries a few, and per-haps some of your friends subscribe to one or two more. Sometimes the larger financial newspapers or magazines will carry offers where you can get a free sample of one issue of various newsletters. Even if they don't advertise the free sample, many of them will give you a free sample if you call and ask. Figure out for yourself whether you under-stand what the author is saying. Does it appear to be logical and clear? You can get help with this from a specialized publication called *Hulbert Financial Digest.* That is a publication devoted to rating the value and quality of a lot of investment newsletters. It is excellent, and your nearby college business library should have a copy.

No one else can forecast for you what value you should get from one of these newsletters. They offer a lot of investment advice ranging from the very specific: "buy Coca-Cola, sell Ford"; to the very vague: "be cautious." Some of the investment newsletters are particularly offensive in presenting opinions that are simpleminded. For example, many of them rely on such "advice" as: "The technology area may be putting in a significant near-term top" or "The Dow-Jones Industrial Average could pull back to the 4500 area if it fails to finish at a new high next week." May be putting in a near-term top? Could pull back to 4500 if…? Those kinds of statements are so vague they are of no value to anyone. Nonetheless, some of those newsletters make interesting read-ing; just approach them with a critical eye. None of them guarantee to make you wealthy if you follow their advice.

I rarely study investment newsletters because they rarely show spe-cific advice on stocks or funds that I am interested in at that moment. Also, I feel that there are numerous other publications that give a bet-ter payback for my time and attention, such as *Barron's.* Some of the newsletters may have value for general market education, and some may offer a path to profit if you follow their specific recommendations. They are a mixed bag.

As a special case, *Grant's Interest Rate Observer* is certainly of value as general education. It is expensive and not elementary. But if you choose to get into serious study of interest rates and their effects on markets, it may be essential.

There is another class of periodicals that serve the investment community. This includes some of the most famous publications in the field, and I think some of the best. These are larger and more comprehensive than the investment newsletters mentioned above. In this class you should consider:

> *Value Line Investment Survey*
> *Morningstar Mutual Fund Reports*
> *Standard and Poor's Outlook*

There are others. These publications offer in-depth research, analysis, and historical data on many companies or mutual funds. They also offer very specific buy and sell recommendations, or ratings relative to other companies. They are expensive, typically $300 to $600 per year. If you decide to use those publications, and if you are influenced by their recommendations, remember that the writers do not know you, your current financial situation, or how much risk you're willing to accept. You have to balance all the extra factors against the recommendations in the survey. We will come back to these sources again when we deal with buying and selling stocks or mutual funds.

COMPUTERS AND ON-LINE SERVICES

In this section, I'll try to give you some ideas about the possible uses and limitations of computer methods. Keep in mind that software and on-line providers change so fast that anything I write will be at least partially out of date minutes after the ink is dry on the page.

Remember that no computer system has ever been built that is good enough to do your thinking for you. No software program has ever been developed that is good enough to take responsibility for your money. The essential skills are analysis, judgment, decisiveness, nerve. The computer doesn't do those things.

But computers are good for what they can do. Computer tools may help you do some of your investing work. The areas where they might help the small investor include the following:

1. to collect data about a company or the entire market
2. to see other people's opinions about investment choices
3. to do analysis that requires a lot of calculations or graphing of results
4. to track and analyze your investments

The Tool Doesn't Do Your Thinking for You

The first question is what kind of computer, Macintosh or Windows-compatible PC. The Mac is certainly easier to use, but it appears that there is much more software available for Windows machines (what we once called IBM machines, but which are now made by many manufacturers). On cost they appear to be about even now, although the computer makers and sellers are just as bad as mutual funds about hiding the true cost of their products. If your main need for the computer is something other than investing, then let that guide your purchase decision. If you are using investing as an excuse to buy a computer, get a lot of demonstrations before you buy, and make sure you can return it if you are not satisfied.

There are several useful software applications available (in reading any of the financial newspapers or magazines mentioned in this book, you will be unable to avoid the advertisements for such software).

For instance, a news retrieval service provides up-to-the-minute news on companies (or markets) that you want to follow. By dialing into the news agency's computers you can search for stories on particular firms and make copies of anything that interests you.

Some brokerage firms give their clients software for accessing their account records via modem. These services are typically very short on analysis and just show you the current status of your account, or of general market prices. They may also provide some sort of a window into a major news retrieval service such as the Dow-Jones Service.

Value Line and Morningstar offer software that will help you access their computers and copy data. They also include specific screens[16] and controls to help you through searches and analysis of large amounts of data. This is particularly attractive if you want to look at some large data collections but don't want to go so far as developing your own screens and statistical methods.

The Internet has great potential to help you or to waste your time. It is easy to find all manner of information, opinions, data, reports, misinformation, and anything else you might imagine. It is somewhat more difficult to separate the wheat from the chaff. The on-line services such as Prodigy and America On-Line provide financial interest group bulletin boards where you can eavesdrop in discussions or pose your own questions. You will get all manner of replies from people who may or may not know anything. My experience has been that maybe once in ten times you might see something that looks worthwhile. There are supposed "experts" out there in cyberspace who will offer advice and try to sell their services. Just give them as much credence and caution as you would anybody else who was trying to influence your spending. Just because someone can set up an impressive-looking web page doesn't mean they ever made a nickel in the markets.

---

[16] Here "screen" means not what you see on your computer monitor, but a method of sorting out and picking through stocks to find the ones with certain desired characteristics, i.e., screening out the undesired stocks.

One uniquely helpful service on the Worldwide Web comes from the U.S. Securities and Exchange Commission. The SEC has recently taken over responsibility for operation and maintenance of a computer database system called EDGAR. EDGAR has tons of stuff and it's all free. Some examples include recent quarterly reports or annual reports from companies that have registered securities, and new or proposed rules from the SEC that will affect mutual funds, investment companies, and the stock markets. Use EDGAR and SEC as keywords to find it when you start browsing the Internet. The American Association of Individual Investors (AAII) also offers a lot. See them inside the AOL Personal Finance Forum, or at their Web site: www.aaii.org.

BROKERS

The full-service brokerage firms can be excellent sources of research information. Companies like Merrill Lynch or Dean Witter keep large research staffs and produce research on individual companies, bonds, segments of industry, or general business trends. These reports are generally available free to their customers. That is one reason why it may be reasonable to pay their large brokerage fees. You cannot assume that their research is always right, and no one guarantees a profit, but at least you can read the opinions of professionals who have done their best to evaluate the chances. In addition to their research reports, or as part of them, they also give buy, sell, or hold recommendations for individual stocks or mutual funds. For each company that they follow closely, they will at any time have an opinion on the attractiveness of the stock. It is also helpful to keep in mind that some of the new opinions published by the brokerage research departments will influence stock prices. The research doesn't have to be right; just the fact that Dean Witter publishes something may be enough to have an effect on prices.

BOOKS

Most bookstores have a section for investing or personal money management, and your library should have a wide selection as well. It is certainly a matter of choice just how much time you want to spend reading books. Here are just two warnings: some of them contain inaccurate or less-than-useful information or are poorly written, and some others are out-of-date. That said, do *not* reject a book just because it was published a few years ago—or more. Some older titles may still be valuable or interesting, and there's absolutely nothing wrong with having a lot of background information. Just be a critical reader and select for yourself what is helpful to you. Start with the recommended further reading in this book to ensure not wasting your time initially, and then you can branch out to try the rest of the offerings on your library or bookstore shelves.

TELEVISION

There is something of value for the Small Investor out there. There are a few helpful programs running now, and there will probably be more financial news available soon. The current financial news network is CNBC, available in most areas as a cable offering. It offers full-time, all-day tracking and reporting of markets and major business stories, while the markets are open. In the evenings and weekends it offers various business commentary or roundtable discussions. National Public Television also offers several shows such as the *Nightly Business Report* each evening, and *Wall Street Week* on Friday evenings. CNN and C-Span carry regular or irregular business news and analysis programs that may offer valuable commentary or education. All of those have something of value at different times. If you sample them a few times, you will probably find one or two things that suit your areas of interest and experience.

BROKERAGE SEMINARS

Before you attend one, refer to the "No, thank you" exercise at the beginning of chapter 4. Most brokerage firms offer occasional free seminars on different investment topics. These can be interesting and worthwhile. They will probably be advertised in the local paper from time to time if you have a brokerage office in your town. Just be warned that they have their own reason for offering the seminar, and they will get your name and telephone number if you attend. Be prepared for the ensuing sales pitch.

OTHER SOURCES

In chapter 6, we will discuss in greater detail the sources of information that are available for bond investors; in chapters 7 and 8, we'll look at more for stock pickers; and in chapters 9 and 10, yet more for mutual funds investors.

Buy, Sell, or Hold

On television, on the radio, or in the financial papers or other press, you will sometimes encounter interviews or articles in which some financial guru, stockbroker, or analyst is giving advice on whether you should buy, sell, or hold a particular stock. This sort of thing should absolutely always be taken with a grain of salt. Whatever the person is advising may be based on a good analysis, but for every one who says "buy now," there are other, equally credible analysts who say "don't buy now." In fact, if there was unanimity of opinion to sell stock XYZ, then the price would collapse to a more defensible value before you ever got your order in. Don't be unduly influenced by any single broker's or analyst's opinion unless he or she is a professional that you have come to respect.

THE BOTTOM LINE

1. You have to make some decisions for yourself.
2. You have to face the real risk of losing 30 percent to 50 percent of your money.
3. Your decisions cannot be any better than your sources of information and your judgment.
4. There are a great many good sources of information available, and you should take a look at a wide range of them before making any important decisions.
5. Your public library is your best friend.

There are many more complex and sophisticated sources of investment information out there that we have not mentioned. You will start to bump into them if you begin with the ones we *have* mentioned, and can thus best discover what works for you.

Recommended Further Reading

Wall Street Journal

New York Times business section

Barron's

Investor's Business Daily

Financial News Network, CNBC

Morningstar Mutual Funds Reports

Value Line Investment Survey

Kiplinger's Magazine

1996 Mutual Funds Fact Book, published by the Investment Company Institute

CHAPTER 6

Bonds and Bond Markets: The Standards of Comparison and Value

Small Investors need to know:

- What is a bond?
- Can I make money in bonds?
- Can I lose money in bonds?
- How can I figure the value of a bond?
- What are the relationships between price, yield, and risk?
- Why do yields change?
- How do bond markets affect stock markets?
- What are the differences between treasury bonds, state bonds, corporate bonds, municipal bonds?
- What are "ratings" all about?
- How can I decide if bonds are good for me?
- Should I buy bond funds?
- Where can I find more information?

Do Me a Favor, Read This Chapter, Please

Even if you don't care about bonds, even if you expect to never buy a bond, read this chapter anyway.

Anytime that you consider spending or investing money, think about the other choices you have. Think about other things that you might do with the money.

Most other smart investors will be examining their choices. To protect yourself and make sure you understand what is going on, you should, too. It is especially important to remember that if you are considering investing in the stock markets or mutual funds, bonds offer additional reasonable choices.

If the bond market becomes very appealing, other investors may sell stocks and move the money into bonds. That will cause a loss of value in stocks, and may have a great effect on your investments. That is one reason why you should not ignore bond markets, even if you don't want to buy bonds.

Here is another reason. To evaluate the quality and appeal of whatever you might consider buying, you should compare it against some standard. Bonds generally offer a good standard of comparison. Their values and fluctuations are published in newspapers every day. Many of them are relatively stable and predictable. Therefore, the bond markets offer important information, even if you don't deal in bonds. One thing you will soon learn is that the fair market value of stocks is forever debated. Reasonable, intelligent analysts may have widely differing opinions on the fair price of Sara Lee stock, or Amoco, or any other. However, because of the pricing and market mechanisms, people seldom have much dispute about the fair value of a treasury bond or a high-quality corporate bond.

What Is a Bond?

A bond represents a loan. More specifically, it is the promise to repay the loan on a given schedule, with a specified interest rate. If you lend $1,000 to Uncle Jack, and he gives you a signed note promising to repay $10.00 on the first of each month for five years and then repay the original $1,000, his promissory note is a bond of sorts.

In the financial markets, a bond usually represents a loan to the actual United States itself, or to one of its states or counties, to a government agency, or a corporation. The promise to repay becomes a financial instrument (a security) that may then be sold and resold to various investors. Each one in turn acquires the right to enjoy the promised payments and interest rate until the bond matures or is sold to another investor.

The Small Investor Comes to the Aid of His Country

For example, suppose that Mega Oil Corp. had wanted to raise cash in 1986. They might have advertised a bond promising to pay 8.5 percent interest annually until 2006, and at that date repay the full amount of the loan. They would have sold the repayment promises (the bonds) in face amounts of $1,000. If Mega needed to raise $20 million, they would have issued 20,000 bonds for $1,000 each (face amount = $1,000). You could have invested (loaned to them) $10,000 by buying ten of those bonds. Let us suppose that you did that. You could hold the bonds for twenty years. They would pay you 8.5 percent interest (the coupon yield) for each bond for each year. The value of each year's payment (for each bond) would have been $85, which is 8.5 percent of $1,000. However, bonds are usually written so that interest is paid twice a year, so each bond would pay half of $85 twice each year. For your ten bonds, you would receive 10 × ½ × $85.00 twice yearly.[17] That is, $425.00 twice yearly for twenty years. After twenty years, after the final interestpayment, you would have collected a total of 20 × 10 × $85 = $17,000 in interest, and then you would have received your original $10,000 back, too.

---

[17] That is 10 for ten bonds, times one-half because of twice yearly payments, times the interest payment.

To summarize the example on page 107:

initial investment: 10 × $1,000 = $10,000
income from interest: 20 × 10 × $85 = $17,000
return of principal: $10,000

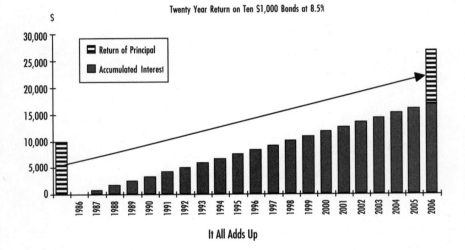

Twenty Year Return on Ten $1,000 Bonds at 8.5%

It All Adds Up

Notice also that you have another chance at profit: while that $17,000 of income is coming to you at the rate of $425 every six months, you have an opportunity to reinvest it to make more. Now let's look at some real-life examples, a couple of bonds that we'll be returning to throughout this chapter, to make a variety of important points.

In early 1994 Sears issued a new bond that was to pay 6.25 percent until January of 2004. The person who bought that bond new could plan to hold the bond for ten years, collect $31.25 every six months, and at the end of the term receive the $1,000 face value back. About the same time, Walmart issued a new bond of their own. The Walmart 7.5 percent bond was to mature in May 2004. If you had bought it in May 1994, you would have ten years of collecting $37.50 every six months and receive $1,000 back on maturity.

CHARACTERISTICS OF BONDS

Many people think of bond investing as staid and conservative. You might have an image of retired people or insurance companies leaving all of their money in bonds. This is true of many bonds. However, bonds can also be wild and exciting, gaining or losing large amounts of their value in a hurry. Bonds can be fairly simple to evaluate or extremely complex. The simplest bonds might be U.S. Treasury notes with no special provisions attached. The wildest bonds might be those issued by an Argentine corporation with a call provision, and a convertible option, where the issuer is in default.[18] That would probably be a bond that you might buy for pennies on the dollar of face value and expect to have large probability of losing it all, or you might have a shot at huge profits if the company improves. The Sears and Walmart bonds mentioned above are examples of generally safe and secure investments that one might very well plan to simply hold until 2004 for the interest payments and return of face value.

The best bonds are relatively safe and predictable if you just buy and hold, while some others offer extreme speculation. You can blend a mixture of risk and reward prospects to suit your personal investment strategy by selecting the right mix of bonds. Or you can just stay out of the bond markets, but use them as a standard of performance for other investments.

I have several standards of performance for my risk-oriented investing, and one of them is directly tied to the bond market. I feel that if my annual profit in the markets stays ahead of the total return I could have earned on long-term treasury bonds, that is one indication of moderate success. I also use several other standards, but the bond markets offer one that is easy to check.

THE LANGUAGE OF BONDS

If you are buying lumber at Home Depot, you should know the difference between a landscape timber and a slat. Well in the bond markets,

---

[18] Don't give up; these terms will be explained as you go along in the chapter.

you need to learn a special language too. It's not difficult. We'll start here with the basics. In the example above, each individual loan (bond) had a loan amount, or *face value*, of $1,000. Most of the bonds that we will deal with will have the face value of $1,000. Occasionally you may see a government bond or some other bond for higher face value, but $1,000 is by far the most common. The interest rate specified for the bond, 8.5 percent in the Mega Oil loan agreement, is the *coupon rate* (or *coupon yield*). After a bond is issued, the coupon rate is fixed and unchanging for that bond. Coupon rates for different bonds vary depending on current interest rates in the economy when the bond is issued, as well as the length of the loan and the credit worthiness of the borrower. It is easy to find bonds still in circulation that have coupon rates of interest anywhere between 5 percent and 20 percent. The loan interest rate is called a *coupon rate* because in prior years the lenders actually got paper certificates for the bonds, and each certificate had the proper number of tear-off coupons that could be turned in to receive the interest. Such coupons are no longer used except for old bonds. These days the records are kept in computers that hold numbered accounts. Finally, the length of the loan period is called the *term*, which is twenty years in our example. The year of the final payment on the bond is the *maturity* of the bond.

The Sears and Walmart bonds mentioned above have face values of $1,000, and maturities of 2004. The Sears coupon yield is 6.25 percent and the Walmart coupon yield is 7.5 percent

So the simplest possible view of a bond is this: a loan agreement for a specified term, with a specified maturity date and fixed schedule of interest payments. It promises a constant series of interest payments, and after the last interest payment, it promises to repay the original principal, usually $1,000.

Changing Prices and Yields

Bonds may be bought and sold another way, too. If for whatever reason you decide to sell your bonds before maturity, your broker will go into the bond markets where they are sold after initial issue. That market is called the secondary (or resale) market. Current market conditions may affect the prices and rates of bonds in the resale markets. To fully understand price and yield changes requires more mathematics than I want to discuss in this book. In the real world, thousands of computers do the math, and all the brokers and newspapers have access to the information every day.

It may happen someday that you decide to sell a 6 percent bond that you bought new for $1,000. The buyer will be getting almost the same thing you bought. You sell her the continuing stream of interest payments and also the final return of capital at the end of the term. The distinctions are that the time period and prevailing market rates have changed and you have already received some of the interest payments. Because of those changes, the buyer may only offer you a lower price; suppose it is $950 and you accept that price. Let us see what has happened to the yield: the bond with 6 percent coupon pays $60 per year, but for the new owner that is 6.32 percent ($60/950 = .0632$) of her price. At the time of sale that is the new yield on the bond. It is given a name, *current yield*. So the lesson here is that current yield changes with market conditions and the price of the bond, while the coupon yield is always the same fixed value.

Price also changes. In the above example, the price changed to $950. If you decide to sell your bond, the market will pay what it will pay. You cannot influence that. The original $1,000 is written in history as the first price or *par value*, but when we speak of *bond price,* that means the current market value of the bond. It can be less than or greater than par value. Now let's look at some specific examples.

In September of 1995, the Sears bond had a market price of $956.25 for a current yield of 6.54 percent (that's $62.50/956.25$). The Walmart bond sold for $1048.75 with a current yield of 7.15 percent. Over the same time period, from early 1994 to September 1995, the price of the Sears bond went below par value, while the price of the Walmart bond went above par. There are many factors that affect the price and yield of bonds, and we will look at them in the rest of this chapter.

Words

Let's pause for a couple more definitions: *prevailing rates* and *market rates,* which are generally used to mean the same thing. A market rate is the interest rate for which people are willing to buy and sell a particular bond on a particular day. The bond market is a free and open market, and people can ask or offer whatever prices they choose, but the price at which the bond is actually exchanged is the market rate: a price at which both the buyers and the sellers of the bond agree. For example, one day people may be willing to buy and sell U.S. Treasury bonds that mature in 2007 and yield interest on the price of 6.96 percent. However no one is willing to buy for a higher price that would give an interest any lower than that, and no one is willing to sell for a lower price that would give an interest rate higher than that. Thus 6.96 percent becomes the market (prevailing) rate for that bond on that day. A New York City revenue bond might require 8.33 percent to reach agreement among buyers and sellers, so that would be its market rate on that day. Each of those rates is likely to change the next day, and in fact will probably change during the day as people hear news or rumors about the economy. Each of those rates is likely to change substantially over a period of months or years, as inflation or business conditions change.

Ratings

How will you protect yourself from the risk of market erosion of prices? You can't do anything after you buy the bond except sell it, because the markets are not responsive to your needs. You can do a few things about choosing the characteristics of the bonds you buy.

The safety or riskiness of your investment is to a great extent, but not entirely, a function of the quality and strength of the corporation or government that issued it. It is difficult to evaluate the relative strength of different organizations. Two prominent businesses that do that for us are Standard & Poor's and Moody's. They regularly publish and update their opinions about the relative strength and quality of corporations, their stocks and bonds, and municipal bonds. The ratings scales are

S&P (best to worst): AAA, AA, A, BBB, BB, B, CCC, CC, C, D
Moody's (best to worst): Aaa, Aa, A, Baa, Ba, B, Caa, Ca, C

These grades are broken down into finer points, too. S&P sometimes adds + or − to a grade to indicate if it's a little to the strong or weak side of that grade. Moody's adds a 1, 2, or 3 to the grade. For example, Moody's scale includes: A1, ranked better than A2, which is better than A3, which is better than Baa1, etc. The corresponding ratings on each scale are nearly equivalent; that is, AAA is nearly the same as Aaa, and BB+ is nearly the same as Ba1.

The first four grades (AAA to BBB, or Aaa to Baa) on each scale are considered "investment grade," which means they are considered to be suitable for conservative investors and to have less fluctuation and risk. But remember that even a AAA bond is still subject to the risk of market value fluctuation. The ratings agencies deal only in the strength of the original bond and the relative safety that the issuer will both pay the interest and repay the face value. They do not try to promise you anything about the future market value of the bond.

The grades below BBB or Baa are sometimes referred to as junk bonds. The pejorative term refers to the attendant risk. But notice that there are relative levels of junk. A bond rated Ba is only slightly riskier than a Baa bond, and may carry nearly the same yield. By comparison, a C bond is much riskier than a AA bond and must offer much higher compensating yield. It is not enough to simply evaluate bonds as either junk or investment grade.

The Sears 6.25 percent '04 was initially rated Baa1 when it was new, but had been upgraded to A2 by September 1995. The Walmart 7.5 percent '04 was issued new with Aa1 rating, and has held that rating. The Sears bond is investment grade, but the Walmart bond is very high quality investment grade.

Types of Bonds

Each individual bond is relatively straightforward, but the bond markets as a whole are extremely complex. There are many different types of bonds with different characteristics. Some bonds, even U.S. Treasury bonds, come with special conditions. Remember that the bond is basically a contract for repayment, and as such it may have various contractual rules attached. For example, some U.S. Treasury bonds come with a provision that says, in effect, "maybe this bond matures in 2006 and maybe it matures in 2012; we'll let you know later." You should get a higher yield for a bond like that. Some bonds come with a provision that says, "this bond matures in 2013; however, if it is convenient for us, we may pay it off in 2007." That last one is a *call provision*.

These conditions may have a strong effect on the value and safety of your bond. If you plan to buy a bond through a broker, ask him to explain to you any special conditions attached. If you buy mutual funds[19] that buy bonds, make sure you know what kinds of bonds and what kinds of conditions fall within the charters of your funds (read the prospectus!).

U.S. TREASURY BONDS

These are the safest bonds in the world, but not entirely risk-free.[20] While the U.S. government has never defaulted on its debt in its 220-year history, you have at least the risk that you might someday have to sell into unfavorable market conditions. These bonds are given the strongest guarantee in the world, and have the added advantage that the interest is exempt from your state and local taxes. If you sell the bond for a profit or a loss, this will affect your taxes and must be reported. Treasury bonds are called *notes* when issued for two to ten years, and called *bills* when issued for one year or less. You have the opportunity to buy bonds directly from the Treasury if you want to avoid brokers. Look in the government pages of your telephone book to find a number for Treasury direct sales, or you can call your regional federal reserve office.

One standout distinction of the U.S. Treasury savings bond is that there is no secondary market for these. It is restricted to the buy-and-hold investor until you return it to the Treasury.

MUNICIPAL BONDS

These are bonds issued by local or state governments or agencies acting under the auspices of a local government. They are generally exempt from that state's and federal taxes. Because of the tax saving, they will normally have a lower coupon rate than other bonds of equal quality. Municipal bonds are usually found to have high-quality ratings, because we don't expect to see governments defaulting on debt. However, there is no uniform rule on this. Some municipalities do have poor debt ratings.

---

[19] We'll talk about mutual funds and prospectuses in chapter 9.

[20] Remember, there are no risk-free investments. Anytime you let go of your money, there is a chance you may never see it again.

Even as I am writing this, the world of municipal bond investing is changing. There has been a long-standing presumption in our financial markets that governments don't default on their bonds. For many years people have looked to municipal bonds as a source of stability and safety for the small investor. Then along came Orange County, California, apparently prepared to wreck all of that. To make a sad story short, the government of Orange County borrowed money from a lot of people and other agencies who were looking for a safe haven, and then closed their eyes while others gambled with the money. The gamblers lost, big time! The other innocents stood to lose also unless Orange County would step up to their responsibility to stand behind their bonds. It appears that they will not. It doesn't matter why. The jury is still out, but if you grew up thinking that municipal bonds were always a safe haven, wake up and look around.

Municipal bonds are also available with extra insurance of repayment. The issuing agency may buy insurance for their bonds from private companies set up for just that purpose. You pay a little more for that kind of protection, but its value is highly debatable. None of the private insurers have ever been tested in a real crunch situation, such as a massive default of local governments. Since the state and local governments are also rated by the ratings agencies, it might be wise to confine your bonds business to those who have AA or AAA ratings, and forego the insurance.

CORPORATE BONDS

A corporate bond is issued by any private business. The business must get approval and registration from the Securities and Exchange Commission to take the bonds to market, but basically they are just going out to get a loan for ten, twenty, eighty million dollars or whatever. Corporate bonds usually pay higher yield than government or municipal bonds because they presumably carry higher risk and the earnings are fully taxable.

CONVERTIBLES

Certain corporate bonds may carry a provision that under specified conditions they may be traded into the company's common stock; in other words, they can be converted to stock.

What's the point? The conversion privilege is worth something to the buyers, therefore the corporation can offer a lower yield on the bonds. Bond buyers may or may not find that appealing, depending on the terms of the conversion offer and the attractiveness of the company's stock. Here is an example: say Wellfarm Corporation issues a bond with maturity in 2008, and coupon at 10 percent. In order to make it more appealing to buyers, they offer a conversion option with the bond that says: "Anytime after January 1, 1998, this bond may be converted into 45 shares of our common stock." Suppose the common stock is currently trading at $18.50, and for the past two years has varied in price from $16 to $23.75.

There are Many Ways to Go, Including the Convertible

If you hold the bond and keep it until sometime after January 1, 1998, you would have several choices:

1. Keep the bond; continue to collect $100 annual interest, and plan to collect $1,000 face value at maturity.
2. Sell the bond—it would bring a higher price because it carries the conversion option with it.
3. Convert to the stock.

The value of the stock may have gone up or down. If the stock is high, say, $34, your conversion stock would be worth 45 × $34 = $1,530. That might look attractive, but it would be reflected in the current market value of your bond. The bond would have a $1,530 straight conversion value plus some value relative to the yield and the continuing conversion choice. Its price would certainly be above $1,600, and you might sell it in the bond market.

If, however, the stock has fallen, say, to $17, the 45 shares would just be worth $765, which is not attractive. However, you would still hold a bond, which had the value of a normal bond investment, and you could hold it for its bond value. The final analysis is that if the company were sound, you would never have less than the value of a normal bond, and if the stock were strong, you might have a great deal more.

ZERO COUPON BONDS

Remember my Florida Federal bonds? A zero is a bond that does not pay its interest every six months, but instead saves up everything and pays it all at once at the maturity. U.S. savings bonds are like zeros in many ways. Your friends at the IRS call them "Original Issue Discount Instruments." They will be happy to give you a copy of their publication #1212 that lists a lot of them. That publication serves three purposes: to help you identify zeros that are in the markets; to help your broker understand their responsibilities in reporting the investments to the IRS; and to explain tax rules related to them. There are tax complications with zeros that you or your tax advisor must consider when you plan to buy them, when you sell them, and even while you are holding them. Do not buy zeros until you read and understand the tax requirements.

Alright, so how do zeros work? Let me show you the growth of an investment that is earning compound annual interest of 7 percent. Just for the sake of argument let us begin with $508.35. Look at the value if the interest is kept in the investment and compounds each year: start with $508.35.

after 1 year	543.93	after 5 years	712.99
after 2 years	582.01	after 8 years	873.44
after 3 years	622.75	after 10 years	1,000

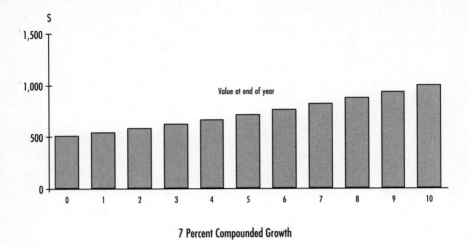

7 Percent Compounded Growth

What if they sold you a $1,000 face value bond for $508.35, but never paid you any interest? That's the zero coupon, and after ten years they would repay the bond face value of $1,000. Then you would have the results of 7 percent compound growth over the ten years. The price that you paid is $491.65 less than the face value, and that is the *original issue discount*.

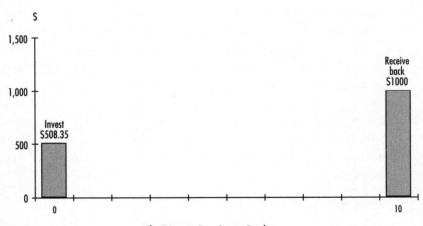

The 7 Percent Zero Coupon Bond

A zero coupon bond is a bond that is sold at a discount to the face value, and does not pay any interest before maturity. It will be priced to yield a specified equivalent compound interest on maturity.

CALL PROVISIONS

Sometimes when companies or governments issue new bonds, they want to build in an extra feature to protect themselves from the long-term repayment requirement. For example, ABCD Goldfish Corporation may want to sell bonds when the prevailing long-term interest rate is 13 percent. That would force them to pay 13 percent interest for the life of the bonds. If, sometime after a few years, prevailing interest rates fell to 8 percent, they would like to issue new bonds at 8 percent, repay the old 13 percent bonds, and save a bundle on interest payments. They cannot do that unless you agree to sell back your 13 percent bonds. A call provision is a contractual provision added to the bond contract that says you will agree to give it up after some specified date, at the company's choice. If the bond has a call provision you may have to give up your right to collect the 13 percent coupon sooner than the bond's maturity. You should get paid extra for that. ABCD might offer to pay you more than the $1,000 face value if they call the bond, or they might offer some other inducement like higher yield or convertibility to make the bond attractive to you. At any rate, you need to know if there is a call provision, and remember it was put in there for the pleasure of the bond issuer, not for yours.

JUNK BONDS

These are bonds that carry higher-than-average risk of default, and usually bring along a higher yield. See the section on bond ratings, page 114.

INVESTMENT GRADE BONDS

These are bonds for which the repayment of interest and principal is more secure than average, according to the opinions of Moody and Standard & Poor's.

Buy and Hold

That's all folks! If you have a good broker who can select them for you, and if you will simply buy and hold the bonds until maturity, that's all there is to it. Do try to become comfortable with the information in the first half of this chapter; it is the foundation of further knowledge.

Risk and Reward

So far we have a simple view of bonds that should appear appealing to many of us. But in risk-oriented investing, bonds can be a great deal more exciting and complex than the first view we saw above. Suppose that you or your broker do a lot of very fine analysis and you find and buy a batch of bonds that mature in the year 2009 and pay you $4,000, twice yearly, in interest. So you're happy and content to hold them to maturity and plan on the steady income stream. The risk to consider is that you have an unanticipated emergency need for the money. (This is not just a risk of bonds, but one that comes along with every investment you make.) But you are not worried, because there are efficient markets for bonds that allow your broker to sell your bonds for a fair price.

The Small Investor Is Laid Up

The risk is that the fair price might be less than what you paid. If the bonds each cost $1,000 when you bought them at issue, the current market value might be considerably lower or higher depending on market conditions. There is a chance that you might sell your bonds for more than you paid, but for now let's look at the risk side: you might lose money on the sale.

Here's how that might work.[21] Say you have 100 bonds with coupon rate of 8 percent maturing in 2009. That makes $4,000 every six months, right? (8 percent of $1,000 = $80 per year for each of the 100 bonds). The risk is in current fair-market interest rates. If the markets, in their collective wisdom, have settled on a current long-term interest rate of 10 percent, they will not buy your bonds that only pay 8 percent unless you adjust the price to meet the buyer's needs. In this case the bond market computers may have agreed that an 8 percent coupon bond maturing in 2009 is currently worth only $900. That leaves you looking at $100 per bond in loss. We will return to these bonds in a moment.

Here is the deal: If you buy good bonds and hold them to maturity, you may reasonably expect to collect the interest and return of principal that you bought in the bond. However, if for any reason you have to sell the bonds before maturity, you are at the mercy of market conditions to set the price of your bonds.

The primary risk in bond markets is that market conditions may change the value of your bonds, and you may lose money if you have to sell them.

Here are some prices from a recent issue of *Barron's*:

A 3.5% U.S. Treasury bond that matures in 1998 may be sold for $972.60; the current yield is 3.6%.

A 6.75% AT&T bond that matures in 2004 may be sold for $1015.00; the current yield is 6.65%.

A 10.95% Chrysler bond that matures in 2017 may be sold for $1111.25; the current yield is 8.2%.

A 6.0625% Cray Research bond that matures in 2011 may be sold for $770.00; the current yield is 7.9%.

---

[21] In this example, we will ignore the date of sale, because I want to keep the example as simple as possible.

Each of them has face value of $1,000. Why are these prices adjusted up or down from face value? That is a more complex question that we can only begin to deal with in this book, but the first lesson is that bond prices do change with market conditions, and you have no control over those conditions.

Your main concern is how to value your bonds, or bonds you are considering buying. Do this in two ways. The first valuation focuses on a bond's value as a continuing stream of income, and the second focuses on a bond's value as a marketable security. Both valuation methods are valid, and different investors may have good reasons for placing greater emphasis on one or the other. You should always consider both of them, although one or the other may seem more important to you at various times.[22]

There are two numbers we use to judge those two valuations. The first way uses *current yield*, which means the coupon payment divided by the current price. The second way looks at the current yield plus the return of par value at the end. It is called *yield to maturity*.

It is easy to calculate current yield. It is more complex to accurately calculate the yield to maturity. What we do, instead, is simply look it up in the *Wall Street Journal* or another publication, or ask a stock broker.[23]

Now let us return to the matter of those bonds that you sold for $900 each. For each bond, the buyer gets the $80 each year of interest plus some growth in principal (they will get back $1,000 at maturity), which is an extra $100 in profit. *The current yield describes the interest payments in terms of the current price.* In our example, the current yield becomes $80/$900 = 8.89 percent. *Current yield is the coupon payment divided by the current price.* That may be either higher or lower than the original coupon yield.

Examples:

If a 4 percent bond sells for $800, on that date the current yield is $40/$800 = 5 percent.

---

[22] Your tax status may affect which aspect of bond value is more important to you. I can not cover that in this book, so you should see a tax accountant, tax lawyer, or certified financial planner, if tax considerations must be part of your plans.

[23] I will discuss how to look it up later in this chapter.

If a 10 percent bond sells for $700, on that date the current yield is $100/$700 = 14.28 percent.

If a 14 percent bond sells for $1,250, on that date the current yield is $140/$1,250 = 11.20 percent.

All of the current yields will change whenever the prices change.

For our earlier example where the 8 percent bond sold for $900, the yield to maturity would depend on the date, which I have not mentioned yet. If the date was exactly 11 years before maturity, the yield to maturity would be 9.4 percent. This should seem reasonable, because the buyer gets the stream of payments worth 8.89 percent (current yield), plus $100 extra growth in principal with the $1,000 return of par value.

If the date of sale was exactly five years before maturity, the yield to maturity would be 10.5 percent. The extra $100 gained in five years is better return than $100 gained in eleven years.

When you need information on a bond, you can calculate the current yield easily. For the yield to maturity, ask your broker, or look in a financial publication. Of course, the financial publication will have only the old value for the day before its publication. You could also check with your broker for the current yield if you don't want to do the calculation.

As a bond investor or as a stock investor who is comparing choices, you should evaluate bonds by considering both current yield and yield to maturity. When you look in a newspaper, you may see bonds listed in several ways. The first trick is to be able to identify the bond. For Treasury bonds, the listing will show something like:

bond description	bid	asked	yield
10 3/4 Aug.05	132:29	133:01	6.23

This means: a 10.75 percent bond, that matures in August of 2005. The :29 and the :01 represent 32nds of a dollar, so 132:29 means $132 and $^{29}/_{32}$, that is $132.90625, the 133:01 means $133 and $^{1}/_{32}$, or $133.03125. The bid and asked values are per $100 of par value. So for a $1,000 par bond, you would multiply by ten. The yield shown here is yield to maturity. What is the payment stream? It is 10.75 percent of $1,000 = $107.50 yearly, and paid twice each year as $53.75 for each $1,000 bond.

Now we can read the example line: a U.S. Treasury bond with 10.75 percent coupon rate is maturing in August of 2005 with buyers bidding $1,329.0625 for $1,000 face value, and sellers are asking $1,330.3125 for $1,000 face value. At the asking price, the yield to maturity would be 6.23 percent. The final payment at maturity is $1,000 per bond.

Here is another:

bond description	bid	asked	yield
11 3/4 Feb 01	126:18	126:22	5.91

This is an 11.75 percent Treasury bond maturing in February of 2001. Buyers offer $1,265.6250 and sellers want $1,266.8750 per $1,000 face value. At the asking price the yield to maturity is 5.91 percent. The payment stream is ½ × $117.50 = $58.75 paid every six months. Again, the final payment at maturity is $1,000 per bond.

If the Treasury bond has a term of one year or less, it is called a *bill*, and if the term is two to ten years, it is called a *note*. One distinguishing characteristic of bills is that they are sold in $10,000 or larger face value. Usually the bills will be listed separately, and the notes will be listed with the longer bonds, but denoted with an (n).

Corporate bonds are listed differently. They should show at least the following and perhaps more.

name & coupon	current yield	high	low	last
Cleveland Electric 8 3/8 12	9.0	94	91 3/4	93 1/2

This is a Cleveland Electric Corporation bond with 8⅜ percent coupon maturing in 2012. On the previous day, it traded between $91.75 (low) and $94.00 (high) and the last transaction was at $93.50, per $100 value. The actual final price on a $1,000 face bond was $935.00. The current yield is 9 percent. If you want to know the yield to maturity, call your broker, or check the *WSJ*. If the listing was exactly fifteen years before maturity, and you paid the 93½ price, the yield to maturity would be about 9.1 percent. What is the income stream? 8.375 percent of $1,000 per year, paid half every six months. That is $41.875 every six months for each bond you hold. The final payment will be the $1,000 face value.

It would be instructive to pick up a newspaper and read a few of these things, just to sense the flavor of it. Be aware that no newspaper is likely to list all of the bonds in the market, as there are just too many of them. The papers will list the recently traded bonds. If you want to know about others, call your broker or head to your library business reference section.

If you have read and understood everything up to this point, you have a basic working knowledge of bonds. Many people go through life and even invest in financial markets without ever knowing as much as you know now. The rest of the story is one complication after another. Financial people are clever and creative, so they invent all kinds of bonds, as well as things that act like bonds, bonds that can be changed into something else, and on and on. Each of those special cases requires its own separate study if you intend to invest with them. We cannot cover all of that in this book. In the remainder of the chapter, we will look at some of the risks and special cases and mention how they differ and how they might be useful to you.

A little knowledge is a dangerous thing. So be careful out there!

Risk-Oriented Investing

Bond yield rates are set in more or less open market negotiations between all of the bond issuers and all of the bond sellers or buyers. This whole process is just like the way things operate in most businesses, in that everything is negotiable. When Big Soap Suds Corporation decides that they need to raise $50 million through a bond offering, they will talk to their preferred financial services company and negotiate an offering of the bonds where they discuss yield, term, maturity, seniority, and special conditions on the bond. But one over-riding factor is that if they want to stretch out the term to repayment, they will have to raise the coupon yield. Repayment after a greater amount of time is a greater risk for investors than repayment soon, so the investment markets demand higher interest payments for longer-term bonds. Generally speaking, if all other factors are equal, an issuer's short-term bond should pay a lower yield than the same issuer's long-term bond.

VARIATIONS IN PRICE: THE RISKS

When you buy a bond you buy a promise to pay two things: the twice yearly payment of interest, and the final repayment of principal.[24] Anything that threatens either of those is a threat to your investment success. Furthermore, you might want to sell the bond sometime to raise money. The sale price that you receive may be higher or lower than what you paid or what you would like. Those are the primary risks.

What could threaten the payment of interest or repayment of face value? The issuer of the bonds might go bankrupt. Or they may decide they are in such trouble that they just won't pay the interest. Or they may pay other people or other bonds before they pay yours, and not have enough left to pay you. If the company is short on funds, they will pay their suppliers before they pay the bonds, and they may have a contractual clause that says some bonds get paid before others. That last condition is referred to as seniority of the debt. Senior debt will be paid first. Subordinated debt will be paid when they get to it, if there is money left to pay out.

How can you protect yourself from this kind of risk? You or your broker can evaluate the financial strength of the company and check the bond conditions to discover whether there is any senior debt. You might consider the long-term history of the firm's payment of their debts. You might consider overall economic conditions and the health of their markets. If the company relies on selling record-player turntables, this will not generate a reliable stream of income, so maybe you shouldn't buy their bonds. Fortunately, there is a lot of help available. Standard and Poor's and Moody's regularly evaluate companies and bonds to predict which are safe and which are not so safe. It is almost guaranteed that they can do that better than you or your broker, so you should rely heavily on those ratings. The main point there is that if the rating for a bond is high (A or better), then you should feel quite safe that the interest payments will be met.

That is not a guarantee. Penn-Central was one of the largest and strongest firms in the United States in 1969 and had the highest ratings from several rating agencies. They went bankrupt with little warning

---

[24] A zero coupon bond only promises the final payment.

to anyone, and the bond holders were severely hurt. Up until nearly the time of the bankruptcy, in June of 1970, their bonds were rated as investment grade by the major ratings agencies. This is not intended as a criticism of Standard & Poor's or Moody's. They do a lot of fine work and give us a lot of valuable information. The point is that when they publish their ratings, they do not guarantee the safety of your investments. They publish opinions, not gospel.

BOND VALUES AND INTEREST RATES

To carry risk study further, we need to look at the relationships of bond values and prevailing interest rates. For example, consider a fictional AA (very safe) rated corporate bond that pays 8 percent and matures in 2005. The original value was par, or $1,000. Suppose you want to sell it when there are six years left to maturity and at that time the prevailing market interest rate is 12 percent for AA-rated corporates maturing in '05. The market will impose a fair price on your bond so that the yield to maturity becomes 12 percent. That means that your bond must sell for $823 to make a fair market. You have lost $177 in the value of the bond due to the rise in market interest rates from 8 percent to 12 percent.

When prevailing rates rise, the price of preexisting bonds will fall.

Let's look at the same bond, but change the scenario. Suppose the prevailing fair market rates on new AA bonds maturing in 2005 actually fell to 6 percent at the day of your sale. The market will impose a new price on your bond to make it pay 6 percent yield to maturity. However, in this case, your bond is paying more than new bonds coming to market, so the market will bid up to higher prices to get your bond— $1,102. What did you get? You have had the interest payments for however long you held it, and you got more than your original investment back. What did the buyer get? The buyer got a higher coupon than new bonds which would be only $60.00. The buyer's current yield is 7.26 percent, and he is looking at a loss of principal since the bond will still only return $1,000 at maturity. The coupon payments plus the projected loss on the principal combine to give the buyer a yield to maturity of 6 percent.

When prevailing rates fall, the price of preexisting bonds will rise.

So You See, It's Very Simple!

Here is the essential characteristic of bond price fluctuation, which you must remember if you want to trade bonds, or just wish to follow bond market action. *Bond prices move opposite to current interest rates.* How much do they move? Usually bonds with longer times left to maturity will react to interest movements more than bonds with shorter times left to maturity. Here are some real-life examples. Each of these is an actual U.S. Treasury bond, and I am comparing prices at three times: early September of 1992, mid-October 1993, and mid-September 1995. (YTM stands for *yield to maturity.*)

bond's maturity date	coupon rate	Sept. 1992 price	Sept. 1992 YTM	Oct. 1993 price	Oct. 1993 YTM	Sept. 1995 price	Sept. 1995 YTM
Nov. 1998	3.5%	99:08	3.64%	101:00	3.28%	98:26	3.9%
August 2005	10.75%	133:22	6.79%	146:22	5.37%	133:01	6.23%
August 2020	8.75%	116:19	7.34%	135:29	6.03%	125:11	6.65%

All of those bonds maintain a constant $1,000 face value to be repaid on maturity. The Nov/98 maintains a constant $35 annual coupon payment, the Aug/05 maintains a constant $107.50 coupon payment, and the Aug/20 maintains a constant $87.50 payout. Also observe that the shorter bonds (1998 maturity) have lower YTM than the longer bonds. That is usually true because of the time value of money and opportunity cost of holding an asset, but occasionally, a situation develops where shorter bonds pay more.[25]

In September of 1995 the Sears 6.25 percent '04 had a price of 95:20, which gave a yield to maturity of 6.94 percent. The Walmart 7.5 percent, '04 had a price of 104:28 for yield to maturity of 6.74 percent. We saw before that the Sears bond in September had a lower current yield, and yet their relative positions on YTM are reversed. Each of those bonds might appeal more to different investors for different reasons, depending on whether the investor wanted current yield or yield to maturity.

Normally, earlier maturity bonds should pay lower YTM than later maturity bonds of the same quality and terms. Whenever new earlier maturity bonds pay more yield to maturity than new later maturity bonds, the term used is *interest rate inversion.*

For example, we would have an interest rate inversion if the government issued a new ninety-day Treasury bill which paid 5 percent, and a new ten-year Treasury note paying 4.9 percent.

There are many theories and opinions about what inversion means, and how investors should behave when an interest rate inversion occurs, but for our purposes, it is sufficient to say that an inversion is a warning that something strange is going on in financial markets, and we should be alert to more danger and change than normal.

BOND FUNDS

There are mutual funds that buy and sell bonds, and there are thousands of different ways that they select them or mix them with other investments. If you plan to spend less than about $20,000, it is probably smarter and more economical to buy bond funds rather than individual bonds. See chapters 9 and 10.

---

[25] When your money is not available to you, as in a long bond investment, there is an *opportunity cost*, which means that you forego the alternative of investing it elsewhere or spending it.

Interest Rates

Here is the truth. If you don't believe anything else I said, believe this:

No one can consistently, accurately, and reliably predict interest rates.

Anyone who says she can is not your friend. Therefore, no one can accurately guarantee the market prices of your bonds. This leads to some lessons about investing:

1. The only guarantee you get is the guarantee of the government or the corporation that issued the bonds, which in turn is no stronger than that organization's finances and management (except for Uncle Sam, who can simply print more money to pay you).
2. Planning for safety in bonds means planning to buy and hold.
3. Diversify, by purchasing bonds that will behave differently in different situations, or at least add diversity to your other investments.

To look further at the buy-and-hold strategy, it does not mean that you have to hold them. It just means that you buy bonds that you think you would feel comfortable holding to maturity. Remember our earlier discussion about plans? You need a plan because that is better than no plan, but you don't have to stick with the plan if surprises develop later on. For example, in January of 1995 I bought some 7.25 percent U.S. treasuries maturing in May of 2016 at the price of 92.4062. Current yield was 7.8 percent. I expected to hold those babies to maturity. But luckily, pretty soon prevailing interest rates started to fall and by July, I could get 104 for each bond. Current yield was down to 7 percent. I decided to grab the profits and run. I made 3.9 percent on one interest payment plus 12.55 percent profit on the sale, so the whole thing paid over 16 percent in six months, a tidy return. [26]

---

[26]Today, in hindsight, I see that I could have done better by holding the bonds another year, but that's okay; hindsight never made a profit for anyone, and nobody ever went broke by grabbing profits.

Recommended Further Reading

Nichols's book is outstanding, and I would recommend it as the next place to study if you really want to be up on bonds. It has ten times as much information as I had room for in this chapter and is quite well written.

Moody's Bond Record, in your library, frequently updated. Call (212) 553-0300 for more information.

Moody's Credit Survey, in your library, frequently updated. Call (212) 553-0300 for more information.

Nichols, Donald. *The Personal Investor's Complete Book of Bonds*. Chicago: Dearborn Financial Publishers, 1990.

Renberg, Werner. *All About Bond Funds*. New York: John Wiley, 1995.

Standard & Poor's Bond Guide, in your library, updated monthly.

CHAPTER 7

Investing in Stocks

Small Investors need to know:

- What is a stock market?
- Why do people go to that kind of market?
- Is it all just a great den of gambling?
- Can everybody win? Does everybody win?
- Can I win?
- How do people pick stocks?
- What are sectors, caps, P/E, and trends?
- Do the prices of these things go up and down?

The Stock Markets...at Last!

All right! Here you are. You put up with the stuff about risk and diversification and bonds and the other sermons, but what you really wanted to learn about was the stock markets, wasn't it? Don't apologize, that's the most fun for me to write about, too. However, if anyone skipped any of the preceding chapters to rush into this one, shame on you! You are asking for trouble, and I will not be accountable for your subsequent grief.

Studying the stock markets will help you to be a better investor, even if you never intend to buy individual stocks. If, for example, you plan to put all of your investing money into mutual funds, you still want to be able to make some judgments about selecting stock funds, diversifying amongst them, and judging risk.

The Small Investor in the Market

What should you reasonably expect from the stock markets? It's hard to say. I don't know you or whether you will work hard, or buy large or small stocks, or utilities or software companies. But we can make a guess that you will do average. That's what averages are for, after all.

As a representative of some kind of average performance, we can look at the most widely reported average, the Dow-Jones Industrial Average (the DJIA). It represents the stock price performance for thirty of the best-known companies with some of the most widely traded stocks. The thirty include GE, IBM, GM, AT&T, McDonalds, and twenty-five other such stalwarts of American business. The Dow-Jones Industrial Average is not a straight average of stock prices, but is a weighted average that in some sense also figures in the relative size of these corporations in the market. The DJIA numbers are widely reported and regarded by many as an indicator of overall stock market performance. The number does not reflect performance for all stocks in general, but it probably is a fair indicator of the performance of large, well-known firms that are traded on the NYSE. Such large, established firms are collectively labeled "blue chips."

The Long View

The long-term investment view of American stock markets is pretty good. That means that if you choose to invest in American companies by buying stocks and holding them for a long time, there is a strong expectation that you will make good profits. How good? We don't exactly know, but the evidence is that it probably would be better than other long-term investments.

How long is long term? Again, nobody can say exactly how long you'll need to hold onto any given stock or stocks. Statistically, the long run means however long it takes. If you don't have that long, you'll have to compromise. A fair view of long run for many investors might be placed at five or ten years. Most folks need to think about getting their money back after ten years or so.

I am going to illustrate with some numbers that roughly indicate what kinds of results you may have gotten if you (the collective average you) had invested in the DJIA stocks at their average price each year, held them for five years and sold at average prices in the fifth year, or held for ten years and sold at average prices in the tenth year. It is unlikely that anyone would ever do that, or ever want to, but the calculations indicate something about the average results for the average investor who chooses to invest principally in large and well-known American firms on the NYSE.

If, on the other hand, you invest in different kinds of stocks, say, only small companies, the DJIA doesn't say much about the results you might expect. There are other published averages that address the results and history of other groups of stocks: the Dow-Jones Utilities Average; the S&P 500, which is based on 500 of the biggest firms rather than just 30; the Wilshire 5000, which covers most of the stocks publicly traded on stock exchanges; or the Russell 2000, which includes 2000 small company stocks.

The chart below shows what the results would have been if a person had invested $1,000 in the Dow-Jones Industrial stocks on thirteen occasions during the past seventy-five years. It shows the results for buying at average prices each year and selling at the average prices during the year of sale.

Results of $1,000 invested in the Dow-Jones Industrial stocks
(buy and sell at the years' average prices)

Year of investment	Value of investment if held for		Compound annual rate of growth in investment	
	5 years	10 years	5 years	10 years
1927	$370	$950	–18%	–0.6%
1936	750	1,190	–6%	2%
1940	1,330	1,600	5%	5%
1945	1,270	2,610	5%	10%
1948	1,530	2,730	9%	11%
1952	1,760	2,360	12%	9%
1959	1,320	1,390	6%	3%
1963	1,270	1,290	5%	3%
1968	1,002	910	0.4%	–1%
1973	890	1,290	–2%	3%
1979	1,400	2,970	7%	12%
1982	2,560	3,780	21%	14%
1988	1,710	*	11%	*

data not yet available
Numbers are rounded

These numbers do not include brokers' commissions, which would drag down the profits by a little, and they do not include dividends that the companies pay to shareholders. Dividend payments would increase the rate of return each year by anywhere from 2 percent to 7 percent. For example, during the years 1988 to 1993, the dividend yield on the DJIA stocks averaged close to 3 percent. You might reasonably claim that the *overall* five year rate of return for the 1988 purchase should be figured as 11 percent + 3 percent = 14 percent. The first table only addresses gains or losses on the stock prices. Let's look at the effect of adding in dividend payments.

Dividends are handled differently by different investors, and for a variety of good reasons. Some folks want to take the money and use it for living or playing expenses. Others reinvest the dividends in more stock. Any calculation of the effect of dividends has to make some assumption as to what the investor does with the dividends. Over a period as short as five years it can make a big difference. For this example, I am going to assume that the investor takes the dividend as regular income and spends it.

Now the profits over the five-year and ten-year periods are increased. They look like this:

Total percent gain or loss from investment

Year of investment	From price of stock held for		From price of stock and dividends received	
	5 years	10 years	5 years	10 years
1927	−63%	−5%	*	*
1936	−25%	19%	2%	68%
1940	33%	60%	58%	114%
1945	27%	161%	56%	216%
1948	53%	173%	83%	225%
1952	76%	136%	100%	177%
1959	32%	39%	49%	74%
1963	27%	29%	43%	65%
1968	2%	-9%	21%	36%
1973	−11%	29%	16%	83%
1979	40%	197%	67%	242%
1982	156%	278%	177%	316%
1988	71%	**	87%	**

* figures not readily available
** figures not yet available

If Uncle Jack bought $1,000 worth of the DJIA in 1959 and sold it in 1969 at average prices, he would have sold for $1,390. The gain from the stock prices would have been $390; the gain from stock prices plus dividends would have been $740.

Is there any lesson in this? Well, it's like beauty—it's in the eyes of the beholder, but let me suggest a lesson:

On average, the patient, long-term investor who buys stock in large American corporations may expect to earn some profits on the stock values plus 3 percent to 6 percent each year from the dividends. And that is not bad.

The Small Investor Is In for the Long Haul

Stock Markets

Corporations often want to sell stock to raise money. Investors want to buy stocks because history shows us that it is the best way to build a nest egg. However, the investors will not buy much stock unless they are certain that there is a dependable way to get their money back. Therefore, the corporations can't sell much stock unless a dependable secondary market exists. Luckily, or through the collective genius of democracy and capitalism, such markets do exist. In spirit, they're like a farmers' market. Somebody provides a space for the sellers and buyers to come together, and charges a fee for the convenience. But in financial markets, the sellers and the buyers are generally not acquainted, and are many miles apart, so the market is a place for a bunch of middlemen to set up shop and just bring the buy requests and the sell requests together. The middlemen are brokers. In the New York Stock Exchange or American Stock Exchange, they all pay a steep fee for the privilege of coming in to do business. A stock market is a professional organization of the people and firms who offer the brokerage service. There are many similar organizations in every economically strong country in the world, but in the United States the largest exchanges are the New York Stock Exchange (NYSE) and the American Stock Exchange (ASE).

One stock market is a special case. It is the NASDAQ (National Association of Securities Dealers Automated Quotation) System. The NASD (National Association of Securities Dealers) is one of the prominent, non-government securities regulatory organizations, and NASDAQ is their creature. NASDAQ is not like a farmers' market. NASDAQ exists only as a computer network, and the people and agencies who use the network for pricing and sales information. NASDAQ labors under some controversy. There are people who say that small investors get ill-treated by the NASDAQ. There are people who say that NASDAQ gives small investors the best deal they could possibly ask for in trading small or new companies that aren't big enough to get into the NYSE. It is also true that there has been more rumor and smoke swirling around NASDAQ operations than the other major exchanges.

I have traded stocks using the NYSE, the ASE, and the NASDAQ, and I have never had any cause to doubt the efficiency or honesty of anyone handling any of my trades. There have been occasions when I paid a slightly higher spread[28] on a trade through the NASDAQ, but I always got exactly what the broker said I would get, and I never had any reason to doubt the fairness of it. Based on the complexity and volume of their business, and the extent of and strains on their computer networks, it seems rather remarkable that NASDAQ can offer all the service and information they do for the large number of low-priced, thinly traded stocks that they service.

Stock markets offer the greatest combination of fun and excitement, risk and reward, and roller-coaster emotional rides of anything that is likely to make money for you. The markets have the potential to

---

[28] The spread on a trade is the difference in the bid and asked prices. If a stock is bid at 20.75 and asking 21.25, then the spread is 50¢.

set you up for life, or knock you down for life. They may even contribute something to your social life, particularly if you have been at a loss for conversational entrees. But be observant about how much of your advice people want to hear before you let someone else share an opinion.

Of course, if you really want to mark yourself as a most desired guest and great wit, ask others for their ideas and recent experiences. If they don't have any opinions, they will hand the baton back to you and you are awarded the cachet of an expert. If they do have opinions and you listen attentively, you will be regarded as a genius!

So stock markets offer fun and gains. As long as you care to bring your money, there will be people there who are eager to trade with you. If you ever quit bringing money, for whatever reason, they will pitch you out and forget you. The market that loved you as a buyer will not provide a friend or counselor in time of need. As in much of our daily toils, many want to share your success, but only a few stick around to share your failure.

Investment Clubs

An investment club is a legal partnership. It consists of a group of people who have agreed to share their money, knowledge, and work in investing. If you want to know the rules, methods, or how to get started, contact the National Association of Investors Corporation (810-583-6242). They will send you information about how clubs work, how to get started, and clubs in your area. Investment clubs generally have fairly good records. They tend to put more time into individual stocks, rather than bonds or mutual funds. I would urge anyone who lacks experience with stock markets to find an investment club in your area, or to start one. It is likely that some local broker or investment advisor would be willing to offer free advice to your club. That's a good way for them to meet potential customers.

Investment clubs offer another method for diversification, too. Everybody knows something about business. But some people know more about other businesses than you do. Think about an investment club where there were six members who individually had five years experience in computers, telecommunications, the grocery business, retail sales, newspapers, and raising kids.[29] What a wealth of knowledge and experience to help analyze products or services! They would bring different points of view to each stock you might analyze. It is almost guaranteed that the group would consistently make better decisions about stocks than any one of them individually. The group working together would certainly recognize and evaluate risks better than any one working alone.

When you form a club or join an existing club, look for diversity in experience, social background, and education. Don't start a club with just engineers who work for the same employer and have worked there for years. They have all started thinking alike. Be attentive that the members share the workload. Some clubs fall into a habit of letting some dominant person do all the research and bully people into buy and sell decisions. Such clubs would offer none of the intended benefits of investment clubs, and always fail as social outlets. Make sure that all of the members agree and are comfortable with the contributions level ($20 per month? $100 per month?) and the general philosophy (aggressive investing, conservative investing, stocks only, stocks and bonds). It would do more harm than good to bring someone in who shortly turned out to be unhappy about the ground rules.

If you intend to explore stocks, and if you have the small investor's usual healthy fear and suspicion, there may be nothing better suited to a good introduction than an investment club.

Why Stocks?

It's easy: that's where the rewards are. But it's difficult: that is also where the most work and the greatest risks are.

Make no mistake about it, in the long run, common stocks on the whole will outperform[30] every other type of investment. That's the

---

[29] Let's make certain that there is no one out there saying, "Not me, I don't know anything about anything." You do, you do. You probably use as many different products as anyone else. You know which ones you and your friends like or hate. You know if business is good at the local grocery. If you live on this planet, then you have regular contact with the economy, and you derive some knowledge that would help in evaluating investments.

[30] When I say "will outperform," this is just an extension of the historic record, but it is based on a lot of history, so that's good scientific method.

good news. The bad news is that you won't just go out and buy the market, and among individual stocks there will be huge variations as to results. Besides, in the long run most of us will be dead.

Does the long run do us any good? Does it do you any good if you buy stocks near a market high and the market declines for two years, followed by another six years of modest growth? Did it do any good for your grandparents who bought stocks in 1927, lost badly in 1929 and 1930, and then hardly made any profits until 1946? Did the long-term upward trend of the market do any good for people who bought Wang Labs in 1983 at $30 a share, or in 1987 at $15, or in 1990 at $4? (Answer: no, Wang went bankrupt.)

Let's Play the Market

Play the market? Let's not. If you treat this as play, you will lose your shirt. Playing the market is a concept created by stockbrokers to make you think it's not really dangerous. It is dangerous and you play for keeps.

Let's Work the Market

We are going to get into some ideas about managing (risk-oriented) money that is allocated for (risk-oriented) investments in individual stocks. Back in 1990, I was sitting around watching Unisys Corporation (symbol UIS on NYSE). Unisys makes computers and provides all manner of services and support to people who use computer systems. Their stock had been through an awful slide from around $40 per share in 1987 to a low of $16 in 1989, and down to $1 in 1990. They were victims of slumping mainframe sales, and the popular story of that day that mainframes were dead. Nobody liked Unisys. However, I knew that they had an active and productive service organization that stood to gain from the current trends to farm out more computer support from large companies. I figured that the service organization was a good bet, and the death of mainframes was a hoax, and somehow this company ought to be worth more than $1 a share. Pretty smart thinking, right? But I didn't buy. I couldn't ever make up my mind and get off the dime. At the end of 1991 UIS was $6 a share, and at the end of 1992 it was $10. In 1994 it got as high as $16 for a few days and then settled in around $7–$10.

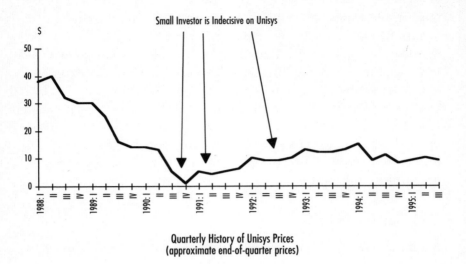

Small Investor is Indecisive on Unisys

Quarterly History of Unisys Prices
(approximate end-of-quarter prices)

Lessons learned: It is possible to make good money in stocks, but there will come a point when somebody has to make a decision. It is not always easy. Second lesson: there are probably some people, probably even some big-time money managers, who bought Unisys around $30 a share in 1988 and have held it ever since. Tough luck. It's a jungle out there.

In late 1991, Ford was clunking along (their stock, that is, not the cars). The country was in an economic slowdown and car sales were not holding up. Also, the popular wisdom was that Americans could not build and sell cars in a worldwide competitive market. So there sits Ford. In 1989 the price had hovered around $50 a share and revenues had been $96 billion. In 1990 the price fell as low as $25 per share, and revenues were up a little. In 1991 the price bounced between $25 and $38, but it ended the year on a pronounced downslide. The revenues were off to about $88 billion. Net profits of the firm went from $4.3 billion profit in '89 to $860 million profit in 1990 to $2.3 billion loss in 1991. Things looked pretty bad for Ford.

I took a look at it and had my own opinions. I thought they built great cars, and the company had a history of commitment to a strong dividend, which was interrupted by a dividend reduction in 1991. I liked it. So I bought Ford in November of 1991 at $27.50. I sold it in July of '92 at $42 and collected $1.20 per share in dividend payments along the way. Good deal, right? At the time there were any number of prominent prognosticators who were preaching against Ford. In fact, I have a signed letter from one of them telling me to sell my Ford in the fall of 1991. But I held on and made a good profit. The people who held on longer made more money than I. I ended up two years later buying Ford again at $29, but that was after a two-for-one stock split, meaning its value was comparable to $58.

Lessons learned: It is possible to make money in stocks, but there will come a point when somebody has to make a decision. It is not always easy. Second lesson: there are probably some people, probably even some big-time money managers, who passed on Ford until late in 1993 and missed the plum. There are probably some long-term investors who bought Ford at $48 in 1987, and still hold it at a split-adjusted value of $60, so they have had a lot of grief with Ford and haven't made much money (up 25 percent in eight years). It requires some decisiveness to either buy or sell if you're going to take profits out of the market. Third lesson: Long-term investors in blue chip stocks do not always get rich.

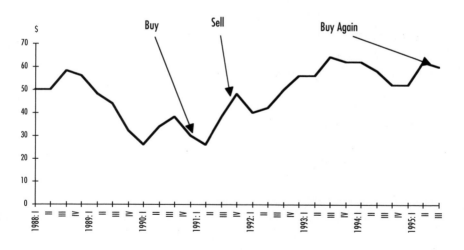

Quarterly History of Ford Prices
(approximate end-of-quarter prices shown based on presplit prices)

You can look at the chart and make all kinds of judgments as to whether I did well or not very well. However, I made decisions, I made commitments, *and* I made money. Good enough!

But sometimes even a blind pig can make money. In late 1992, I heard about a local company that was preparing for its initial public stock offering. I felt like writing a story, so I hustled the idea to the Chapel Hill News, and went out to do my research on the company, CREE Research (symbol CREE on the NASDAQ). I wrote a good story and learned a lot. I liked it. The initial price was $8, and by the time I finished my story it was $16, so I passed, and waited, and watched. Pretty soon it was $25, so I waited. Pretty soon it was $14, and I bought CREE at $12 in September of 1993. Over the next eighteen months it really bounced around, but I liked the company and the people and I thought I partially understood their markets, so I bought more. The price bounced between $6 and $15, and I ended up with six purchases at an average price of $11. After my last buy, at $9.25, the stock went through the roof, to $20 per share. I had made plans to take some profits at $20 per share, but changed my mind because of the strength and speed of the rally; it then increased to $25, then to $30; I sold some, just to get some money off of the table. It had gotten to the point where nearly half of my total investments was in CREE, and that is just not good diversification for a small investor like me. It climbed further, to $35, then to $40. There was one day when the market took an awful jolt for a while, especially the high-tech stocks, so I decided to take some more money out, so I sold some at the market that morning and got $36.50. The stock climbed back up to 44, and the company split its stock. Since then it has gone as high as 30 again, and then went on a severe downslide. I have sold all of mine, and ended up making a profit.

Lessons learned: It is possible to make good money in stocks, but there will come a point when somebody has to make a decision. It is not always easy. Second lesson: there are probably some people, probably even some big-time money managers, who bought CREE at 22 or 23 or 24 after the split and are looking at no gain, probable loss now. On the other hand, there are probably some people who bought CREE at 6 in December of '94 and sold double the number of shares in the high twenties in late 95.[31] But it takes nerve and decisiveness.

---

[31] That means that each dollar invested returned about $8 or $9.

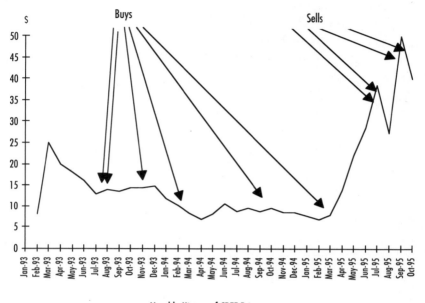

Monthly History of CREE Prices
(approximate end-of-month prices, presplit basis)

CREE is an interesting case in speculation. Unlike Ford or Unisys, these guys have virtually never made a profit. The bet is on their potential. I put in as much as I was willing to expose to high risk, and took money back out when I got nervous. They have never paid a dividend and probably will not for a long time. Paying a dividend wouldn't make any sense. They should be putting their money into research and development, not just returning it to the shareholders. The market capitalization at the time I was buying was not over $80 million, and the staff and working digs are correspondingly small. But the potential for reward was, and still is, immense.

At the time that I first decided to get serious about the stock markets and make some bigger moves, the first stock I bought was Potomac Electric Corporation (symbol POM on NYSE), at $23.875. It was very big, safe, and secure, and had an immensely strong track record as to profits and dividend payments. The yield ran around 7–8 percent depending on price fluctuations. I planned to hold POM for the rest of my life. In late 1993 all of the electric utilities were quite popular and the price had been pushed up substantially. The dividend rate at that point fell below 6 percent. I was nervous about the overall stock market and decided to take some money out. I sold POM at $27⅜ after having collected about $1.60 per share dividends each year while I held it. This turned out to be a good move. It quickly went into a swoon, along with all the other electric companies and dropped to $22. I bought it again at $22 and watched it fall to $18 before coming back up to $27. All the while, on the second ride, I was collecting about 9 percent yield on my investment.

Lessons learned: It is possible to make money in stocks, but there will come a point when somebody has to make a decision. Making decisions is not easy. Second lesson: there are probably some people, probably even some mutual fund managers, who held POM all the way, and failed to grab the profit when they had a chance. Even conservative, buy-and-hold, long-term small investors like us can sometimes make a profit by being decisive and taking some money back out of the markets.

Buying and Selling

So I hope that the examples along with whatever you hear from the news and your friends have convinced you that it is possible to make money and to lose money. Sometimes it may happen that two investors will buy the same stock at the same time, for the same price, and one will end up making it profitable while the other will not. This is because it's not just which stocks you pick, it's when and how you sell.

Even the conservative, long-term, buy-and-hold small investor like us should be looking at the sell side. Because almost every stock is a winner and almost every stock is a loser. You have to make decisions and take action sometimes if you want to be a winner.

It's a Stock Picker's World

Sometimes, especially if the major market averages are not moving much, you will hear commentators say, "It's not a stock market; it's a market of stocks." That means that you can't just safely go out and buy the market, instead you have to pick and choose stocks to buy in order to get ahead. But how?

The next few sections are going to review some of the popular notions about how. There is no consensus as to what works best. There are a thousand other more or less reasonable schemes besides what I will mention here. This is an introduction only. I want you to get some idea as to whether any of this makes sense to you. By the end of this chapter, you should have some well-formed thoughts as to whether you will study some of these ideas in other books, seek other theories, or just chuck it all and avoid buying individual stocks. Find something that you will be comfortable with. I think this stuff is interesting and worth the risk; you may feel otherwise.

Investing in Common Stocks

Let's focus. *To invest*: my big unabridged dictionary says first, "**1a**: to array in the symbols of office or honor"; that's not what we want. The second definition has "to commit money for a long period in order to earn a financial return." That's better. But see those key words: *long period* and *earn*. That is not necessarily the stock trader's view, either the long period, or the earning. Well, my point is there are different views of the practice, or art, or work, or fortune of investing, particularly investing in stocks.

You can do whatever you want, and I won't pass judgment, regardless, but let's distinguish two popular views of stock investments. Any investor certainly wants to make a profit. Profits can be tied to two sources. They are the stock markets' changes in prices, and the earnings of a company whose stock you own. Generally, when I invest, I look for companies that are likely to reward me on both counts. The first, stock market price changes, is in some sense an unearned reward, or at best earned by your analytical insights into the stock. The second, company operational profits and dividends, are most assuredly earned by the management, labor, and sales of the company. Much of their fruits flow to the owners, the stockholders. Some investors devote most of their attention and plans to the price changes in the market. I think that is foolish, but it is certainly widely practiced and somebody makes a profit at it. Others, the more conservative investors, focus more on the earnings and dividends. They are expecting to derive profits through someone's labor, and not rely on the more speculative variations in the markets.

You may sympathize with either view and manage your money accordingly, but you should consider both avenues to profits, and be aware of how other investors regard them.

Earnings and Dividends

What do you get when you buy common stock? You may or may not get the piece of paper, but there is something in the company's (or your broker's) records that says you own a piece of the company. If anyone wants to buy your company, they may have to deal with you, or your co-shareholders. You probably get a right to vote for the directors, but sometimes not. You also probably earn a share of the profits. The company earns some revenues from sales, and after taking out the costs of administration, operations, and taxes, they should have a profit. That profit belongs to the shareholders and will go into two buckets: part into dividends paid to shareholders, and part for the company to retain to improve operations or initiate new product lines.

Both of those two earnings buckets work for you, the shareholder. The dividend comes directly to you as cash, and the retained earnings increase the value of the company and your shares. Therefore many investors are particularly concerned about how the earnings and the dividends look compared to the price of a share.

The *price/earnings (P/E)* ratio is the price of one share divided by the total earnings per share. Generally speaking, lower values of the P/E ratio are considered safer than higher values. If a company's stock shows a P/E ratio of 10, each share of stock is earning one-tenth of its price. For each dollar you invest, the company earns 10¢. If another company has a P/E ratio equal to 18, each share earns one-eighteenth of its price. For each dollar you put into that stock, the earnings will be about 5.6¢.

Stock buyers and sellers use P/E ratio numbers to estimate where prices might go. The rule of thumb is: the estimated fair price for the stock = the estimated fair P/E ratio times the estimate of earnings.

Early in 1994, Emerson Electric was selling for $62 a share and had earnings for the year of $3.52 per share. That gave it a P/E ratio of 62 ÷ 3.52 = 18 (with a little rounding). Suppose some investors thought that 18 was a proper and fair P/E value for Emerson (symbol EMR on the NYSE). In other words, they thought it was a fair buy at that level. If they forecast sales for the next year of $4.50, they would decide the price could reasonably rise up to 18 × $4.50 = $81.

For those investors, this view of the P/E ratio would indicate that they should buy Emerson for $62 and have it rise next year to close to $81. Other investors would have other opinions, which is why the markets stay active.

Another group of investors might decide that Emerson did not deserve any higher P/E ratio than General Electric. GE at that time had a P/E close to 14. These investors think that Emerson should have a P/E close to 14 also. This second group thinks the fair price of Emerson should be closer to 14 × $3.52 = $49 this year, and just 14 times next year's earnings, next year. This group would not buy Emerson at $62, and in fact would sell it if they had it.

It takes all kinds to make a market. Given the price in late 1994 of $62 and earnings of $3.52, a sample of investors might consider these kinds of actions for Emerson:

Jake thinks that the P/E = 18 is fair, but the earnings next year will only be $4. He forecasts a future price for the stock of 18 × $4 = $72 and acts accordingly.

Sarah thinks that the P/E should be fairly set at 20 and the earnings next year will hit $5. She forecasts a stock price of 20 × $5 = $100 for next year and acts accordingly.

Jim knows that the average P/E for all companies in similar business is 15, and guesses that Emerson should get about the same. He figures that Emerson is really only worth 15 × $3.52 = $53 today.

Lynn buys the stock at $62 just because she likes the products and their balance sheet. Eight months later, the forecasts become quite specific that Emerson will earn $4.20 in 1995, and the market still gives them a P/E value of 18. Then the stock price grows to 18 × $4.20 = $75.60.

Betty has held the stock for eight years and has no intention of selling. However, the mood of the market turns pessimistic, and all stocks get priced downward to lower P/E values. The market decides that Emerson now will only sell for 13 times the 1995 earnings of $4.20. So Betty's stock falls in value to 13 × $4.20 = $54.60. She is a long-term investor who sticks with Emerson because of their very strong long-term record. She is willing to wait and see what the long run will bring her.

Look at three fictional companies, ACO, BCO and C3PO, which each earn $1 per year in earnings per share. Suppose the market has decided, as the collective wisdom of all investors, that ACO deserves a P/E of 28, BCO deserves 19, and C3PO deserves 7. Then ACO should sell for $28 a share, BCO for $19, and C3PO for $7. If you thought that the businesses and the prospects for those three were about the same, you should buy C3PO stock.

Imagine you have $5,000 to invest. In ACO that gets you 178 shares and earns $178 per year. In BCO, you could buy 263 shares and get $263 per year in company earnings. But in C3PO you would buy 714 shares and control $714 per year in corporate earnings. If all other factors can be considered equal or nearly equal, the stock with the lower P/E ratio will earn more for the investor.

Many investors adopt a practice that they will not buy a stock unless the P/E ratio is below some value they consider safe. That imagined "safe" P/E value might be 8, 10, 14, or the market average, or whatever they like, but it does influence the thinking and buying decisions of many. For that reason, a low P/E ratio does help to support, or justify, the price of a stock.

The *yield ratio* (or simply, the yield) is the dividend per share divided by the price per share. Higher yield ratios are considered better than lower. Many investors adopt a practice that they will only buy stocks that have a yield ratio above some acceptable number. That imagined "safe" yield may be 2 percent, 4 percent, 6 percent, or the market average, or the yield on ten-year Treasury notes, or whatever they want, but it does influence the thinking and decisions of many investors. Therefore, a higher yield number helps to support the value of a stock and provide some assurance against loss of value.

Here are a few examples:

In 1992 KO (Coca-Cola) had a price of $40, earnings of $1.43 per share and dividend of 56¢. So the P/E was $40.00 \div 1.43 = 28$, and the yield ratio was $0.56 \div 40 = 1.4\%$.

At the end of 1991, Potomac Electric (POM) had a price of about $24, earnings of $1.87, and dividend for the year of $1.56; thus the P/E ratio was $24 \div 1.87 = 13$, and the yield ratio was $1.56 \div 24 = 6.5\%$.

From this perspective, Potomac Electric may have appeared to be a sounder investment than Coca-Cola because it had much higher yield (6.5 percent compared to 1.4 percent) and much lower P/E ratio (13 compared to 28). That is only one way of looking at the stocks, and many other factors need to be considered, but it is a view that has a strong influence on some investors.

The numbers become important to investors who say that they are only in it for the profit, and the most dependable sources of profit are earnings and yield. When Coca-Cola's P/E was 28, that meant that the investor would pay about $28 for each dollar of earnings. With a stock that had P/E = 13, the investor would only pay about $13 to get $1 of earnings. Most investors feel that the stock price to get a dollar of earnings should be a factor in their decisions.

If you were looking at two stocks, say KO and POM, as candidates to buy, you could do a little risk analysis as follows. Both of these are large profitable companies with long histories of solid earnings and dividend payments. With KO I get lower yield now, but faster growth of earnings and share price. With POM I expect larger dividends now, but more stable earnings and share price.

Another point to consider is the market's overall average yield or price/earnings ratio. Let's say that, on average, large blue-chip companies were paying 4 percent yield with a P/E ratio of 15. What if the rest of investors decided that Coca-Cola was no longer such a great growth vehicle? If the other investors decided that they had to have 4 percent yield or a P/E closer to the market average of 15, that might hurt the price of KO.

The stock market cannot change Coca-Cola's earnings or dividends, so they change what they can, the price of the stock. For instance, if KO had earnings of $2 per share this year and dividend of 65¢, in order to have a P/E of 15, they would need a price of 15 × 2 = $30. Investors might decide to reduce KO's price to the point where the P/E was only 15, which makes the stock price $30. In order to have a yield of 4 percent the price would fall to 65¢/.04 = $16.25. If the market demanded[32] a yield ratio of 4 percent for KO, people would bid the price down to $16.25. Both of those potential changes in price *might be interpreted by some investors* as showing a risk of lower stock price for Coca-Cola.

On the other hand, if POM were to be purchased at price of $24, with earnings of $1.87 and dividend of $1.56, and if the market were to reprice it towards a P/E of 15 and yield of 4 percent, those would both tend to move the price up. The P/E = 15 would imply a price of 15 × $1.87 = $28, and the yield = 4 percent requirement would imply a price of $39. Both of those *might be interpreted* as showing a possible price appreciation for Potomac Electric.

This sort of analysis is summed up in the chart below:

	POM	KO
actual market price	$24.00	$40.00
earnings	$1.87	$2.00
dividend	$1.56	$0.65
implied price if P/E has to be 15	$28.00	$30.00
implied price if yield has to be 4%	$39.00	$16.25

This is of interest to some investors who think that in the long run many stocks will tend to be evaluated and priced equivalently. That kind of thinking indicates that KO is overpriced and POM may be underpriced[33] relative to other very large corporations. In the final analysis, a good stock picker[34] has to do some figuring and thinking, and then decide whether there really is any good reason for Coca-Cola to have a much higher P/E and a much lower yield than the average Dow-Jones Industrial stock.

---

[32] When the "market decides," it just means most investors think that way and act accordingly.

[33] I do not intend to imply that the conclusions are necessarily correct, but that this is one way of looking at P/E ratios and yield ratios.

[34] Warren Buffett is one of the most respected and successful stock analysts of all time. It is instructive to read in his biography how he approached the analysis of Coca-Cola. See *Buffett, The Making of an American Capitalist* by Roger Lowenstein.

The yield ratio tells you how fast your investment is coming back to you. If the yield ratio is 1.4 percent, then each year you get back 1.4 percent of what you have invested in the stock. When the yield ratio is 6.5 percent, then each year you could get back 6.5 percent of your investment. The astute and careful investors will also compare this with the yield return that they might get on buying bonds. A good bond might return 7 percent or 8 percent with very little risk or opportunity for price fluctuation.

So what is best to buy? There is no automatic answer. For some people the choice is to buy Coca-Cola, pay the high price for earnings and yield, but expect a steady strong growth in earnings, yield, and share price over the coming years. The KO buyers accept a risk of share price loss that is implied by the high current P/E ratio. For some investors the choice is buy Potomac Electric shares at a lower price, and get strong assurance (from their history) that the dividend will be maintained at or above this good yield of 6.5 percent. They have a long, well-established history of raising the dividend year by year. The POM buyers accept the risk of share price loss that is implied just by being in the stock markets, but they are encouraged by the safe market of the company. The high-dividend yield also helps to provide a prop for the stock. If it started to fall in price, the yield would go so high as to certainly attract new buyers.[35] For others, the best choice is buy a ten-year Treasury note that pays 6.5 percent, and rest secure in the government's promise to pay the yield every year, and return exactly $1,000 at the end of the ten years.

Your position, as an independent small investor, is that you do not have to prove which decision is best or justify your decision to the world. Just find something that works well for you.

You may not want to be married to any particular guidelines or rules on how to use the P/E ratio or the yield ratio, but it would be foolish to ignore them.[36] Both of them tell you something about the value of the stock and its relative attractiveness compared to other stocks.

---

[35] This is about what happened in 1995.

[36] There is a nice, easy-to-read, and helpful book on investing driven by dividends: *The Dividend Investor*, Knowles and Petty, Probus Publishing Co., 1995. It presents a simple and easy method for choosing stocks that might appeal to some small investors.

Most of the financial news sources will frequently publicize the market average P/E, or perhaps the average yield for the DJIA, or the average for the S&P 500 or some other group of stocks. Those numbers help value-conscious investors look at stocks relative to what other investments offer.

Compounding the Growth by Reinvesting Dividends

Look at two hypothetical investors Bill and Jane, who owned 100 shares of the same stock for 10 years. Here are the numbers:

year	1	2	3	4	5	6	7	8	9	10
price ($)	22	23	24	21	25	26	24	23	26	27
dividend per share	88¢	92¢	96¢	92¢	1.00	1.10	1.10	1.00	1.10	1.15

Bill collects his dividends in cash and spends them on current necessities. Jane collects her dividends and converts the money back into stock.[37] Where do they stand at the end of the ten years?

What did they collect each year?

Bill collected cash for his 100 shares: $88 + 92 + 96 + 92 + 100 + 110 + 110 + 100 + 110 + 115 = $1,013, and he still has his 100 shares worth $2700. A good, neat profit.

Jane bought new shares:

year	shares held	dividend earned	new shares bought
1	100	$88.00	4
2	104	95.68	4.2
3	108.2	103.87	4.3
4	112.5	103.50	4.9
5	117.4	117.40	4.7
6	122.1	134.31	5.2
7	127.3	140.03	5.8
8	133.1	133.10	5.8
9	138.9	152.79	5.9
10	144.8	166.52	6.2

[37] Many companies offer dividend reinvestment plans whereby instead of paying the dividend, they will just give you the equivalent in new stock. This has an added benefit of avoiding brokerage fees. In addition some of the companies even offer the new stock at a small discount from the market price.

At the end of ten years, Jane owns 151 shares at $27 each for a total value of $4,077. Jane's investment grew by 85 percent, while Bill's grew by 23 percent.[38] Of course, Bill also had some money from dividends to work with along the way. If Bill reinvested the dividends elsewhere, he might be as well off, but if he simply spent the dividends, he is way behind where he might be.

Many investors have good and sufficient reasons to spend their dividends, and maybe you do, too. However, there is no denying that if you can reinvest dividends, the compound growth should pay off greatly in a few years.

Looking for Value or Growth?

The value theory of investing emphasizes that there are certain fundamentals about a company that will determine its ultimate success or failure, and its level of sales and profits. Value investing leans on fundamental analysis that requires doing research in the financial reports and profit and loss statements. It requires analyzing the products or services of the company and its competitors. A value investor wants to know something about the management and their plan, as well as the company's history. A great book to read to pursue this further is *The Intelligent Investor* by Benjamin Graham. The bottom line is that if you want to make money, you have to do it the old-fashioned way: work for it. The methods of Graham and his disciples require work. They also require some understanding of financial statements and the ability to judge products and management. Those things are not precise sciences, and may require more background or more analysis than is suitable for some investors.

There is a legitimate point of view that if you can't handle any of that, then maybe you should just stay out of the stock markets. A better course would be to join an investment club and share the burden with someone whose experience and education are different from yours. You might decide instead to find a good broker or advisor and follow their advice. Or go back to school and study some financial management or accounting.

---

[38] Note that these returns depend on a case in which you have both strong dividend payments and a rising stock price, but I assume that if you hold a stock for ten years, then it must be doing something right.

What's called growth investing is sometimes put forward as the counterpoint to value investing. There is no essential contradiction between value investing and growth investing, but the value-oriented investor will be more impressed by the financial ratios and the dividends and price/earnings ratio of a company, while the growth investor is concentrating his attention on the rates of change of the total sales and earnings, as well as the stock price. The premise of growth investing is that trends in revenues and profits can carry a company into or out of a slump. For example, in 1991 Chrysler was a mess. The company's stock was selling for about $10. But then the automobile market started to come back. Anyone who could have discerned the trends of car sales or in Chrysler's revenues and sales could have done very well over the next few years. The (strict) value investor would have rejected Chrysler throughout 1991 and 1992, and maybe even still today. Some smart folks figured out the trends and the momentum in Chrysler's sales and stock price and stock market volume early on and have made a pile of money.

CREE Research is an example of a growth-oriented investment.[39] With very small current sales or profits, it has nothing to offer the value investor, but if it ever gets up to $15 per share in revenue and maybe $1 a share in earnings, it will probably attract value investors plus all manner of growth investors who will make assumptions about the trend continuing.

Growth investing can apply to all kinds of companies. For example, Coca-Cola is pretty well known and fixed in their rut. But it's still regarded as a growth investment. The logic is that even though their stock price is pretty high (at $69 for a company that only earns around $2 per share this year), the trend is your friend. Look at Coke's share price for the years 1990, 1992, and 1994: it was around $40 until late 1994, when it ran up to about $48. The profits per share for the same three years were $1.02, $1.43, and then $1.98, and the paid dividend grew from 40¢ to 78¢. Some people thought Coke was too expensive at 40 times earnings in 1990, and again in 1992 at 28 times earnings, and again in 94 at 24 times earnings. Maybe so, but the growth-oriented investors who bought it have taken a very good profit, with good dividend yield

---

[39] I guess; it may turn out to be a no-growth oriented investment, but the theory to support it is the growth theory.

and a rock-steady upward price trend. And if a billion Chinese people love Coca-Cola, which apparently they do, the company doesn't need to do anything different.

You might find that Coca-Cola also qualifies as a value investment in terms of finances, management, markets, and almost everything except price, but the purist value investor is reluctant to buy stocks when the price/earnings ratio is much higher than the rest of the market. The bottom line of value investing is that most stocks represent good companies with good markets, but any stock can be just plain overpriced.

Investing for value and investing for growth are not antithetical. Some financial specialists prefer one over the other, or apply different methods at different times. A savvy stock picker will consider both. Anytime you prepare to make an investment, you should think about other things you might be doing with the money. If most of your money were invested in growth stocks, it might make sense to diversify some by buying a couple with higher dividends and lower price/earnings ratios.

Sectors

If you get into picking stocks, there will be many times when you are only concerned with a small part of the stock market as a whole. For example, you might be particularly interested in electric utilities. Electric utilities form a sector of the market. Other sectors would include perhaps only automobile companies, or perhaps just department stores, or just small cap companies. *Cap* is the standard market jargon for the total market capitalization of a company, the product of the price per share times the number of shares. It is, in a sense, what someone might pay if they tried to buy the entire company.

Examples:

Coca-Cola has a price of $69 and 1.25 billion shares. That gives a market capitalization of around $86 billion.

POM had a price of $24 and 119 million shares. That gave POM a market cap of $2.9 billion.

CREE started out with price at $8 and 4 million shares for a market cap of $32 million.

So investors sometimes look at *sectors* of the market. These might include electric utilities, automobile, biotechnology, retail stores, small cap, medium cap, large cap, blue chips, growth, etc. There are thousands of different sectors.

Each sector requires its own approach to stock picking. Certain sectors are naturally full of value stocks, some are naturally full of growth stocks, some are composed of out-of-favor stocks, some tend towards higher or lower P/E values, and some tend towards higher or lower yield values. The electric utilities sector tends to show higher yield and lower P/E than others. The computer software sector is full of supposedly growth-oriented stocks that typically have very high P/E and little or no dividends.

TOP-DOWN INVESTING: CHOOSE A SECTOR, THEN PICK A STOCK

Sometimes it is helpful to an investor to start out by selecting a sector before thinking about an individual company. For example, I have a personal prejudice in favor of electric utilities that operate in the southeastern U.S. That gives me a sector of about fifteen stocks that I can study to find one to buy.

Then my task is to find one of those fifteen in the sector that looks best, so I compare the P/E ratios, the yield ratios, the debt, the dividend histories, and the market area economies before making a choice. But in making that decision, it is not appropriate to compare the P/E of an electric utility with Coca-Cola. Once you make a decision to go into a specific sector, your choice should depend on the relative values in that sector. Or you may decide there is nothing in the sector that is good enough. There may be times when you have good reasons to only be interested in local banks in Alabama, so you study that sector to find one to buy. It's still okay if you decide that all of them are overpriced. That kind of thing has happened to me a couple of times when I was just too late in deciding to purchase stock. Other investors saw the reasons to buy paper companies before I did, and everything got bid up to excessive prices.

You might also choose to focus on a sector before picking individual stocks in order to improve the diversification of your portfolio. The financial newspapers and stock advisory publications like *The Value Line* will give periodic reports on the average P/E, or average yield, or growth prospects for various sectors. Those numbers can help you pick the particular stock you want to buy. Or they might convince you that the entire sector is weak.

Sometimes the sector analysis can persuade you to stay away from a given stock. If one stock in a sector looks good but the overall sector is weak, it might happen that the market becomes prejudiced against the sector and takes the one good stock down with it. That is a judgment call that you or your advisor will have to wrestle with. If, for instance, at some time General Motors looked good to you while Ford and Chrysler looked bad, you would have to make a decision: is GM about to get socked with the same bad economic conditions that are hurting Ford and Chrysler, or is GM really doing a great job and stealing the market from the other two?

Large Cap, Small Cap

Usually a company with a market capitalization of more than $2 billion would be regarded as a large cap, and one with market cap below $200 million would be small cap. Beyond that, people have different ideas of how to define the two terms. What *is* important is the tendency for larger and smaller companies to behave differently.

Both large and small caps have certain characteristics and advantages. History shows that the smaller caps outperform the large caps over the long term, but they also carry greater risk. The smaller caps are usually considered to be the higher-risk group, although there are great variations among individual companies.

Think about a situation where an engineer had a brilliant idea that led to a new product line estimated to have market potential of $20 million in sales, producing $6 million in profits. If he worked for General Motors (market capitalization = $35 billion), the increase in revenues is 0.013 percent, and the increase in profits is 0.1 percent (using 1995 data). So that one invention should not have a huge impact on the stock price. However, if he worked for Checkpoint Systems (CKP on the NYSE), the growth in revenues would be 10 percent and the growth in profits would be 60 percent. The invention would have a dramatic impact on their stock price. Even without any great new invention, you could imagine a case where Checkpoint might be able to double their market share over the next few years. It is difficult to imagine the GM behemoth doing that. However, the smaller companies are exposed to more risk, too. If a company only has a modest amount of capital goods to support their operations, a competitor could enter their market and take away sales easier than if the investments were huge. It is difficult to imagine a new American automobile manufacturer making much headway against Ford, GM, and Chrysler, but it is easy to imagine new strong competition for the fast-food chains, an auto parts manufacturer, or CREE Research, where the original investment might require less than $50 million.

Generally, the small caps offer potentially greater growth, but also greater risks. It is probably an idea to use in your diversification scheme, if you can stand the risks. Another approach might be to do your own stock picking for some blue chips or utilities, and invest in a mutual fund that specializes in small caps. The mutual fund would diversify among 50 to 100 small companies and save you the trouble of studying a lot of them.

Technical Analysis

Technical analysis is an attempt to learn from the numbers and the history of a stock. It relies on interpreting price history as a reflection of collective market judgment. It is easiest to see what is involved by looking at charts of stock prices. You may not care to use it or study it, but many people do. It is worthwhile for you to recognize some of the words and ideas.

Technical analysts have studied the history of price movements and other measurements of market activity and found trends and patterns that they believe will help them forecast coming developments. Of course, no one is so foolish as to promise certainty in such forecasting, but some analysts believe there is enough consistency and rational basis in the patterns to make them useful guides. Most stock market investors agree that there is some validity in technical analysis, although the amount of value in it is debated.

The following is a true story. The company name is withheld so we can concentrate on the technical analysis. In the middle of 1988, some analysts might have looked at the price chart for a company on the NASDAQ and seen this:

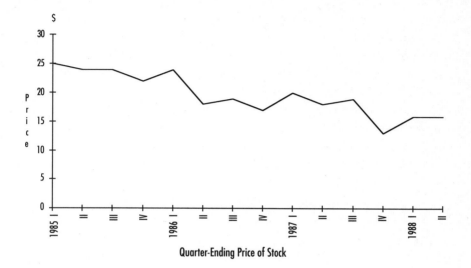

Quarter-Ending Price of Stock

This is not very pretty, but almost any stock is a winner if you can buy at the right time, and maybe this one is sufficiently low that it's ready for the big turnaround. Should we buy now? The technical analysts will take out a ruler and draw some "trend lines" on the graph:

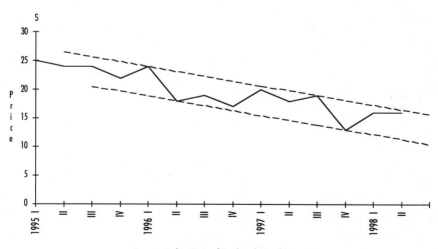

Quarter-Ending Price of Stock with Trend Lines

The trend lines draw attention to the succeeding lower values of each attempt to rally, and the succeeding lower values of each intermediate low point, leading to lower highs and lower lows. This is an ugly trend. Technical analysis would indicate against buying this stock in the middle of 1988.

If the analyst came back to the same stock in the middle of 1992, the picture (below) would show some new features. The downtrend continued, and in fact got worse, as indicated by the new trend lines, but there is an interesting feature in the third quarter of 1991 where the upper and lower trend lines converge. That pattern is thought to foretell the end of the downtrend. The graph here seems to confirm that. Some technical analysts would have felt very tempted to buy this stock in late 1991.

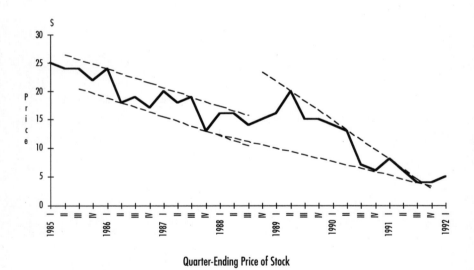

Quarter-Ending Price of Stock

If we leap forward to the middle of 1995, you can see that a new uptrend was established in early 1992 or late 1991. Also, in early 1995, the stock was breaking away from its 1993–94 trends. I have added a new line (the dotted curve) which is a moving average for the stock price. It represents the average price over the past four quarters.

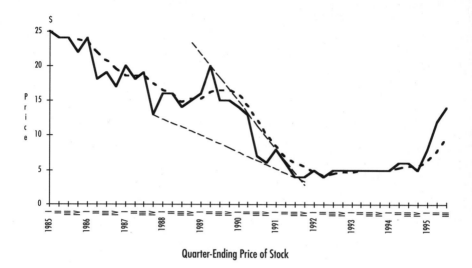

Quarter-Ending Price of Stock

One theory in technical analysis is that when a price breaks signif-icantly below, or above, its moving average, that is a *sell signal* or a *buy signal,* respectively. In this case the chart has given a strong signal in late 1991 that the downtrend was over, and a strong buy signal in early 1995 by breaking out above its moving average. A confirmed chart watcher would be very eager to own this stock in early 1995. Within six months, his or her money would have doubled. However, notice also that the moving average line gave a buy signal in early 1989, so these things are not infallible. Another interesting idea that comes out of technical analysis is *volume momentum,* which postulates that a price change on heavy share volume is more predictive than a price change on light volume. I don't think anyone disputes the valid-ity of this theory.

Technical analysis is one of many tools that a stock picker might use. Some people say it is foolishness, and others say it can be relied upon for almost all buy or sell decisions. I say it is a tool. It won't do your thinking for you, but it might deserve some consideration. Some investors are successful relying completely on technical analysis, and some are successful while ignoring it. You can decide for yourself whether it deserves any of your time and attention.

Dollar Cost Averaging

Some people think that there is a magic method to guarantee that you come out ahead on investments. There is not. However, there is a method to take advantage of the long-term upward trend of the market if you can stay in long enough for the long-term trend to outweigh the short-term setbacks.

The rule of dollar cost averaging is that you decide on some fixed amount that you will put into your investments every month, every quarter, or whatever time period you like. The benefits of dollar cost averaging are that you have a regular practice and discipline in your investing, and price breaks become opportunities to buy more stock than you would have acquired at the higher prices.

Let us say that you have decided to invest $1,000 every quarter in your favorite stock, and (we ignore brokerage fees for the moment) the price of the stock over four quarters went like this: $18, 16, 18, 19. If you bought as many shares as you could with the $1,000 each quarter, and held the extra cash to put into next quarter's purchase, your four quarters' purchases would buy 55, 63, 55, 53 shares, respectively. At the end you would have 226 shares worth $4,294. The dollar cost averaging procedure kept you in the market, and in fact buying more shares, when the price took the dip to $16. This is better than you would have done if you had invested the entire $4,000 either in the first or last month, and far better than you would have done if you had been scared and sold out on the price dip in the second quarter.

However, if the price had gone down, say $18, 16, 16, 15, you would end up with 247 shares worth $3,705, which is a loss. Dollar cost averaging depends on the long-term uptrend in the price of the stock. If the uptrend is not there, or if you can't wait for it, dollar cost averaging will not make you a winner. This method is applicable to any kind of investment as long as you can make regular fixed payments that are large enough to make the accompanying brokerage fees or sales loads not too painful. That is easiest if you work with an investment club or a mutual fund, but it also works with individual stocks if you can manage the discipline and fees.[40]

---

[40] Buying $1,000 worth on four occasions will run you much higher brokerage fees than a single $4,000 purchase.

There is no scheme, formula, or magic key to the stock markets that will make up for buying bad companies or for buying into long-term bear markets. But you say, "Aha! This is the new millennium, and there are no more long-term bear markets." I say, "It's extremely doubtful." Dollar cost averaging in a bear market will lose money until the market turns.

Recommended Further Reading

Band, Richard. *Contrary Investing for the '90s: How to Profit by Going Against the Crowd.* New York: St. Martin's, 1991.

Dreman, David. *The New Contrarian Investment Strategy: The Psychology of Stock Market Success.* New York: Random House, 1982.

Engel, Louis, and Henry Hecht. *How to Buy Stocks.* New York: Little, Brown, and Co., 1994.

Lowenstein, Louis. *What's Wrong with Wall Street.* Reading, MA: Addison-Wesley, 1989.

Mamis, Justin. *When to Sell for the '90s: Inside Strategies for Stock Market Profits.* Burlington, VT: Fraser Publishing Co., 1994.

O'Neil, William. *How to Make Money in Stocks: A Winning System in Good Times or Bad.* New York: McGraw-Hill, 1994.

Zweig, Martin. *Winning on Wall Street.* New York: Warner Books, 1994.

CHAPTER 8

More on Stocks: Selling, and Losing, and Taking Profits

Small Investors need to know:
- What kinds of fees and expenses will I pay?
- Can I take profits?
- What does the smart money do?
- What does the dumb money do?
- What effect does the Dow-Jones Average have on my stocks?
- If not "buy and hold," then what?
- How can I manage selling to protect profits or limit losses?
- What happens in stock market manias, panics, and crash?

Good News

A lot of people make money by trading in stocks.

Bad News

A lot of people get badly hurt by trading in stocks. There are clever and ambitious people out there who would like to take your money. And bad stuff happens. Not all the time, of course, but sometimes. The miracle of capitalism is that while all of the money is changing hands, there is also real work going on, so it is possible for everyone to win. But not everyone will win.

Brokerage Expenses and Churning

Brokers have to make a living, too. But they are working for their bosses to generate sales and commissions, not just feather your nest. Sometimes they may take a lot of commissions out of your account. It may be perfectly honest, but it pays to keep your eyes on those commissions. Almost any week, you can read in the *Wall Street Journal* about some case of disciplinary or legal action against a broker who has been accused of leading clients into excessive trading action in order to generate sales commissions. The majority of brokers are reasonable and fair businesspeople, but sharks *will* get your telephone number. When that happens, be prepared to give a very firm "no" to a very fast hustle. If you can't handle that, say your prayers, and lock away your money.

Check up on your regular broker, too. If you are willing to consistently let 6 to 10 percent of your portfolio disappear in commissions each year, why should your broker complain? Study your account statements month by month and year by year. Be vigilant about keeping track of how much you are spending in brokerage fees or account management fees, and how much trading is being done in your name.

The Small Investor Reviews His Statements

By way of an example, suppose you had $20,000 in a brokerage account, and during the year you made the following trades:

1. buy 200 XYZ at $23	broker fee = $90
2. buy 300 GHL at $6.50	broker fee = $60
3. buy $4,000 of AZGTX fund with 3.5% load	sales commission = $140
4. sell 200 XYZ at $21	broker fee = $90
5. buy 200 ABC at $33	broker fee = $120
6. buy 150 RST at $40	broker fee = $120
7. sell 300 GHL at $8.50	broker fee = $60
8. buy $2,000 of AZGTX	sales commission = $70
9. sell 200 ABC at $37	broker fee = $120

That makes nine trades in a year. Generally successful. But the total of fees has been $870, which is over 4 percent of your capital. It will be tough to make a living that way. These figures are representative of what brokers might charge. With some discount brokers you might expect to pay half as much, but you wouldn't get any help. With full-service brokers, you might pay higher and get the support that goes along with it. But no matter where or how you trade, the brokerage fees can be a significant part of your money, and you have to watch where they are going. *You* have to watch and control the fees; no one else will do it for you.

Bear Markets, Panics, and Crashes

In any market, goods change hands and prices go up and down. Most of the time we expect to see fairly orderly and rational changes in stock prices. We expect that either we, our brokers, or the gurus on the mountaintops can make sense out of what is going on, and relate the price changes to economic news. But sometimes things run wild and you may run into manias, panics, and crashes.[41] The crashes will be all over the news, and everyone will be talking about them, but the manias and panics are not always so clearly defined. It is important to recognize the manias and panics because they are the warnings of coming crashes.

---

[41] There are a number of well-written books in the area. I like *Manias, Panics, and Crashes* by Professor of Economics Emeritus Charles Kindleberger of MIT (Basic Books, 1989).

A mania is an excessive and unjustified rapid increase in prices. Sometimes, especially when the market has been going up strongly for a while, people seem to fear that the opportunity to make a lot of money is running away from them. Even professional money managers can worry that they may not be keeping up with their competitors. Then they may rush into buying just for the sake of buying. The panic phase can set in after investors have spent all of their ready cash, and people realize that price levels are excessive. If too many people want to take their profits quickly, or need to get out of the markets and back to cash, that may set off a panic of sellers. The markets as of early 1996 appear to be in a mania that some people think can go on for a long time. Whether there is a selling panic will depend on when, and how suddenly, people quit contributing their retirement money to stock market mutual funds.

The Small Investor Gets Off the Bull

Experienced stock market seers have been predicting for the past three years that the end was near, the market was overpriced, and trouble was just around the corner. They might have had good reasons for thinking so, but the market has just kept on marching along. That may go on for five years more, or it might end tomorrow. No one can fore-tell that with certainty.

The smart money on Wall Street is supposed to be in the hands of people who usually make money, avoid the big trouble, and hear the hot news first. The "dumb money" is supposed to be in the hands of people who usually get into a hot stock too late, waste too much on brokerage fees, or buy into last month's winners just when the smart money wants to sell.

It may be that we are just going through another transfer of money out of dumb hands into smart hands. It is too soon to make a definite judgment call on that, but if a lot of working people suddenly decide to stop or decrease their contributions to retirement plans, we will find out in a hurry. Even if they just decide to switch the money out of stocks and back to certificates of deposit, the stock markets would go into great weakness or possibly an actual crash.

It well may be that we are in a buying mania phase now, and possibly have been for several years. The rate of increases of prices of all stock markets in the U.S. for this sustained period is unprecedented. Even the mania before the 1929 crash only lasted a couple of years, and although the bull market of 1935 and 36 roughly doubled prices, that was a lull between two storms. The Dow Jones Industrial Average lost about half of its value between the first quarter of 1937 and the first quarter of 1938, and did not recover the loss until 1946. The current markets have roughly quintupled, from 1000 to 5000 on the DJIA in thirteen years; 1995 action appears to be beyond all precedent. There may be good strong economic factors to support most of that price rise. Many commentators say there are, but we may also be in a buying mania. One of the dependable signs of a mania is that people start to feel compelled to rush their money into the markets. They feel as though the markets may leave them behind, and that there is not much time left to grab the prize.

One of the things that we might worry about is whether this is smart money or stupid money coming into the markets. Certainly, the prices that people pay for stocks are running up well ahead of the rewards that they take out. A lot of the new money is coming from retirement accounts. When must those retirement-oriented investors start withdrawing their money to buy food and pay medical bills?

Whenever they need to take money back, it must come from either dividends or sale of stock. The dividend rate for most of the major American markets is so low that few will find it satisfactory for long.

It is important to see the distinctions between real money and stock ownership. Stock ownership can show all kinds of wondrous "paper" profits based on current market prices and percentage increases in share profits, but when people have to pay the mortgage, or send the kids to college, or pay for surgery, they must have real money. That means that stock must be sold or the dividends must be substantial.

But you may hear that it's different this time. Sure it is. It was different last time, too, but it never supported stock prices that only paid 2.3 percent average yield from dividends, like now. If this market keeps going up, one of three things must happen: dividends must be substantially increased, the companies must demonstrate that their underlying values are greater and will produce greater earnings, or investors must settle for a lower dividend yield and earnings level. In the past, the investing public has never settled for as low a dividend yield and relative earnings power as they are buying now. Not for long, anyway.

What might persuade our fellow investors to stop buying stocks? What if the interest rate paid on long-term Treasury bonds got up to 8 percent, 9 percent, 10 percent? That would certainly draw some money away from the stock markets. What if inflation got out of hand and people could no longer keep putting money into their retirement programs? Any of those things, or a hundred others, might cause the supply of new money into the market to fall off. Then the next seller would have to lower his price in order to attract new buyers. That might be the start of an orderly retreat of prices, or it might degenerate into a panic or even, perhaps, a crash. In 1987, the market (DJIA price average) went up from about 1900 to near 2800 in less than a year. The yield fell to about 2.5 percent, while good long-term bonds were paying much higher. When the selling pressure was strong, the market panicked, crashed, and lost approximately one-third of its value in a few days.

Neither I nor anyone else can tell you with perfect assurance how close we might be to the end of the mania, or the next panic. But it certainly pays to be cautious when the yield is at or near an all-time low, and prices have been pushed up rapidly to all-time highs. Think about what kind of defensive measures you can use, or how you will manage your selling tactics to get money out.

The Small Investor Joins the Bears

Selling, Attitude, and Discipline

If you bought 200 shares of NationsBank in October of 1991 and sold in June of 1994, you would have earned $796 in dividends and made about $3,400 on the stock price. You might have paid between $100 and $300 in commissions. Some clever small investors have held on until today, and expanded their profits on the value of the stock by another $2,000.

If you had bought 300 shares of Ford in January of 1988 and sold in January of 1995, you would have earned $2,252 in dividends and about $2,400 on the price of the stock, and paid maybe $100 to $300 in brokerage commissions. A smart operator might have sold in early 1994 at about $33 per share. The lost 1994 dividend would have been $270, but the extra price appreciation would have been $1,200. It nets out to an additional $900 for a well-timed sell.

If you had held 200 shares of IBM from February of 1990 until April of 1994, you would have earned $3,220 in dividends and taken about $10,000 loss on the price of the stock. The disciplined investor might have sold in December of 1991. Then the dividends would have only been $1,936, but the loss would shrink to $4,000. Net advantage from a smart sale looks like close to $4,000. Who has the discipline to sell at a terrible price and take a $4,000 loss?

What's the point? Earnings from dividends are significant, but that should not mean that we neglect the potential profit or loss from the price of the stock. Managing your potential profits or losses into real profits and minimal losses requires some kind of selling discipline.

Buy and hold is fine, when it works. Buy and hold is better than a series of frequent trades that erode your principal through trading fees. Buy and hold may even be better than no plan at all. But what is really good is smart selling. And it is difficult. Of course, we cannot expect that everyone is going to be sharp enough to identify those three optimal selling points (for Ford, NationsBank, and IBM) above. It's not that easy. But there are people who make good money in the markets. They don't make it by wearing bags over their heads with "Buy and Hold" written on the outside.

Working stocks is like playing bridge, in a sense. In bridge everyone likes to talk about bidding, because it's fun and pretty easy. The difficult work is in playing the hands, and not so many people know as much about that. Same thing with stock picking. It's fun, and you can always speculate on success or the potential for success. The harder part of the work comes in selling, and not so many people care to study that.

Some people fall into a self-imposed trap of treating selling as an admission of failure. Either you quit and give up on the potential gains you foresaw when you bought it, or you admit that your great gains could have been better, if you had only known then. And we get attached to our stocks. Everybody does. Almost every person who trades stocks loves to try to convince others that the last pick is the real gem, the best of all possible current investments. The point of sale is always some kind of emotional trial, both for our winners and our losers.

Lesson #1: Selling is important to your profit and loss results. Lesson #2: Selling is difficult and complicated and emotional.

Selling

There is no single well-defined discipline or formula that will make everyone a smart seller, just as there is no one investment strategy or one buying formula that makes everyone a winner. It doesn't do you any good to read the best possible selling strategy if you don't have the inner fortitude to follow through on it. However, there are some ideas that are worth looking at, and maybe one or two of them will work for you.

VARIATIONS ON BUY & SELL

Buy or Sell at Your Price

It is okay for you to specify a price that you want to obtain on any order. You can tell your broker to sell Sears (symbol S on NYSE) at $45, and the broker will do his best to complete the deal at that price. However, if the stock is currently being bid up, it might happen that the market is offering $46 just when you come in at 45, you might lose a dollar per share by specifying 45; or on the other hand the best offer might be $44¾,which leaves you holding the stock. The advantage of buying or selling at your specified price is that you can be confident that you will get your price or no deal. The disadvantages are that you may pay more than you had to on a purchase or sell too low on a sale. You might also simply miss the deal when it could have been completed at very close to your price.

Market Orders

You can instruct your broker to buy or sell a stock at the current market price level, whatever it is. This is the most common way of entering orders. It has advantages and disadvantages. On September 20, 1995, AT&T announced the breakup of the company into three new independent companies. I thought that was a great idea. I saw the news before the market opened, called my broker, and told him to buy AT&T at the market price. I knew that the price had been hanging between 48 and 55 for a long time, but I didn't have any idea what would happen to it that day. I just wanted to buy it. I ended up buying it for $63 a share. If I had said buy at $55, I would have been shut out. If I had said buy at $65, I would have paid too much. At that time I was willing to trust in the collective rationality of the New York Stock Exchange and the good service history of my broker. The advantage that I gained was getting the stock I wanted at a fair price. The risk I took was that I might have gotten into paying a higher price than I expected.

If you are dealing with very large and well-known companies on the NYSE, this sort of risk is probably just about always going to be acceptable. If you are dealing with small cap companies for which the price and liquidity are highly variable, on the other hand, this might be too much risk. NETSCAPE (symbol NSCP on NASDAQ) went to market in September of 1995 after an initial public stock offering that set the price at $28 a share. The first day of public trading, people went crazy over it. This was certainly part of a buying mania for high-tech stocks. The price got up to $75 and quickly retreated. Some people who put in market orders to buy got the stock at over $70 and were facing a $20 per share loss by the end of the week.[42] Use market orders when you have a high degree of confidence in the market you are using, the stability of the share price, and the customer service history of your broker.

The most common use of the market order is a case where you would have an interest in a particular stock, and then ask your broker what bids and offers[43] are currently active in the market. The answer might be, say, that the stock is at $34.25 bid, $34.75 asked. If you feel that is a fair range, you can put in a market order to buy the stock. That means that the broker should buy the stock for you at the best price (lowest price for a buy) that he can get. Usually the broker should be able to confirm within minutes that you have bought it at $34.50 or something in the range. If the stock is volatile that day, you would expect the worst case would be that you buy a little higher, perhaps at $35.00. Market sell orders work the same way—the broker should get the best price he can get for you, and it should be very close to the stated range.

---

[42] Netscape went back up, well over the $75 of the first day, but if there was ever an example of a buying panic, this is it.

[43] A bid is a price proposed by a buyer; an offer is a price proposed by a seller.

Limit Orders

You can tell your broker that you want to buy or sell a stock at a certain price or better. That is called a limit order. For example, if GM is selling today at $47, you might decide that you would be happy to sell at $50, but you don't want to sit around watching CNBC all day to see when it hits, so you tell your broker: sell 200 shares of GM at $50, a limit order. The broker, or the stock exchange specialist, has to watch GM and as soon as someone offers $50 they should try to sell your stock. If the stock is on a run-up, they might even get $50½ for it. The limit sell order can be used to try to ensure that you get out of the stock position if the price rises enough to give the price you want. It does not give guaranteed results. If somebody ahead of you sold GM at $50, and then there were no more buyers at $50, you would not get your sell price even though the target was hit. That problem is rare. One of our advantages as small investors is that if the market hits a certain price, we can generally feel safe that there is enough action and sales volume at that price to soak up whatever we want to buy or sell. If the manager of the Strong American Utilities Fund is trying to move 50,000 shares of GTE, he has no such assurance.

Stop Orders (or Stop Loss)

A stop order is somewhat related to a limit order, but there is an important difference. The stop order becomes a market order when the target price is achieved. The stop order is basically a protective, or defensive, order to keep the market from running away from you. For instance, the first time I bought IBM, at $85¼ in 1992, I was lucky and it ran up to $100 in a hurry. I didn't want to sell, and I didn't want to take much risk, so I put in a stop loss order at $93. That was planned to save me from losing all of the profit. Pretty quickly it plunged and my broker sold it and got a price of $92⅞. So I had a good profit on a short-term holding. If I had not had the stop loss order in, it is very likely that I would not have even known about the drop in price until it was down to $85 or less. You see, I, like most of you, have a life to live. I can't sit around watching the markets all the time. The stop loss order sets a broker in place to act for us.

Notice that the price I received for IBM was not the $93 that was in the order. The stop order says to the broker, "If the price hits $93, sell this boy at the market." On that day if I had said sell at $93, I might never have found a buyer.

There is one more potential catch with the stop loss order. You had better be serious. Don't put in a stop loss order and think you will have a chance to back out. You may have to live with some mistakes. For example, in the summer of 1992, the stock price of Hewlett Packard (symbol HWP)was going down the drain. I recognized that as an opportunity (right) and bought at $61¼. However, at the time I was very nervous about the market in general, and was trying to be very defensive. To protect against too much erosion of capital, I put in a defensive stop loss order at $54. HWP continued to slide and pretty soon hit $54, and my broker got me out at $54. Good service, bad judgment. The stock immediately turned around and a year later it was near $80. If I had the nerve to avoid the stop order, or if I had the nerve to set the stop at $52, I would have kept the stock and made a good profit instead of $8 per share loss (counting commissions). Tough luck. A year later, I held IBM again, purchased at $67⅜, and put in a stop loss at $54. We hit the stop and got out at $53¾. Right at the worst possible time. After I sold IBM, it went up quickly to back over $90. I got what I asked for: I avoided the risk and avoided the profit. So the stop loss order better be serious before you put it in.

There you see three transactions made through stop loss orders, two with IBM and one with Hewlett Packard. One made a good profit, two made substantial losses. You don't get any guarantees in the stock markets, only opportunity. And the opportunity cuts both ways. In those three cases, I was practicing a selling discipline that was an absolutely essential ingredient of my personal investing strategy. When you hold a stock, it is perfectly reasonable to plan to hold it for a long time, but you should not just stick your head in the sand. Watch your stocks. Determine where you want to take profits or cut losses. Then take action to make those things happen.

We should also discuss the concept of the *mental stop*. This is when an investor makes up his mind to sell if the market price falls to a certain level, but does not actually place a stop order with his broker. Instead, he keeps his eyes open, planning to put in a sell order when the stock falls to some critical price. Fine, but remember, the road to ruin is paved with good intentions. With a mental stop, you run at least two risks: first, the market may get away from you. You plan to sell at $25 and the stock hits $20 before you hear about it. Or you plan to sell at $25, you see the report of sales at 24, but by the time you get to a telephone, the stock is down to $22. Now what? There will be a gut reaction to not sell. "Don't accept this terrible price. Wait for it to come back to $24 or $25." Good luck! It won't come back.

The second risk is that of waiting too long. People who wait are liable to find themselves in a mess. The markets will never wait on you. The most dangerous words in the language of any investor are "I'm just waiting for it to come back to my cost level, and then I will sell it." People hold losers forever waiting for them to come back. If your dearest friend says to you, "I am just waiting for it to come back up to $25," tell her, "Don't wait. Sell it. Let go of the worry. Find something else." If she ever again says, "I am just waiting for...," counsel her to get out of the stock markets and look into Gamblers Anonymous. If you hold a stock that you have truly lost confidence in, sell it!

There is a popular theory that says: "Cut your losers, and let your winners run." It means get rid of the bad stocks and hang onto the good ones. But we know that every stock can be both a winner *and* a loser. What to do? Well I told you what to do with stocks that you have no confidence in, but what about the good stocks that are down in price. It happens all the time. Almost every stock that I have ever held was down in price at some point. I had an average cost of $12 in CREE and it fell to $6. What to do? It went back up to $60, on a presplit basis.[4] What to do? It fell back down to $40 on the presplit basis. What to do? Well, if you had a good reason for buying the stock in the first place, reexamine whether the stock still satisfies your criteria. If it does, then maybe you should hold on. A stock that was good at $27 may still be good at $22. It can be a difficult call. If it was easy, *everyone* would be rich.

Taking Profits

Whenever you own a stock that goes up, you will imagine that it could go up forever. But profits come from collecting dividends or selling, not from watching. Whenever you buy a stock you should have done enough work that you will have some idea about the markets,

---

[4] *Presplit basis* means at the comparable price per share before the split. If a stock just had a 2-for-1 split, and it is selling at $15 today, then the comparable presplit price would be $30.

and revenues and profits of the firm. Those things should enable you to imagine a good price level that is fair for the stock. When you buy, set an idea of the price you expect to achieve before selling. If the price gets close to that level, either give your broker a limit sell order (sell at X price or better), or reexamine the company's results and see if that is still the proper target price. At any rate, don't just sit idly by, expecting that the price will grow forever, beyond your original hoped-for value. The price may keep going, or it may not, but you should have some idea about reasonable expectations just as you did when you bought it.

It is no disgrace to take profits. Some people make money that way. It is no disgrace to take losses, some people stay healthy that way. The only disgrace is to put your hard-earned money into the stock markets and forget about it. Even if you practice buy and hold, which may be right for some people, you cannot buy and *forget*. If you expected to hold a stock for a long time, but it takes a dive, should you just hold on? If you expected to hold a stock for a long time, but it has a dramatic run-up in price, should you sell and grab the profits? Maybe yes, maybe no, but never just ignore the situation. The toughest part of the whole business may be to make decisions and take action.

The Small Investor Collects Profits

In 1988, a lot of people held IBM stock at average prices of $100 to $125 a share. The ones who just bought and forgot it have had some real pain with it. They may all come out well. I hope they do, but there has been some pain along the way.

You can set up fixed guidelines, if you don't want to keep working at reevaluating your stocks. Suppose you tried this as a rule: Whenever I buy a stock, I will put in a stop loss order 10 percent below the buying price, and a sell order 20 percent above the buying price.

For example, you might buy MASCO Corp. (symbol MAS on the NYSE) at $30. Give your broker a stop loss order at $27, and a limit sell order at $36. If the stock ever falls to $27, the broker will sell it at the market; if it ever rises to $36, the broker will sell for the best price he can get at or above $36.

With that rule, all of your stock purchases will fit into one of three classes: either they fall 10 percent and you get out with a 10 percent loss, or they go up 20 percent and you make a 20 percent profit, or they stay within −10 percent to +20 percent of the purchase price and you just hold on until you feel like reevaluating them. With that rule, in a generally rising market you might expect to make fairly consistent profits, and in case of a generally falling market, you might expect to restrict your losses on each stock to not more than 10 percent plus whatever brokerage costs you have. (Of course this is based on average cases—exceptions will occur. But it's a pretty good rule of thumb.)

> **Warning: This is not a recommendation that anyone should adopt the rule above. It is only an example of how an investor might try putting some discipline and rules into their investing strategy.**
>
> **Even if you did adopt this rule, or any other, you would still have some risk of long-term substantial losses. There are no risk-free investments. If you buy bad stocks and consistently lose 10 percent on each and pay brokerage fees, you might lose almost all of your money pretty quickly.**

Hustlers

The Small Investor Gets Hustled

This very morning, as I sat here writing, a stockbroker called me. It was some guy I have never met, although he had called once before. He wanted to do me a favor; put me into "the single best idea" his firm had going this morning, and he was going to make only a small ($50) commission on the buy. He didn't tell me what commission they would extract on the sell. I wonder how big it might have been.

His idea was Calloway Golf. "Jim," he says, "Jim, have you heard about Gerber Food, and Dr. Pepper?" He says: "They were recently bought out and the stock went through the roof. Well, American Brands is currently sitting on a large cash stockpile and they need to buy a golf equipment manufacturer. We are convinced that American Brands is going to take over Calloway Golf." Insider buying is strong. The CEO and President of Calloway recently bought large amounts of stock on the open market; the average daily trading volume has recently doubled; there is a massive short squeeze going on. The shorts[45] will have to buy in their sales to cover, and that will put immense upward pressure on the stock price. He needed to "put me in 1,000 shares," then a little later 500 shares, then a little later 200 shares. He said we could use a stop loss order to limit the losses in case the stock fell.[46] Then he wanted to know my overall investment portfolio size. I said it was none of his business. Then he wanted to know if it was at least $300,000. I said it was none of his business. Then he said, "Are you really that small?" I said it was none of his business. He said, "Good-day, Jim," and hung up. All through the pitch, I kept telling him I would not buy anything until I had done my own homework, and I wasn't going to do it on a schedule to please him. He never seemed to hear that. You're right, I could have hung up in the first thirty seconds, but right away I knew I was going to use the example here.

This was a hard sell. At least in my league it looked like a hard sell. The guy said a number of things that sounded like legitimate reasons to buy Calloway (its price that day was $15½), if they were all true. His claims that I could check out quickly and easily were true. But I passed.

Why pass? Well, first thing is when you get to the point, somebody has to make a decision. To buy, to sell, somebody has to make a decision. I don't let strangers just call out of the blue on Monday morning and make my decisions for me. I also have a fixed practice that I don't buy on impulse, no matter how great the story sounds. In fact, I almost never buy a stock unless I have spent several weeks, or months, thinking about it and gathering information. Remember, I'm one of us. I am not a full-time professional stock trader and don't intend to let it become the focus of my life. And finally, if someone offers us a deal that sounds too good to be true, that means that we just don't understand all of the risks.

---

[45] Short sellers, or shorts, are stock traders who make a bet on a stock going down. In a short sale, they will borrow stock they did not own to sell at current prices. They expect to later buy it back at lower prices to close the loan of stock. If they can actually buy it back cheaper than they sold it, then they make a profit on a "sell high, buy low" deal.

[46] This was where he was telling me something that was not true, although maybe he didn't understand it. A stop loss order is an instruction to your broker to sell a stock at once if the price ever falls to a certain value. It is intended to limit your loss to whatever it might be at a certain point. In fact, a stop loss is not guaranteed to get the stated price for you, but only to sell the stock after it hits that price.

Go look in today's newspaper, or call your broker. How's Calloway today (its symbol is ELY on the NYSE)? Did I avoid a loss? Did I miss a great opportunity? Either way, I don't intend to worry about it, and I won't feel any pain over it. I will go on about my investing practices in the same old slow and cautious way. It works for me, and Mrs. Investor. Find something that works for you. Don't let anyone rattle you into decisions before you have examined the facts. Adopt your own rules or practices for safety and stick to them.

Gurus

John Wayne did what he did better than anybody. Peter Lynch managed mutual funds better than anybody, and Joe Montana won football games better than anybody. In your business there are some people you know who are simply the best, or among the best. It's also true in investing. There are a few people in the world who are generally acknowledged as being masters of investing, and among them there are a number who are master stock pickers. We would all pay a good price for their advice. But we don't have to. It's free. Many of them regularly appear on TV or in newspapers and magazines and give away their opinions about some current good buys in the stock markets.

One supposes that this enhances their reputations for selling their mutual funds or personalized advice. If you want to be cynical, you might even guess that their published views are self-serving—maybe they have already bought the stocks they are recommending and want you to rush out and bid up the prices. But let us adopt a more charitable view. Those people are already wealthy, by my standards at least, and they probably enjoy having a chance to pontificate before a mass audience. So the point is you can get advice from real experts for free. It would be foolish to ignore it. But it might be equally as foolish to follow them blindly.

In July of 1993, *Barron's* had an article from a continuing series they call their Roundtable. Once every six months or so, they call together five, or ten, or fifteen of the biggest names in the business to have a wide-open discussion on the economy and where the markets might be going. One of the things you can pick up in those articles is a list of names of recommended stocks. In July of 1993, one of the experts recommended 50-Off Stores. It doesn't matter who did it. Those folks really are good and nobody promises 100 percent accuracy in picking stocks.

50-Off Stores (symbol FOFF on NASDAQ) is a chain of small discount stores that sells mostly apparel, along with a few other odds and ends. During 1989 and 1990 the earnings had been between 20¢ and 33¢ per share and the share price bounced around between about $1 and $4. In 1991 the earnings doubled, but the stock price flew up to over $25. In 1992 it hit as high as $32 at one point. Well, the company was doing very well, but with a P/E ratio over 30 and no yield, it had to look pretty expensive. Definitely not a value-oriented investment. From early 1992 until mid-1993, the price fell pretty much in a straight line to $6 per share. Sales were up but earnings completely disappeared. They had a net loss for 1993.

Well, the Roundtable expert came in and reviewed the situation. He saw something that foretold a turnaround and prescribed buy at $6. The stock finished 1993 above $8, fell to $3 in early 1994 and finished 1994 below $4. The current price level is under $2.

Okay, fair enough. This is risk-oriented investing and nobody ever said it would be easy. As small investors we have to remember that not every investment is equally attractive to everyone. What may offer fair risk and better diversification for one investor should be viewed as poison to another. In fact, in deference to the great man's track record, we should say that 50-Off was a reasonable risk and considered buy for him, or for his mutual funds at the time. That doesn't mean that it was a good recommendation for everyone who heard about it. The expert had no doubt considered the risk level and cash level and current mix of stocks in his portfolio. For some reason the risk/reward potential of 50-Off looked appealing to him. That does not mean that it represented good diversification and good risk and reward mix for us.

When the small investor learns that Mr. Hot Money is buying a stock, this should be taken as part of a never-ending avalanche of available information. The small investor should consider how and where he heard about it. Is it, in fact, a reliable source of information?[47] If so,

---

[47] *Barron's* Roundtable, by the way, is reliable information of the very highest order.

maybe you should check it out. Find out some of the reasoning behind the position. If you can't learn the supporting reasoning, what you have is nothing more than rumor.

After you get that far, you have to decide whether this particular stocks fits anything you might need. Check your own current stock holdings. If you already own one firm in the same business, maybe you don't need both of them. What's good diversification and fair risk for Mr. Hot Money may be a walk on the wild side for you. Even if it is still interesting to you, do your homework. Check the Value Line Report on the stock, if there is one. If you use a full-service broker, ask for his firm's written opinion on the stock. Check the date on the report. You'll be surprised at how many old reports get handed around. Write to the company and ask for their latest annual or quarterly reports.

And take your time. If you think you have such hot information that you have to buy right now, you are almost certainly kidding yourself. Except in the rarest instances, we small investors simply will not get information when it is hot. If the stock is good today, it should be good tomorrow. Gurus serve a valid role in this world. They stimulate good conversation. They make money, they spend money. It does not necessarily follow that you should turn over your thinking to them, nor follow them blindly.

Beating the Averages

It is not profitable to give too much time and attention to how everyone else is doing. Take care of your money and let the others take care of theirs. What do we care what the averages are doing? What do we care how the mutual funds in general are doing? If you find out that the Dow Jones Industrial Average was up 14 percent last year, that won't put any money in your pocket unless you owned the stocks. And if you find out the S&P 500 was down 11 percent last quarter, that won't take any money out of your pocket. Forget the averages. Take care of yourself and your money. I finished 1995 with a better investment return than most of the 7,000 mutual funds being sold, but who cares? That knowledge is not going to make a nickel for me next week, or preserve my hard-earned gains. I still have to practice the defensive role of the cautious and insecure small investor.

Recommended Further Reading

Investors Beware is pretty much just anecdotal and may be a bit one-sided in view, but the author has some experience in the business and has presumably seen much of what he reports. *The Intelligent Investor* is one of the true classics of this business and is must reading for anyone who expects to be a stock picker.

Allen, John. *Investors Beware: Protecting Yourself Against Stockbroker Abuse While Protecting Your Money*. New York: John Wiley & Sons, 1993.

Graham, Benjamin. *The Intelligent Investor*. New York: HarperCollins, 1986.

Weiss, Martin. *How to Survive the Coming Money Panic*. New York: Sure Sellers, 1995.

CHAPTER 9

Mutual Funds

Small Investors need to know:
- Do mutual funds belong in my personal investment strategy?
- What is a mutual fund? How does it work?
- What are the benefits?
- What are the costs and risks?
- What are the factors I need to evaluate when choosing among mutual funds?
- How can I buy them?
- How can I get my money back?
- How do they calculate and report their gains or losses?
- Where should I look for more information and more in-depth research?

To Begin With—What Is a Mutual Fund, and Who Cares?

Part of what separates us from the professional money managers is that we have our own lives to live, and other priorities apart from the financial markets. You might do as well as the average money manager if you wanted to commit eight hours a day for two years to studying markets, and you could get your hands on a few million dollars for educational purposes in the Wall Street Laboratory. But you don't want to. You can't. You won't. You're reading this book instead. You want to keep your money management as simple as possible and not devote too much time to it.

When I set out to manage an IRA, I had a lot of motivation to overdo the research angle. Managing money, writing about it, and market research all happen to be fun for me. Even with all that, it took a year before I felt comfortable enough to be 75 percent invested. During that time I bought nineteen stocks, sold six of them (five at a profit), and bought three rather conservative mutual funds. Buying the mutual funds was the easiest part. Each stock that I bought was studied carefully for weeks or months before the purchase, and followed with at least weekly review. You may be willing to do as much work. Some may even enjoy it. Others want an easier way.

Mutual funds were invented to solve several concerns of the individual investor. Their track records have been good. To a great extent, mutual funds achieve better results with less work for small investors. The biggest and most famous of them all has been the mighty Magellan Fund of Fidelity Distributors Corporation of Boston. Magellan, primarily under the guidance of Peter Lynch, achieved an average compound rate of return of over 18 percent for ten years. That's incredible; those guys made money faster than the government could spend it!

In 1965, individual investors owned over 80 percent of the value of U.S. stocks. In 1991 that had fallen to just over 50 percent. Today mutual funds and pension funds and other institutional investors control much more of the markets. In 1960 there were 4 million individual accounts in mutual funds, in 1980 that had grown to 12 million, and today, over 90 million.

WHAT IS A MUTUAL FUND?

A mutual fund is a pool of investment money under professional management. Many investors put in their money; a few professionals manage it. The benefits of mutual funds are

- less work for the individual investor
- probably less risk for the individual investor
- a good chance at more profit for the individual investor

All of us should consider using mutual funds instead of direct purchases of stocks and bonds. But there is an area of concern to keep in mind. The mutual fund business is changing so rapidly that it is becoming difficult to balance the benefits against the costs of mutual fund investment. So you get a kind of "good news, bad news" situation: the advantages of mutual funds, and the risks involved in new developments. I'm sorry about that, but there are always some tough points to consider.

HOW DOES A MUTUAL FUND WORK?

A good starting point is to look at a bank money market account. The money market account is a type of mutual fund where all of the investors' money goes into a pool for buying short-term bonds. The bonds belong to the bank, not the depositor. The bank probably earns 3 to 7 percent annually on the money and pays out a little less to account holders. The majority of the account holders have little interest in investing directly in bonds. They prefer to let the bank do the work.

A mutual fund management company (also known as an investment company) is similar to the bank: they want to hold and invest your money; they plan to make a profit with it, and they will keep part of the profit.

Investing in a mutual fund partially resembles buying shares in any other company that would use your money to run their business and pay you some dividends out of the profits. You may also profit from share price appreciation. With mutual funds, the share price is based directly on the assets that the fund owns. If you own General Motors stock, it is difficult to determine each day just exactly what the company is worth but, by contrast, if you own shares in the Financial Industrial Income Fund, there is a well-understood, consistent formula for determining the fair price of the shares each day. We'll get to that in a few minutes.

One big difference between stocks and funds is that for most mutual funds you do not sell your shares in an open market—instead, you redeem them with the fund company. The company stands ready to buy back (or redeem) shares at the current asset value at any time (with a few exceptions such as closed-end funds, discussed later in this chapter).

The Small Investor Takes the Easy Way

Among the important advantages of buying mutual funds are *efficiency*, *management*, and *diversification* (lower risk). We will look at each of those separately. They are factors that you should consider in evaluating funds you might buy (more on choosing funds in chapter 10).

MUTUAL FUND EFFICIENCY

The mutual fund will manage the investments at lower costs than a lot of small investors acting independently. If a thousand of us each had $5,000 to invest in the stock market, we would probably end up buying two or three stocks each. Acting separately, we might buy 500 different stocks and pay $400,000 (very rough estimate) in brokerage fees, counting commissions on both purchases and future sales.

But look at how it would work if we put all the money into a mutual fund. The investment company would manage all of that for us. They would collect the entire $5 million (1,000 × $5,000) and keep track of 1,000 separate accounts for us. They would apply their greater research and experience to invest the money in perhaps 50–100 individual stocks. They would also take care of the brokerage fees. In exchange for this service and the potential gains, they might charge us 3 percent of the amount invested when we buy in, and maybe 1 percent annual management expenses. If we all held our accounts for three years, and if the total assets value didn't change much, expenses would amount to $300,000. That looks like about $100,000 saving in expenses for the investors (as a group) and income of $300,000 for the fund management.

In some cases, the initial expense for buying the fund shares might be lower than 3 percent, perhaps even zero. Then the amount saved by the investors might get up to $250,000; that's $250 apiece out of their original $5,000. That's 5 percent, which is a very significant saving on expenses.

The numbers above were just made up for this discussion; however, the numbers are realistic. They represent fair estimates of what might happen with some mutual funds. With mutual funds, economies of scale act to benefit the individual investors. (I ignored growth and profit here, to focus on the fees alone.)

Mutual Fund Diversification

Remember that in chapter 3 we talked about the problem of diversification for the Small Investor. There was a difficulty in choosing to spread your money among several stocks or trying to reduce brokerage fees. But we can get excellent diversification through a few mutual funds. For example, if you want to invest $50,000 on your own, you might buy five to ten stocks or four or five bonds; quite aside from the research involved, that could set you back $500 to $1,000 (or easily more) in brokers' fees when you buy, and that much again when you sell. But $50,000 might be distributed among four mutual funds as follows:

- $10,000 in a blue-chip fund holding 100 stocks
- $10,000 in a small-capitalization fund holding 100 stocks
- $15,000 in a bond fund holding 50 bonds
- $15,000 in a mortgage fund investing in government-
  guaranteed mortgage certificates

You'd pay far lower fees compared to buying the stocks.

In this way you would only need to select the four mutual funds. The fund managers would take care of the work, time, and expense of diversifying, and buying and selling stocks or bonds.

MUTUAL FUND MANAGEMENT AND RESEARCH

The mutual fund should bring strong analysis and management to the investments. Instead of the $5 million total investment we talked about before, an operating mutual fund would probably have something much larger to work with. If they had $500 million of investors' money and produced $10 million a year in revenue for the fund's management, they could hire a few bright, energetic analysts to do their research. In addition to the analysts, the mutual fund would have a senior manager who had final authority over what they would buy or sell. That overseer should be a seasoned financial expert who had proven his good judgment and decisiveness through years of Wall Street guerilla warfare. Once again, we have to allow for variations from one fund to another, but you can see there is a presumptive case that the mutual fund gets better research and better decision making than the individual investor. Before you buy a fund, check that presumption by reading the fund's objectives, reviewing their current portfolio, and reviewing their performance record over the past five years.

Mutual fund performance has been an area of ongoing dispute. Certainly the longest-lived and most-advertised funds have been generally successful. But that is a biased sample, and it rides on a trend of rising markets for the past fifteen years. There is research that tends to a conclusion that stock mutual funds generally do not outperform the overall market averages.[49] On the other hand, you have the indisputable real-world example of the Magellan Fund: choosing the right fund can be extremely profitable. My own conclusion is that for those of us who decide to get into the markets, picking a mutual fund is easier than picking a good stock or bond, less risky, and has as good a chance at success.

---

[49] *The Quarterly Review of Economics & Business*, vol. 31, no. 4, Winter 1991.

Let's look at results. In the January 1995 issue of *Barron's Quarterly Mutual Fund Reports*, I randomly selected forty-six bond and equity funds and checked their results for one-year and five-year performances.[50] The results[51] are summarized below:

- the average result for the year 1994 was a 2 percent loss
- the best result for 1994 was a 20 percent gain
- the worst result for 1994 was a 13 percent loss and for the five-year period
- the average result was 48 percent gain (about 8 percent per year)
- the best result was 130 percent gain
- the worst result was 3 percent loss

The Small Investor Can Relax and Enjoy Life

---

[50] *Barron's* gets their data from Lipper Analytical Services. This was a random sample from a biased sample, because all of the funds that I used had actually survived for five years. It also excludes municipal bond funds, which have to be evaluated on a tax-exempt basis.

[51] These results are calculated after deducting loads and management fees.

The average for the one-year period is about in line with overall market averages, and the five-year period shows a very low chance of loss. On average you can expect the promises of efficiency and better management to produce some results. And it was achieved with less work for the individual investors and greater diversification. The results for calendar year 1995 are much stronger, but not far removed from the market averages.

THERE ARE DIFFERENT KINDS OF MUTUAL FUNDS

By the time you read this there will be over 8,000 mutual funds. Selecting one or two to buy can be a daunting task, but it is simpler than picking individual stocks. What are the differences among the funds, and how are they labeled? Funds can be studied by the kinds of things they invest in, the way they structure fees to shareholders, their risk levels, and other ways. In fact, there are clever and ambitious people in New York right now who are inventing new mutual funds with original features that can be advertised as filling a niche for some class of neglected investors. The more you study, the more variety and complexity you will find. Remember Rule #2: Don't get bogged down in a search for perfect information.

Types of Investments

The most obvious description of funds is according to what kinds of things they buy. Some examples are *stock funds*, which invest in various stock markets; *bond funds*, which invest primarily in bonds; *balanced funds*, which buy stocks seeking a combination of income and growth; and *funds of funds*, which invest in other mutual funds.

THE STOCK FUND

The simplest idea is the stock fund. A stock fund will typically invest between 60 and 95 percent of its money in stocks. Each fund will have a prospectus, which is a pamphlet that describes the fund's rules and objectives. The fund is required to show the prospectus to each new investor so you may know where the money is going. The statement of the fund's objective in the prospectus should help you gauge the risk and reward associated with a given fund.

Here is an example of some information (lifted out of context) from the prospectus of the Axe-Houghton Growth Fund, which was one of the USF&G family of funds.[52] This excerpt is not a complete nor adequate description of the prospectus of the fund; it is only a sample of some information that may be found in a prospectus.

INVESTMENT OBJECTIVE AND POLICIES

The Fund's primary investment objective is long-term capital growth. The Fund also seeks to protect capital values. The Fund's investment objective is a fundamental policy and may only be changed with the approval of shareholders. Other investment policies and practices are not fundamental and may be changed by the Board of Directors of the Company without shareholder approval. Due to the uncertainty inherent in all investments, there can be no assurance that the Fund will be able to achieve its investment objective.

The Fund's assets are normally invested in common and convertible preferred stocks. It is anticipated that the Fund's portfolio will be heavily weighted in stocks of companies that have above-average earnings growth potential. In selecting such stocks, the Fund's investment adviser will consider factors such as the issuer's financial condition, management, earnings momentum, and the position of the issuer in its industry. Investments are sometimes made in securities not currently paying dividends but believed to have good income and growth prospects. Under normal circumstances, at least 65 percent of the value of the Fund's total assets will be invested in stocks.

---

[52] In August of 1992, the Axe-Houghton Growth Fund was merged into the T. Rowe Price New American Growth Fund.

Some key phrases to pick up include *long-term capital growth; normally invested in common and convertible preferred stocks; at least 65 percent invested in stocks.* This fund may fairly be described as a stock fund. If you were interested in this fund, you should ask them for a copy of their latest report to shareholders.[53] That would include a listing of stocks and bonds that they owned just prior to the date of the report. You could examine that list to see that it conforms to the full statement of objectives in the prospectus, and to see if their particular selection of stocks appeals to your risk and reward standards.

Among stock funds there are many, many variations. Here are examples of a few you'll be running into:

Blue Chip Funds

This refers to stock funds that focus on large, solid, well-known companies; they probably hold GE and Potomac Electric and Merck. Examples include the AIM Value Fund and the Founders Blue Chip Fund.

Small-Cap Funds

These funds focus on companies whose market capitalization (total market value of all shares) is below a threshold value, such as $200 million or $600 million. They probably own a mix of well-known and lesser-known companies. They might own Wal-Mart and some new biotechnology firms. Wal-Mart gets in here because if the manager was very clever, he bought Wal-Mart in 1989 and has held it ever since. Examples include the CAPP-Rush Emerging Growth Fund, the Dreyfus New Leaders Fund, and the Oppenheimer Discovery Fund.

Growth Funds

These funds may not give much attention to company size; they focus instead on growing revenues and earnings. Part of the theory is that a high price for today's earnings may be a bargain for next year's, or the year after. These funds might hold Coca-Cola, Philip Morris and Office Depot, and many companies that are not yet household names. Examples include the AIM Weingarten Fund, the Common Sense Growth Fund, and the IDS Growth Fund.

---

[53] Most of the magazines and ratings services mentioned in this book will show addresses and phone numbers for the fund management companies.

Income Funds

These are the foils to the growth funds. The income funds are designed to serve investors who are more concerned about immediate income rather than pie-in-the-sky several years away. Theinvestors who like income funds may be retirees who want to collect regular income from their nest eggs, or other investors who don't believe that long-term earnings can be forecast reliably. Examples include Capstone Government Income Fund, the Value Line Income Fund, and the Kemper High Yield Fund.

Fee Structure Load, No-load, Other Fees

Some funds require you to pay a sales commission initially. This kind of fee is called a *load,* or *front-end load*. It must be shown in the prospectus and may be as high as 8.5 percent. This commission is expressed as a percentage of the amount invested and normally deducted from the amount that you intend to invest.

If the fund has a 3 percent load, the fee will be 3 percent of the amount that goes into the fund. For example, if you want to spend $5,000, they will split this into $4,854 that actually goes into fund shares and $146 that is the sales fee. The fee, $146, is 3 percent of the $4,854 amount invested.

If you actually want exactly $5,000 worth of shares, they will charge you an additional $150 (3 percent of 5,000) for the sales fee.

Almost everyone classifies funds as being load or no-load, although this distinction is becoming blurred as the investment industry invents more ways to split up their fees into confusing options. Some funds may also require a back-end load, which is a percentage fee based on the amount the investor redeems when he sells his shares. Usually the simplest view is load or no-load referring to a front-end load.

If you want to buy a fund with a 4 percent front-load and a 1 percent redemption fee (back-end load), and if you send them a check for $8,000, they will first deduct $308 from the $8,000, and buy you $7,692 worth of shares. That works out so the fee ($308) is 4 percent of the amount invested ($7,692). Two years later if you decide to sell after your shares have appreciated to $9,000 in value, the fund will deduct $90 (that's 1 percent) from the redemption amount, and send you a check for $8,910.

One of the absolute curses of the mutual fund business has become their development of new ways to describe hidden costs and present them in the prospectus in ways that are difficult to understand. If you plan to buy a mutual fund, read the prospectus. Especially read the section on fees. If you don't understand it, don't buy the fund; they don't deserve your business. If you are working through a broker, insist that he give you a written summary of *all of the fees* that the fund charges or takes out of earnings. If he won't do it, or if the summary is confusing, take your business elsewhere.

The Family of Funds

Mutual funds can be grouped according to the managing investment company. For purposes of planning your investments you might want to focus your attention on which investment company runs the mutual fund. Fidelity Investment Company operates over two hundred different funds. They are spoken of collectively as the Fidelity Family. Other groups include the Dreyfus Family and the Pennsylvania Family. There are two reasons why an investor might want to keep all funds in the same family. First, the investment company should send a unified report, which would make it easy to compare the results of several investments. Second, the investment company would probably give you a break on fees if you transfer your money from one of their funds to another. The downside of that is that you might miss out on some good opportunities by staying in one family.

The Risk Level

When you begin to consider the risks associated with mutual funds, you find a good news/bad news scene. The good news is that there is a reasonable presumption that the professional management and diversification they provide should avoid most of the worst risks. You can assume some degree of safety *relative to the type of investments they use*. In other words, an international stock fund should be safer than what we could do buying foreign stocks on our own, but it would still be riskier than an American blue-chip stock fund. The bad news is that there is no clear and simple measurement of risk that can be relied upon totally. In the ideal case, we would like to see something like a scale of values from 1 to 10 so that we could look at the scale and say the Amoeba Fund has risk rating 8 and the Protozoa Fund has risk rating 4, so therefore I know that the Protozoa Fund is safer. We would like for all of the magazines and newspapers and brokers to provide those numbers to us so that we could evaluate risk. No such luck!

What you can find, though, are fairly consistent opinions about the relative risk levels of different funds. For example, the *Mutual Fund Forecaster* will rank funds as to risk level in five grades: very high, high, medium, low, and very low, based on their previous volatility history. *Kiplinger's Personal Finance* magazine uses a volatility ranking from 1 to 10 (10 is the highest volatility). *Your Money* magazine gives a risk rating from 0 up to a maximum of about 2, where value 1 means that the fund has had the same volatility as the average of its peer group, and 1.3 means the fund is 30 percent more volatile than its peer group. These publications are not totally consistent. I have found occasional contradictions among them, but since there is no certain scientific method of determining risk, they do give us the best indicators available.

My advice is that you cannot expect any guarantees on risk level. What you can expect is some amount of reasonably consistent opinion on the volatility of a given fund compared to other funds that have similar investments.

The Socially Responsible Funds

When I looked into this group, I learned something about doing my homework on mutual funds. Even though these funds share a common label, there are a lot of differences. They offer you different fees, different objectives, and different results in profitability. Even though each claims to be "responsible," they have different ideas about which stocks they buy and the ways in which they try to be socially responsible.

Here is a group of funds that advertise themselves as supporting the public interests. They choose to adopt the labels "socially responsible" or "environmental"; the label is helpful because it indicates there is something at work beyond just the profit motive. The label is also misleading because one investor's concept of socially responsible is another investor's Three Mile Island.

There is an arguable point of view that all investing is socially responsible. It supports businesses that create jobs. You don't have to feel guilty about non-socially-responsible investing. On the other hand, there is an arguable point of view that no investing is socially responsible. It avoids direct support of all-too-obvious immediate public needs. The money could go to charity, or political action committees, or a landscape architect. Once again, when push comes to shove, it's your money and you take your choice.

A few socially responsible funds are

- Dreyfus Third Century Fund
- PAX World Fund Inc.
- Progressive Environmental Fund
- The Rightime Social Awareness Fund

There are others. It's unlikely that any two investors would agree on which is most responsible. Even though all of these funds fall in the category of socially responsible, they vary in their objectives and investments.

The Dreyfus Third Century Fund invests according to four social criteria which in their opinion enhance the quality of life in America: (1) protection of environment and natural resources; (2) consumer protection; (3) occupational health and safety; (4) equal opportunity employment. In November of 1995, their holdings included Imperial Oil, Merck, Hewlett Packard, City Corp, and GTE.

Four years ago, the PAX World Fund Inc. advertised that the fund invests according to six social criteria: (1) life-supportive goods and services; (2) non-war-related; (3) fair employment; (4) sound environmental record; (5) some international development; (6) non-liquor, tobacco, and firearms. In December 1991, their portfolio included Advanced Computer Logic, Walt Disney, Maytag, Bay State Gas, and Campbell's Soup. In 1995, things had changed a bit: "the fund seeks investments in companies that are not to any degree engaged in manufacturing defense or weapons related products." In June of 1995, their largest holdings included Merck, Bristol-Meyers, Brooklyn Union Gas Co., Nynex, and General Mills. They also held about $130 million of U.S. government agency bonds.

The Progressive Environmental Fund seeks long-term capital appreciation by investing principally in companies engaged in contributing to a cleaner and healthier environment. In June of 1995, their investments included Archer-Daniels-Midland, Kenetech Corp, Calgon Carbon Corp, Whirlpool Corp, and CasTech Aluminum Group Inc.

The Rightime Social Awareness Fund invests in companies that show evidence, *relative to other companies in the same industry*, of contributing to the enhancement of the quality of human life (emphasis mine). In April 1995, their portfolio included Arco Chemical, Apple Computer, Hershey Foods, Bank of America, Coca-Cola, and Procter & Gamble.

Even if you are socially responsible, you probably also want to make a profit. The following table shows some of the expenses and results for those four funds. The performance numbers indicate annualized total return (dividends and capital appreciation, after deducting expenses) in the year ending 9/30/95, or the five years ending 9/30/95. The results have been rounded to the nearest whole percent.

	Fees (%)			Total Return (%)	
	Load	**Expense**	**Redemption**	**1 year**	**5 years**
Dreyfus	0	1.17	0	29	103
PAX	0	0.98	0	18	62
Prog. Env.	4	1.85	0	5	5
Rightime	4.75	0.50	0	21	63

The above is not enough to show you whether any of these funds is a good investment for you. The point is you need to do more work than simply ask for a socially responsible fund. These funds would not all have the same appeal to investors. When you decide to invest in these or any others, you should read and compare the prospectuses and the recent results of several funds.

Closed-End Funds

There is a separate class of funds that are handled differently from most that we will discuss. The *closed-end funds* do not sell and redeem shares whenever customers want. Instead, they sell a fixed lot of shares once to raise investing capital, and then those shares may be sold on the open markets, along with stocks, just like the shares of any other publicly owned company. Investing in a closed-end company or fund is very much like buying individual stocks. The investors can determine an asset value for the shares just as we show below, but the selling price of shares is fixed by market demand as for stocks. The selling price will generally be close to the net asset value. Sometimes people speak of "open-end" funds to indicate those that sell and redeem shares on demand, but the common jargon seems to indicate that "mutual fund" assumes open-end. The closed-end funds are frequently just referred to as investment companies or publicly traded funds. The (open-end) mutual funds are by far the more common in the press reports and in individual investors' strategies.

There is no way to describe all of the types of funds. Just assume that if there is anything in the world that moves through markets, there may be a mutual fund that buys and sells those things.[54]

How Do I Get Started?

Individual stock prices are set directly by the market action during each day, but the funds' prices are a little different. To understand the pricing mechanisms you need to know about two numbers, called the *public offering price* and the *net asset value*.

The amount you will pay for a share of a fund is given by the *public offering price* (POP), which is computed at the close of each business day for each mutual fund. The public offering price is the net value (per share) of the fund's investments, plus a little extra for the sales commission, if they have a load. *Net asset value* (NAV) is the sum of values of everything the fund owns, minus the liabilities, divided by the number of shares outstanding. The public offering price is equal to, or slightly higher than, the net asset value.

Think of the NAV as the true intrinsic worth of each share, and POP as the market price.

---

[54] The most interesting exception is zero coupon bonds—there are tax complications that make zeros specifically unattractive to mutual funds.

Suppose you bought a fund called the Fine Fund, and it had net assets of $258,700, and 29,750 shares outstanding. Then the net asset value of the Fine Fund, on that day, would be $258,700 ÷ 29,750 = $8.749 per share. This value is good from one day's market closing until the markets open the next morning.

To get the POP, for public sales, the fund management would calculate the NAV based on stock market prices at the end of the day, and add an adjustment to compensate for the sales load. If Fine Fund had a sales load of 2 percent, the POP would be $8.924. For each share you bought you would pay $8.749 for actual share value and an additional $0.175 for the sales fee ($0.175 is 2 percent of $8.749). For no-load funds, the POP is equal to the NAV. The essential rule to know is that you can buy shares at the cost of POP and redeem them at the price of NAV.

Your cost to buy shares = number of shares x POP
Your redemption value = number of shares x NAV

When the fund has a redemption fee, back-end load, that will be deducted from your redemption value.

Buying and Redeeming Mutual Funds

If you decide to buy a mutual fund, it can be as simple as buying an individual stock. You can call your broker and tell him you have $2,000 to buy the Fine Fund. The broker would purchase the shares at a price determined by the POP at the close of trading on that day.

Suppose the Net Asset Value at the close of that day was $8.749.

If there was no initial sales charge (no load), then POP = NAV and your $2,000 would buy 228.6 shares (2,000 ÷ 8.749 = 228.6).

If there was an initial sales load of 2 percent as we calculated above, you would buy shares at the public offering price of $8.924. You would get 224.1 shares (2,000 ÷ 8.924 = 224.1).

In either case, each of your new shares would have equal value with everyone else's shares, $8.749. You can find the values of POP and NAV for many funds listed in the daily business sections of newspapers. Just as with a stock purchase, your shares will be worth more or less the next day, but they will have the same value as everyone else's shares.

The basic facts to remember are:

When you buy,

$$\text{number of new shares} = \frac{\text{amount you spend (\$)}}{\text{POP per share (\$)}}$$

$$\text{NAV per share} = \frac{\text{total of the current assets minus liabilities}}{\text{total number of outstanding shares}}$$

and POP is equal to or slightly higher than the NAV.

Let's say that two years later you still had your 228.6 shares—you looked in the paper one day and saw that the current NAV for Fine Fund was $9.136, and you decided to sell. At the close of business on the day you sold, let us say Fine Fund held:

	total value
1300 shares of A Corp at 10 ½	$ 13,650
3500 shares of B Corp at 42 ½	148,750
6000 shares of R Corp at 14 ⅛	84,750
and $39,000 in cash	39,000
	286,150

So, the net assets on that day would be $286,150. If there were 31,300 shares outstanding and no debt for the fund, you would calculate the NAV like so, per our formula above:

$$\text{NAV} = \frac{\$286,150}{31,300} = \$9.142 \text{ per share}[55]$$

You could redeem your shares that day, at the close of market trading, for $9.142 per share—the same as anyone else who held shares that day. Your 228.6 shares would bring $2,089.90 (228.6 × $9.142).

---

[55] This assumes there are no current liabilities for Fine Fund.

YOU MAY TRADE WITH A BROKER OR THE FUND MANAGEMENT

If you want to buy or redeem mutual fund shares, you have to deal with someone who is in that business. That must be either the management of the fund or another party with whom they have set up a business relationship for buying and redeeming shares. That other party is probably a stockbroker. This is not so simple as we would like for it to be because the brokers will not all handle all of the funds you might like. We talked about this problem in chapter 4 as part of finding professional help. If you plan to buy mutual funds, you might review that section.

Profits and Losses

With a fund investment, you, a broker, and the investment company are going to get their hands on your money. The ideal case is where everyone wins—in the stock and bond markets that is possible. Let's get an idea of how everyone will make out.

Funds Expenses

The fee structure for mutual funds is getting more complicated all the time. **Read the prospectus!** If it's not clear, don't spend your money (Rule #1). Serious people around Wall Street say that the quality and clarity of the prospectus and earnings reports tell a lot about the quality and thinking of the fund's management.[56] If you don't understand the fee structure, be warned! What kind of financial managers would not show their fees clearly?

Mutual funds' fees come in three forms:

- *load* (up-front, advanced, sales fee, front-end load): a one-time charge when you buy shares
- *expense* (ongoing, annual, operational, management, 12b-1 fees[57]): involve some ongoing annual charges

---

[56] The *Hulbert Financial Digest* evaluates funds on the issue of clarity in their reports, among other things.

[57] 12b-1 refers to fees that were specifically authorized in section 12b-1 of a law; since then, everyone refers to them as simply 12b-1 fees. They go toward sales and marketing expenses to help cover the fund's costs of selling shares.

• *back-end load* (redemption fee): a one-time charge when you redeem (sell) your shares

All mutual funds will charge one or more of these fees.[58] That's fair—they have to make a living, too. Their manager deserves to earn $200,000 a year if she is really good, and all of their little analysts scurrying around have to make $60,000 because they live in New York or Boston.

Don't worry about what they keep—concentrate on what you keep. Remember Rule #4. (It's not a contest.)

Let's look at an example. Imagine that we have the choice of two funds, A or B. You put $10,000 into A; I put $10,000 into B. Imagine further that the account values progress as shown below for the next three years:

	Fund A	Fund B
Front load	0%	4%
Amount invested	$10,000	$9,615
Annual fees	0.4%	0.5%
Redemption fee	1%	1%
Value after 3 years	$11,000	$12,000
Return on redemption	$10,890	$11,880
Profit	$890	$1,880
Total three-year expenses	$230	$670

Fund B was much more expensive, but it was still a better investment. You should be happier making money along with the fund management, rather than just muddling by regardless of how cheap the ride was.

But it would be irresponsible to ignore the expenses. Let's look at the three types. First, we consider the infamous front-end load. The mutual fund management may charge you a fee right up front just to set up your account. For this you get in the game—you get your name in their records and you get their earnings reports. The load will be somewhere between 0 and 8.5 percent, paid when you buy shares. It will be distributed as a sales commission to the salesperson or brokerage firm.

---

[58] If a fund is described as no-load, that means they don't charge the first type, the front load.

Second, along the way they may take out various expenses to keep their business operating. These expenses get all kinds of obscure names (including 12b-1), which don't mean a whole lot. It would be impossible for us to review all of the fees—indeed, it would take a whole new book! Just make sure you get a clear statement of the amount. It should be less than 2 percent a year, on an ongoing basis. That's in the prospectus. Might I mention again: **Read the prospectus!** Even as I write this, I have in hand two annual statements from large well-known mutual funds. Both of them show an "investment advisory fee" along with about eight to ten other obscure fees. Both of them will no doubt advertise that their investment advisory fee is fairly small and leave the customer to figure out for himself where the money is actually going.

Third, the redemption fee is an option the fund management has that works like an incentive to stay with them. Sometimes the redemption fee will go away after three, or four, or five years. That will be stated in the prospectus. The logic in this is that it would be difficult for the fund to manage its business if too many people were buying and selling frequently. They encourage you to leave your money in place for a few years.

Here is a view of some hypothetical fund results just to help you learn what to look at. (Finest Fund is a made-up example.)

EXAMPLE OF ONE YEAR WITH THE FINEST FUND

The Finest Fund charges a 2 percent front load, 1.5 percent annual expenses, and 1 percent redemption fee. If you had $10,000 to spend on the fund, initially $196 would go to the broker (salesman) who sold you the fund, and $9,804 ($196 = 2 percent of $9,804) would be invested in stocks (or gold, or whatever the fund trades). In the first year the $9,804 of stocks might grow to $12,000. Then the fund would rake off 1.5 percent for annual expenses, that is, $180. That would leave $11,820.

Reporting Results

The $9,804 has grown to $11,820 assets in the fund. The fund will report that as a 20.6 percent gain (after taking out expenses).

Your actual investment value has grown from $10,000 to $11,820, which is an 18.2 percent return, but the fund only looks at the part of the money they had to work with after the front load.

Here is another fictitious example of how the numbers might work.

EXAMPLE OF FOUR YEARS WITH THE MAGNIFICENT MUTUAL FUND

If you were to put up $10,000 to buy shares in the Magnificent Mutual Fund, you might find something like this: their prospectus shows 3 percent sales load, 1.25 percent annual expenses, and 1 percent redemption fee. Suppose that over the next four years stock prices, as indicated by the S&P 500 Index, show gains of +6 percent, +2 percent, -10 percent, and +8 percent. And let's say that the management at Magnificent Mutual is good enough to buy stocks that give +9 percent, +8 percent, -4 percent, and +15 percent in the four years (that means they are pretty good).

After holding this investment for four years, you could sell and walk away with $11,879. That is a real gain of $1,879 (which is 18.79 percent) in four years, about 4.4 percent compound annual gain.

Is this any good? The investment company has taken a total of $850 in fees over the life of your investment. Let's look at the results three ways:

1. The compound annual gains in values of the stocks they bought gave a total 30 percent gain in the four years, but this ignores fund expenses.
2. Counting in expenses, the fund's reported results for four years are +7.6 percent, +6.7 percent, -5.2 percent, and +13.6 percent. That gives an increase in share values of 24 percent in four years.
3. The results for the investor: $10,000 became $11,879, an 18.79 percent gain in four years.

When you look at it this way, it appears that the fund has raked off a lot of money for poor results. But that is not the whole story. It is more realistic to look at the changes in the S&P 500 Index over four years: +6 percent, +2 percent, -10 percent, and +8 percent. That gives a four-year total growth of +5.1 percent. If you had taken your $10,000 to a pretty good stockbroker, and paid brokerage fees, and worked hard, and been lucky, you might have realized a gain over the four years of between 0 percent and +10 percent.[59]

---

[59] It could have been a whole lot better, or a whole lot worse, but on average, many individual investors buying stocks will come out somewhere close to the S&P 500 results.

By using the Magnificent Mutual Fund you came out ahead (up almost 19 percent) with less work and lower risk. You made good money—they made good money—who is to worry? Of course, if your return from the fund had been much less than the standard of performance,[60] you should consider moving that investment. This has been a purely hypothetical example, but it will give you an idea of how to interpret the funds' statements of results.

Dividends: More Profits

So far we have taken a simple approach to fund profits and just looked at changes in net asset values. There is another way to profit from funds also. Since they are buying stocks or bonds, they will frequently collect some dividends. Those dividends will be paid out to the shareholders in cash, or reinvested as additional shares if you request it. That again will add to your total return from the fund. When the fund management reports their results, they will always include the paid-out dividends as if all of the dividends were immediately reinvested in new shares. You don't have to reinvest the dividends. You could keep them or spend them, but many investors will reinvest and the fund management will do their arithmetic on that basis. Just remember when they claim annual growth of +9.3 percent, this means assets growth *plus dividends reinvested*, minus their expenses. For a growth fund, expect the assets growth to be somewhat greater than dividends; for an income fund expect the dividends to be larger.

Getting Your Money Back

Getting your investment and gains back out of a mutual fund can sometimes be a problem. It should not be. It will not be a problem for you if you address the issue in the beginning. **Don't put any money into a mutual fund until you understand what you will have to do to redeem the shares.**

---

[60] You might also want to compare your profits with some other market index, or the return on U.S. savings bonds (four years at 5.5 percent gives better than 24 percent growth).

In order to regain your capital, reap the profits, or perhaps recognize a loss, you will have to redeem some or all of your shares. Funds have different procedures and rules for handling redemptions. The basic idea is simple enough—they cancel your shares and send you a check. However, in practice it may not be quite so easy, and it may take longer than you care to wait for your money. The time to take care of that and avoid all the hassles is when you first invest in the fund. In January of 1992, I asked PaineWebber to transfer funds from an IRA money market fund to a new account I had set up with another broker. In September, they were still sending me statements showing how they were trying to complete the transaction (yes, I said *September*). The amount of money involved there was insignificant, but it was aggravating.

In the prospectus, the rules must be spelled out in detail on what you have to do to redeem shares. If you purchased the funds through a broker, she should be able to take care of the redemption. When you buy the shares, ask about the requirements and the time period for redeeming shares and getting your money back. There will normally be a delay of a few days for them to process your request.

If you purchased the shares from the fund, they will require either a written request or a telephone call with adequate identification before they will return the money. In either case, there will be some sort of procedure to prove that the request comes from the true owner of the shares. That may require something like a certified signature card on hand, or certification of the letter by a bank officer. There are several ways they can verify authenticity of the request. Your concern is that it all be set up in advance. Don't wait until the day you need the money and then begin an eight- to fifteen-day process of sending letters back and forth to establish the redemption. When you first buy the shares, make sure that all signature cards, code words, or whatever may be required are set up immediately. Then you will know that you can cash in quickly (a few days).

Changes in the Mutual Funds Industry

Lots of brokers, investment managers, and newspaper columnists like to talk about mutual funds. Whenever they need to get down to brass tacks, most of the hard data is based on past performance. Sure, everyone keeps saying, "Past performance is no guarantee of future results," but it is obvious that they want you to believe that past performance is an *indicator* of future results.[61]

It should be clear to any investor whose eyes haven't glazed over that the investment companies and the brokerage firms are, in effect, advertising that "mutual funds have been very, very good to us for the past fifteen years; therefore, buy more mutual funds." How often do they advertise their risk levels? How often do they advertise what's in the portfolio? Never! (Well, hardly ever.) They only advertise past performance.

Examine that logic before committing any money. The question is: "Should we believe that the performance of the past fifteen years is an indicator of future results?" My answer to that question is generally no. My personal investment strategy says that the world and the financial markets have changed too much. The mutual funds industry has certainly changed enormously. The old rules and the old methods may be no longer reliable. I invest in a few carefully selected mutual funds because of what I see or believe about the current economy and future business prospects, and to diversify[62] our investments—not just because the funds industry has had a good track record.

The reason is that the game has changed. The Washington Redskins had a wonderful record in the National Football League for ten years. I would have predicted a few more years of success for them. Wrong! If the League changed to admit twenty new teams, and then developed a new rule book, you wouldn't want to bet on any team's future performance. You wouldn't want to bet on continued growth and success for the NFL.

That's the way it is in the investment industry in 1996. Huge changes are occurring all around; only the naive will assume that the past tells an adequate prologue to that future. Some of those changes are fundamental to the economy and the markets, and will affect all investors. We don't have time to roll out six chapters on economics, but we can look at the investment industry.

---

[61] There is some statistical evidence that past performance may indicate future performance for some funds if you use the data correctly, but that still appears tricky to me (further information in chapter 10).

[62] Part of the diversification scheme is to use other people's ideas, not just my own.

I have mentioned before about the rapid growth of funds, both in numbers and in total assets. Do you believe that the industry is capable of producing talented managers and analysts to staff the new funds and manage the new money according to the standards that we require? Look at any other business or industry that has grown very fast. You may have worked for one. Do they usually succeed in developing competent new management as fast as needed? Do some folks have to get on-the-job training? Is that what you want from your money managers?[63]

REGULATORY CHANGES

Why did Willie Sutton rob banks? That was where the money was! What would Sutton have done if the FBI had announced a plan to reduce the rules and physical security surrounding banks? Well, guess what! The SEC has announced plans for reducing the rules and restrictions on how mutual funds deal with the public. Some of their proposed changes are good, such as allowing more flexibility and competition on sales commissions—that should reduce costs for everyone. But some of their changes may have an effect of inviting more foxes into the henhouse. For example, there is a proposal to modify the requirement that every investor receive a detailed prospectus—this would just open the door to more exaggerated claims and misdirection by salespeople in the industry. When you put enough temptation out there, and reduce the regulations protecting investors, there is a chance of something going wrong.

Another significant change is the increasing tendency towards special niche funds. One of the advantages of mutual funds has been the diversification that a lone small investor could not achieve. That benefit is no longer present in many new funds. The specialized fund automatically sacrifices some of the benefit of diversification. It deliberately takes on some extra risks in order to seek the unique rewards of its niche. How much diversification will you find in a new fund that specializes in Russian automobile companies? It might be cheaper, easier, and safer to simply buy the stocks if a fund's area of specialization becomes too narrow.

---

[63] Hint: the answers are no, yes, and no.

The Wolves Are at the Small Investor's Door

If 3,000 new funds are created in 1996 and '97, as there probably will be, we can guess that many of them will have new and unique objectives. It would be foolhardy to assume that all of those new funds will have strong management, capable well-trained staffs, good profit potential within their niches, and adequate safety through diversification. It may be—but the smart money will not bet on the field.

Given all that, I still think that for most small investors, advantages outweigh the risks. But caution is advised. Please work hard at selecting the funds to buy. Read the next chapter and refer again to chapter 5.

Recommended Further Reading

The business magazines, *Investor's Business Daily,* and the *Wall Street Journal* will continue to give the best up-to-the minute developments in mutual funds. You can also use the Internet to access the Securities and Exchange Commission's web site (key word: EDGAR) for late legal developments.

If you like a lot of facts and figures and history of mutual funds, one outstanding buy is the *Mutual Funds Factbook*, available for $25 from the

Investment Company Institute and updated every year. They also offer many other brochures and books related to the business. Write to: ICI, 1401 H St. NW, Suite 1200, Washington, DC 20005-2148.

There is also a noteworthy television program on cable TV in most areas. The cable station CNBC (the Financial News Network) carries a regular nightly program called (at presstime—its name has been changed several times) *The Money Club,* which is devoted to the financial concerns of individuals. It frequently focuses on mutual funds and gives you an opportunity to hear from the fund managers or other experts who evaluate funds' performance and risk.

Goldberg, Gary, and Donald Korn. *High Powered Investing.* New York: John Wiley & Sons, 1988 (out of print).

CHAPTER 10

Selecting Mutual Funds

Small Investors need to know:

• Should I buy mutual funds?

• It's getting late in the book. What am I going to do?

• Where can I get more information?

• How do the publications describe mutual funds?

• Are mutual funds always safe?

• How can I diversify with mutual funds?

• How can I evaluate and choose among mutual funds?

• Does past performance mean anything?

Should I Buy Mutual Funds?

You have to decide for yourself where to put your money, but I think there is a good case to argue that for the small investors, a large chunk of our risk-oriented investment capital should go into mutual funds. The questions that naturally arise are how to mix this with the other parts of our investing, and how to select the funds. This chapter will deal with those problems. The main themes are why to buy funds, how to use them for diversification, how to understand the reports and reviews that are offered in many different reference sources, and how to evaluate the funds. Luckily, there are a lot of people eager to write about it. There are more sources of information, and probably more good, readable, reliable sources than any of us could keep up with.

Past Performance Is Not a Guarantee of Future Results

During 1994, the twenty-five largest stock mutual funds had an average performance that yielded a small loss on their shareholders' investments. The entire group of U.S. stock funds did worse, U.S. bond funds did worse, overseas stock funds did worse, and overseas bond funds did worse. So I'm going to tell you to buy mutual funds, right? Right!

In 1995, almost every money manager who could even spell Wall Street, let alone understand it, made profits. The funds that owned U.S. stock funds gained over 27 percent on average. Those that owned sector funds specializing in technology, financial services, or biotechnology made over 30 percent on average. Those with income funds made over 12 percent. Even most of the weakest mutual funds during that period were profitable.

So what are you going to do? You have by now read about stocks and bonds and mutual funds, and you have an understanding of some of the basic ideas. Time is running out. There are only a few pages left in the book, and I can warn you that the last chapter is not going to help you make much money. It is time to make some real decisions on mutual funds. You may decide to toss the book in the trash and go back to your garden or your spouse. Very well, go, I wish you well. But for those who think they are going to stick with, or at least try, some investing in financial markets, you have to take a hard look at some mutual funds.

It would be difficult for the average small investor to build a reasonably safe and diversified investment portfolio without using some mutual funds. You may also buy stocks or bonds or some other things, but if you are the true-blue small investor, you need to diversify. We probably don't have enough money to fully diversify through the stock markets, and we almost certainly don't have enough time or research tools to buy and track more than a few stocks. In order to do a good job in buying ten stocks, you might have to study fifty or more. That would be a tremendous toll on your time and attention. You may want to acquire a mix of stocks and stock mutual funds plus bonds or bond mutual funds, but without mutual funds you probably will not attain adequate diversification.

Allocating Your Money

You still have the question of how to allocate your investment capital. I cannot tell you exactly how to do that because I don't know your circumstances. Some of the books and magazines mentioned throughout this book offer guidelines based on your age, finances, expectations, other assets, plans for the money, etc. By all means look at them. *Smart Money* has run fine articles of that nature. *Consumer Reports* also offers similar advice.

There are some variations in opinions on the asset allocation problem. Some financial advisors think that people older than fifty should keep most of their money in safe bonds or bond funds. Now it is becoming more widely advised that even the retired investor might need to continue to plan for growth of capital in order to keep ahead of inflation and provide for a longer retirement. That would point toward putting more money into growth-stock funds and accepting the risk of being in the stock market. The answer for you is a very personal decision that has been thought through by whoever has a stake in the money. It depends on your retirement income, life expectations, and other financial circumstances. The retired couple who owns their home could presumably take a little more risk than a similar couple who did not.

The same kinds of variations apply to any other category of investors, whether old or young, married or single, parents or not. It is all very personal. I want to proceed on an assumption that you have made or will make some decisions about how much money to put into risk-oriented investments in financial markets, and then look at more choices and decisions.

Different Kinds of Funds

In the last chapter we looked briefly at types of funds, just to illustrate that there are different ways to classify them. There are more than 8,000 mutual funds and the number is increasing, so you have a lot of choices out there. In fact, you have enough choices to satisfy almost any whim as far as type of investments, and enough choices to create a lot of trouble. Luckily, it is not necessary to study the entire market of

8,000 funds to make your choices. Each time that you wish to buy a fund, it will probably be sufficient for you to look over performance results for ten to twenty or thirty of them. That's easy. The results are widely published in many newspapers and magazines such as *Business Week*, *Forbes*, or *Fortune*. Out of those that you look at, you might pick a few to study closely, and out of that last group, chances are you will find more than one that suits your needs. In order to get into this process, we need to explore more about the classification of funds.

One classification scheme is used by a newsletter called the *Mutual Funds Forecaster*. They have a scheme for grouping funds by risk rating. The ratings are Very High, High, Medium, Low, and Very Low, and are based on their own methods of looking at volatility. Volatility is an indication of how much the price moves up or down, and is related to the uncertainty you would have about the daily or monthly variation in the value of your investment.

After the *Mutual Funds Forecaster* classifies the stocks as to risk level, within each risk group they indicate which are good buys and which are to be avoided relative to the risk they carry. Obviously, they cannot evaluate and publish recommendations for all 8,000 mutual funds. Usually around 450 funds get into their monthly issue. In their selection process, they will choose funds that are widely owned or have some particular investment strategy that may be of interest to a lot of readers.

This is not to recommend the *Mutual Funds Forecaster* as either a good or bad place to begin, but it is one source you might want to look at. The point is that by looking at their listing for medium-risk funds that were recommended for buying, you might narrow your search field to a few funds that you would study more closely. Or, if you have already identified some fund that you think is interesting, you could look in the *Forecaster* and see what they think about the risk level and desirability of that fund.

There are plenty of other people or publications offering similar types of help. For example, someone might decide to work within the Fidelity family of funds because of the number of funds they offer. Then there is a publication devoted to the needs of Fidelity investors, the *Fidelity Profit Alert* that purports to advise readers on the risks and rewards of specific Fidelity funds and offers buy/sell advice according to their view of changing opportunities and risks.

In chapter 9, we saw five categories of stock funds: blue chip, small cap, growth, income, and socially responsible. But you recall that the socially responsible funds differed widely in their statements of investment objectives, their selection of stocks, and their results. It will be the same for any category of funds you look at. And, just as before, the name of the fund cannot be trusted as a completely adequate description of what they do with your money. We will look at the ways that various ratings agencies or analysts evaluate and describe them.

LOADS AND NO-LOADS

Fees are important, but the distinction between load and no-load is becoming blurred. The mutual funds industry is working hard to deceive us as to what the expenses are, but the expenses will hit you in three ways: up-front fee when you buy the fund, ongoing expenses as they operate the fund, and redemption fee when you sell your shares. Every fund will charge one or more of these fees.

The front load is sometimes described as a "normal load," which probably means 4 percent to 8 percent depending on whom you are talking to, or a "low load," which means less than 4 percent. Either way, it comes directly off of the top of your money. If you invest $1,000 in a fund that has a 4 percent load, and for the first two years it reports total return of 5 percent and 8 percent, first off, the investment cost you $1,040 because of the load. At the end of the two years, you would have $1,134, which is a compound annual rate of return on your $1,040 of just about 4.4 percent,[64] not as good as a bank CD. The front load eats a big hole in your profits. A 4 percent back load would give nearly the same result except for the effect on income yield from the fund.

Many investors and advisors have a firm rule that they will not touch any funds with a sales load or redemption fee. They argue that there are plenty of other choices, with equally attractive objectives and historical results, so why pay the fee? That's pretty good thinking, but itmight not be right for you. For example, if you work with Merrill Lynch for brokerage service, they have to make a living at the business. In order to get some income they will almost certainly only want to

---

[64] The fund will report 13.4 percent total return over those two years, but you just had 9 percent return because of the load. Nine percent in two years is 4.4 percent compound annual rate.

sell you funds with a load, which is a sales commission. If the load is not present on the front end, it might be replaced with a redemption fee on when you sell. And if you don't see either a front or rear load, there would probably be a 12b-1 fee, which is used to cover sales expenses for the fund. The front sales load and redemption fee are pretty obvious. The 12b-1 fee is sneaky because you probably won't see the expense; the funds management company will just take it out of the assets along with their other operational expenses. Just don't forget that the brokers, their sales force, the fund management, and *their* sales force are all hard-working professional people and have to make a living at the business. Read the prospectus to find out where the expenses lie.

Given all that, it still makes sense to look for funds with reasonable expenses. For most small investors, it is probably true that no-load is the preferred way to go, but not with blinders on. For example, here comes the famous Magellan Fund of Fidelity Investment Company, which does carry a front-end load plus a solid 1 percent expense ratio. It may look expensive, but they are the best over a long time period. A twenty-year history of leading the world in what they do, and a 35 percent return for 1995 year-to-date are precious even with a little load added in. Some of the socially responsible funds might work for you even with their loads. The AIM Constellation Fund carries a front load of 5.5 percent plus an ongoing expense ratio of 1.2 percent, and they still manage to show the long-term results for investors that make them one of the best investments you could ask for. So take a hard look at sales loads and expenses, but remember the payoff is in what you keep, not what they keep. If everybody makes good money, you should be happy.

More Classifications of Funds

In the *Mutual Funds Quarterly* printed by *Barron's* with data supplied by Lipper Analytical Services, there are forty-four distinct objectives used to classify the funds shown with their definitions of the objectives. For example, they show:

- Balanced funds: The goal is preserving principal; on average, the funds maintain approximately a 60:40 ratio of stocks to bonds.

- Convertibles funds: Invest primarily in convertible bonds and convertible preferred stocks.
- Emerging markets funds: Invest primarily in stocks of emerging market nations. ("Emerging" is a very loose term; it may include third world, or new or growing capital structures, or new financial markets.)
- Gold funds: Have at least 65 percent of assets in gold, or gold mining, or mining financing related equities.
- Growth funds: Invest principally in companies whose earnings are expected to grow faster than the earnings averages of the major financial average companies. That is, they expect their earnings to grow faster than the average rate for companies in the Dow-Jones Industrial group or the S&P 500. They may buy stocks of the faster-growing DJIA companies, but not all of the thirty industrials.
- Income funds: Seek high current income through stocks, bonds, or money market investments; have no more than 60 percent in stocks and no more than 75 percent in bonds.
- Specialty funds: Limit investments to a specific industry or business, for example, auto, bank, or technology, or funds that simply do not fit any of the other forty-three classifications.

I recommend the review of mutual funds in *Barron's* for your further study. It is published approximately the second week of each calendar quarter. Certainly, *Business Week* and many other periodicals give similar reports.

Another useful reference, that has fewer details, is the *Worth Financial Intelligence* magazine. In a recent issue, their review of equity mutual funds started with just five broad categories of stock (equity) funds; they were:

- Large cap growth funds: The companies these funds invest in have average market capitalization of more than $1.5 billion and average price to book value[65] ratio greater than 2.87.

---

[65] *Book value* is a financial term used to represent what a company is worth in terms of real assets minus debts. It is, in a sense, what the company might bring in a fire sale. In the description of growth or value funds, we are using price per share compared to book value per share. The calculated book value of a firm can vary widely depending on who is doing the calculations and how they choose to value certain assets.

- Large cap value funds: The companies these funds invest in have average market capitalization of more than $1.5 billion and average price to book value ratio less than 2.87.
- Small cap growth funds: The companies these funds invest in have average market capitalization of less than $1.5 billion and average price to book value ratio greater than 2.29.
- Small cap value funds: The companies these funds invest in have average market capitalization of less than $1.5 billion and average price to book value ratio less than 2.29.
- Global funds: These funds invest in stocks of companies around the world; they have at least 40 percent of assets invested in non-U.S. companies.

For this analysis, *Worth* narrowed their attention to 883 funds by restricting it to stock funds that had been in existence for five years or longer and had assets of $25 million or more. What is the use of this? Why the funny choice of numbers? The editors and analysts of *Worth* are trying to offer a breakdown of choices that in their opinion would offer good diversification to investors in stock mutual funds. This has the advantage (or disadvantage) of offering fewer types of funds than the *Barron's*/Lipper list. If an investor had $28,000 to put into stock mutual funds, she might want to divide that money into $6,000 for one fund from each of the first four *Worth* categories, and $4,000 into the global funds. *Worth* has specific suggestions for which funds in each category would be most desirable (ratings indicated as $ for worst, to $$$$$ for best).

Another strategy for your stock market investments might be that you want to pick some individual large cap stocks yourself, and use mutual funds to get the diversification into other types of stocks. Suppose that the investor had $52,000 that she planned to put into risk-oriented investments in the financial markets. The following could be a beginning strategy.[66]

1. I will initially keep half my money in cash, until I see how things are working and develop a better comfort level.

---

[66] This is not a recommended strategy for you; I cannot recommend a strategy for someone I don't know, but just for illustration, we assume it is a reasonable plan for somebody.

2. I will find two or three large cap value stocks and invest $10,000 in them (in total); this will require considerable time and effort in research.
3. I will select one mutual fund from each of the small cap growth and value lists and invest $4,000 in each.
4. I will find a bond fund that specializes in investment-grade bonds and invest $8,000 in it.

So the money is allocated as $26,000 temporary cash reserve, $10,000 for stock picks, $8,000 for stock mutual funds, and $8,000 for bond mutual funds.

Maybe the funds selection part of the investment plan looks easy. You could simply look in *Worth,* pick out a fund with $$$$$ rating from each of the two categories small cap growth and small cap value, and buy them. That would not be a wise approach to funds selection. What would be wise is to look at all of their top-rated funds in each area, consider their load expenses and other expenses, and call their 800 numbers to get copies of the prospectuses and recent annual or semi-annual reports. **Read the prospectuses!!!** If you don't have time to read them, give your money to a charity. Look at their current holdings as shown in the reports. Read their objectives and fees as shown in the prospectuses. Look at the recent and longer-term total-return figures for each as reported in a recent issue of *Worth, Business Week,* the *Wall Street Journal,* or any of the dozen other periodicals that regularly report those numbers. Read the opinions about each fund in *Morningstar Mutual Funds* or the *Value Line Mutual Fund Reports.*

You can do all of that with a few toll-free telephone calls, a trip to your local library, the purchase price of a few magazines, and perhaps ten hours of research. That is not too much work to do if you are going to put $8,000 at risk.

You might go through he same process again in choosing the bonds fund, but you wouldn't start with the same information in *Worth.* Instead, you might start with *Morningstar* or *Business Week* or some other publication that gives information on bonds funds.

All of the reference publications that I have mentioned here offer good helpful starting points. None of them offers a good place to turn off your brain and snooze.

Asset Allocation Funds

Diversification can get difficult, and there are many people and businesses eager to take that burden off of you for a price. If you use a full-service broker, he will certainly offer several plans wherein he might simply manage your money for you, but an interesting alternative is the asset allocation class of funds. Asset allocation funds use a mix of investments, and change their mix according to what they believe offers the best chances at any given time. The mix may include stocks, bonds, money markets, gold, options, futures, or almost anything else. You have to read the prospectus to see where each asset allocation fund draws the line.

The first thing you may notice is that the *Worth* magazine classification of funds that we looked at above doesn't show anything that looks like asset allocation. Right. There are too many funds. Nobody is going to cover all of them. The *Worth* list was restricted to funds that invest primarily in stocks. If we go to a different reference, like the *Charles Schwab Mutual Funds Performance Guide*,[67] there is no specific listing for asset allocation, but there is one for flexible portfolio funds. The description of those says: "The funds invest in stocks, money market instruments, and/or bonds depending on market conditions." Within that category, I see the following funds (* means a no-load fund; these were grabbed randomly from among a long list):

- Baron Growth and Income* (0 percent current yield): Seeks capital appreciation with income as a secondary objective.
- Brinson Global* (2.4 percent current yield): At least 65 percent of assets in securities of at least three different countries.
- Dreyfus Capital Value A (2.4 percent current yield): Seeks capital appreciation by following an asset allocation strategy that contemplates shifts among a wide range of investments and market sectors.[68]
- Strong Corporate Bond Fund (7.1 percent current yield): Invests in fixed-income securities and dividend-paying stocks.

---

[67] They will be happy to send you a copy if you call them at 800-435-4000. Among the brokerage firms, Schwab offers outstanding value and choice in mutual funds.

[68] Definitely read the prospectus. I don't understand "contemplates shifts among a wide range of sectors."

Those yield numbers are current. Next quarter they will change.

There are fifty-one flexible funds in the Schwab list, and there are significant variations among them. Those funds are available if you invest through Schwab. If you use a different broker, he may offer some, but probably not all, of the same funds. There are two asset allocation funds that I use for a total of about 7 percent of our investment money. Those two offer several features that I do not actively practice in my other investments:

- They actively seek to switch money between markets at the best times, which I do not (that tactic is called market timing).

- They actively seek to work contrarian strategies,[69] which I do not.

- They invest, among other things, in precious metals and options, which I do not.

So those funds offer very specific avenues of diversification to my investing, and they offer features that I do not care to pursue on my own.

The asset allocation group may have something to offer you. However, here again you cannot simply close your eyes and throw a dart at the list. These funds, just like the socially responsible funds, the growth funds, or any other group, have a wide range of characteristics that might or might not be good for you. Some of the asset allocation funds are regarded as high-risk funds, and some are quite low risk. Among the group there are very great differences in how they choose to allocate, and great differences in how much yield they pay.

Do the homework. Do the research. Read the prospectuses!!! Be a smart little investor. If you spent six months earning that money, don't risk it on a sudden whim.

ALLOCATING YOUR INVESTMENTS

There are other approaches to asset allocation that may be good for you. You might like to select a mix of four to eight funds that produce an asset allocation mix that appeals to you. You might even decide to

---

69 The contrarian strategy usually means investing contrary to the general consensus in Wall Street. There is ample data to suggest that can pay good rewards in the hands of a smart money manager.

work your own strategy in switching money among different funds and categories. There are some investment companies that will allow you to switch money between various funds at little or no cost.

One approach to choosing your mutual funds is to decide which areas you do not want to work on yourself. You may look in Moody's bond manuals and the newspaper bond-reporting pages and decide they are just too tedious for your further attention. In that case, you should find a mutual fund, or two or three, to handle the portion of your investments that is dedicated to fixed-income investing.

And finally, you may not want to do any of the research in stocks and bonds or make buy/sell decisions yourself, but still want to earn some of the rewards of investment. Then there are asset allocation funds, or mixes of different types of funds, that should give you good diversification and reasonable risk control along with a fair chance at some profits.

The Small Investor Allocates His Assets

The mutual funds you study and buy should be selected to comple-ment the other parts of your investment strategy. If your personal stock picking is going to focus on small cap stocks that carry a higher risk, your mutual funds ought to balance that with some safer funds, such as perhaps utilities funds or municipal bonds funds.

You may choose to study blue chip stocks, and specialize in them for individual stock purchases. That's enough to keep any two people busy. Then it might be best, for diversification, to buy a mutual fund that specializes in small cap stocks. You might think that health care is a promising avenue of investment, but you simply don't know enough about it to evaluate the best choices. Then it might be easier and safer to choose a mutual fund to handle the portion of your risk-oriented investment funds that you want to put into health care. You can find plenty of good mutual funds that specialize in drug companies, health maintenance organizations, biotechnology, or those that span the entire health care field.

There are untold millions of different ways that individual investors might approach the job of selecting funds. I cannot list all of them, so instead let's look at some basic ideas and examples. In the following paragraphs there are some ideas and questions that you might use to get started. Then we look at some specific (fictional) examples of how various investors might proceed. What happens here is that probably none of my examples exactly fit your situation, but some of them should have areas of similarity to your situation or they might suggest approaches to help you get started.

You should have some idea now as to what kinds of investing appeal to you, and how much you are already involved in financial markets. The small investor should answer these questions: Am I going to invest in individual stocks? Stock funds? Individual bonds? Bond funds? Specialized and hybrid funds such as sector funds, balanced funds, or asset allocation funds? How much money do I already have invested in any of those, and how much more do I want to put in? How do I intend to manage risk?

We will start with those questions in two ways. One way is to allocate money across risk levels, and then try to pick investments that work for that allocation; another is to select specific types of investments, and then try to manage risk within those types.

An example of the first approach is that an investor might decide to put 25 percent of his money into totally safe and secure investments, 25 percent into low risk, 25 percent in medium risk, and 25 percent in seeking higher reward with possibly high risk. That might be allocated as $10,000 in a bank CD, $10,000 in a municipal bonds fund, $10,000 in an S&P 500 Index stock fund, and $10,000 in a small cap technology stock fund.

In the second approach, another investor might decide to keep $4,000 in his savings account, $15,000 in mutual funds, and $10,000 in stocks or bonds that he selected on his own. Then this second investor still has the job of allocating among risk levels.

Look at our first case study: Jack Sprat is a thirty-eight-year-old chemist with a reasonably secure career with a large drug company that he has worked with for eight years. He is single, owns his home, and he can manage his debts and mortgage reasonably well out of current income. In his company 401(k) retirement plan, he has $25,000 worth of his company's stock and $15,000 in money market funds. He has no other investments, but has an additional $12,000 of savings that he wishes to allocate to investing. He feels that the company stock is quite safe, so he doesn't want to let go of any of it. That leaves him with the $15,000 in the 401(k) money market account and the $12,000 savings to work on. The $15,000 has to stay in the 401(k). The other two choices his company offers in their 401(k) plan are a long-term bond fund with a good history, and an asset allocation fund. Jack sees that he has a diversification problem: too much of his financial safety is dependent on the success of his employer, that covers both his job and the company stock; however, he has made a decision that the company and his position are solid. The other parts of his investments have to be allocated in ways to give better diversification. He decides that he needs some investments with potential higher return, and certainly exposure to different economic considerations than the drug business. He decides to take the $15,000 in the 401(k) and split it between the bond fund and the asset allocation fund. The bond fund is low risk, and this particular asset allocation fund has some investments that put it in a relatively higher risk category. Now what about the other $12,000? Jack wants more exposure to the stock market, but he does not want the work and trouble of studying individual stocks. That means he will use mutual funds for getting stock market opportunities. He could decide to use a blue chip stock fund and a small cap growth fund for $6,000 each. Jack's investment plans could now be summed up as

low risk	medium risk	high risk
$7,500 in bond fund	$7,500 in asset allocation fund	$6,000 in small cap fund
	$6,000 in blue chip fund	
	$25,000 in company stock	

That leaves him very large exposure to the safety and success of his employer, plus large exposure to the volatility of the stock market.

In terms of types of investments:

individual stocks	$25,000 (the employer's stock)
bond fund	$ 7,500
asset allocation fund	$ 7,500
stock funds (2)	$12,000

The stock funds and the asset allocation fund should carry some extra diversification protection, if he chooses them carefully. In total this appears to be a medium-high-risk investment strategy, with particular dependence on his current employer. If it works for Jack, okay, it works. This is a plan, which is far better than no plan at all. At the very least, in working this out, Jack has had to think through his current situation and make some decisions about risk level and types of investments to use. As an investment advisor, I would not encourage Jack to stick with this plan, but it is better than no plan at all.

Paul and Mary are in their early sixties, both retired, and have $73,000 in savings along with current retirement income of $2,400 per month. That retirement income is secure for the rest of their lives, and they figure that they need about $2,000 per month to just get by. They have no experience in financial markets. Their primary investment goals are safety of their principal, the $73,000, and some growth opportunity. They began their investment strategy by deciding that $55,000 must be kept in very safe investments, and the other $18,000 must be moderately safe but should offer some growth opportunity. They know of a small company in their town that they believe is a good investment, and they've done enough homework to decide to invest $8,000 in the stock of that company. They think of that as a moderate risk investment, but it may in fact be fairly high risk. They should not allocate any more of their money to individual stock selections. Now the picture, in terms of risk looks like this:

low risk	medium risk	high risk
$55,000 yet to be allocated	$10,000 yet to be allocated	$8,000 small cap stock

They are already outside of their strategic planning framework, but people do, unfortunately, fall in love with the stocks that they pick. They need to be very conservative with the rest of the money. The $10,000 could buy them two mutual funds chosen for safety and total return prospects. They choose a large cap growth fund and a balanced fund for $5,000 each. Each of them should be chosen with an eye for high safety ratings, consistent good return, and low volatility over the past five years, without management changes. The low-risk money will be allocated among bond funds and safe stock funds. They chose to keep money in a money market fund and use a low-duration bond fund,[70] a long-term investment-grade corporate bond fund, and an income fund that uses stocks and bonds. After making those decisions, the money is allocated like so:

low risk	medium risk	high risk
$10,000 money market	$5,000 large cap stock fund	$8,000 local company stock
$14,000 low-duration fund	$5,000 balanced fund	
$15,000 corporate bond fund		
$16,000 income fund		

and all of the dividends or yield will be reinvested in the funds.

This is a plan. Maybe not the best plan, but it is most certainly better then no plan at all. Notice that they have not selected any tax-exempt investments. At their income level, their tax rates are low enough that the tax savings would not be good enough to compensate them for the lower return from tax-exempt investments. Notice also that they have not invested in any limited partnerships for parking lot

---

[70] *Duration* is a bond evaluation factor that looks at how much the price of the bond might be affected by changes in interest rates; low-duration bonds are generally safer than higher duration, and there are funds that specialize in these.

developments. First, they don't know anything about the parking lot business, and second, limited partnerships are usually high-risk ventures with uncertainty as to when they might be able to retrieve the money. The parking lot business is good for somebody, else where would we park? But it is not good business for Paul and Mary. Ditto for limited partnerships.

Sally and Jim are a well-off (at least by my standards) forty-something professional couple. Their combined income is $135,000 (before tax). They live very comfortably on that and save $1,600 a month, of which $600 goes into Sally's 401(k) at work and the rest goes in a bank money market account. The balances are currently $37,000 in the 401(k) and $49,000 in the money market account. Sally and Jim are good old small investors. They have the essential fear and suspicion about financial markets, and they have little prior experience with investing. They have decided to look for a good solid combination of growth and income, with a balance between conservative and moderately risky methods. It is worthwhile for them to keep the profits tax free. They agree to take some of the $49,000 from the money market savings and put it to work in more aggressive investments.

The first view of their planning looks like this:

low risk	medium risk	high risk
$37,000 in the 401(k)	$17,000 from current savings	$17,000 from current savings
$15,000 current savings in money market account		
$600 per month into 401(k)	$250 per month into investments	$250 per month into investments
$500 per month into money market savings		

Tax-sheltered investments: the $37,000 in 401(k) and all income-producing selections[71]
Taxable investments: mutual funds selected with an eye for high growth and low distributions, and stock selections

---

[71] The money market account will necessarily generate some taxable income, but that is the cost of having quick access to the money.

Sally's 401(k) offers six investment choices. They are, as follows: company stock, a growth stock fund, a short-term bond fund, a long-term bond fund, a money market fund, and a balanced fund. All of those would be taxable if they were outside of the 401(k), but in the 401(k) they are not taxable as current income. She buys equal parts of the company stock, the growth stock fund, and the long-term bond fund.

What should Jim and Sally do about picking individual stocks in this situation? They are both smart, self-reliant professional people. They think they can handle stock selections, and they want to give it a try. In view of their lack of prior stock-picking or other market experience, they agree to pick two stocks initially and reevaluate those choices and how they performed after six months before buying any more. They decide that because of their technical and business experience they can reasonably evaluate and buy one stock in the retail stores sector and one in the transportation industry. Those both fall in the high-risk category, and they also want to buy a technology-oriented mutual fund. For the high-tech mutual fund they will start with $5,000 and add $100 per month. The other $150 per month in the high-risk area will be held aside while they explore more ideas.

The $17,000 and $250 per month to be invested in the medium-risk area will be allocated equally among four mutual funds chosen for a balanced approach to safety, diversification, and growth potential. They have decided to use an asset allocation fund, a world growth stock fund, a small cap growth stock fund, and an S&P 500 index fund.

Is this a plan? Yes, it is. Is this the best plan in the world? Probably not. There may be a warning light that our imaginary couple should notice blinking over the amount of currently ready cash savings under this set-up. Does the plan, however, address their needs and their situation and show that they have evaluated their investing goals and their risk orientation? Yes, it does. Is this better than no plan at all? You know the answer.

Let's review the outcome for Sally and Jim since it was more complex than the others.

planned investment	income producing?*	taxable?	planned/current amount
Tax-sheltered 401(k) savings area			
company stock	no	no	$14,100
growth stock fund	no	no	$12,500
long bond fund	no	no	$10,400
ongoing contributions			$600/month
Higher risk/higher reward area			
retail sector stock	no	yes	$6,000
transportation stock	no	yes	$6,000
high-tech fund	no	yes	$5,000 + $100/month
set aside for high-return area			
Moderate risk and reward area			
asset allocation fund	no	yes	$4,000 + $50/month
world growth stock fund	no	yes	$4,000 + $50/month
small cap growth stock fund	no	yes	$4,000 + $50/month
S&P 500 Index stock fund	no	yes	$5,000 + $100/month
maintained in ready savings account			$15,000 + $500/month

* Yes or no mean significantly income producing or not; the investments within the 401(k) produce yield that stays in the 401(k), not current income.

There is not much in there that will be taxed until they start to withdraw money from the 401(k) in twenty years.

But as any architect, football coach, or teacher can tell you, having a good plan is not the same as having the job done. Sally and Jim, and Jack and Paul and Mary, now have their real work set out before them. They have to evaluate the stocks, bonds, or mutual funds they wish to use as investments. The focus of this chapter is on funds.

Evaluating Funds

In the earlier sections of this chapter, as well as in chapter 9, we have talked about choosing which funds are best for you as a small investor. We have talked about selecting the funds with the best or most interesting features. That is not easy. There are so many funds and ways to analyze them. Sometimes the differences are obvious and important, sometimes subtle or trivial. In this section we will look at some of the ways you might try to evaluate and discriminate among funds.

When you are evaluating any fund or funds that you might be interested in purchasing, try using the items below as a checklist of things to look at. It is, of course, by no means the only workable list of criteria, but it will definitely give you some framework to work in. We will start with a list of criteria and follow up with more explanation on each.

1. **Objective**: What does this fund do with the money?
2. **Management:** Who is running the show? Are they any good?
3. **Size**: How much money does this fund currently have under management?
4. **Risk**: How much volatility does the fund exhibit, and what are the causes of its volatility?
5. **Fees**: How much of your money are the managers planning to take?
6. **Reports:** Does the fund give clear reports on their results and fees?
7. **Past performance**: What are their profit or loss results over the past few years?
8. **Taxes:** Is the fund's practice going to generate current taxes for you?
9. **Income:** Is the fund going to generate current income for you?
10. **Current holdings:** What do they have in the portfolio now, and is that attractive to you?

The Small Investor Evaluates the Field

1. THE OBJECTIVE OR CLASS OF THE FUND

The first question is always, Why are you looking at this fund, or any fund? What do you want? What kinds of investment service do you need? Then consider whether the fund suits your needs for diversification, tax avoidance, risk and reward balance, whether it buys stocks, bonds, both, options, futures? Are the stocks large cap or small? Are they growth or value oriented? That last distinction is often not obvious because different managers may have different ideas about what makes a value stock. The main sources of help on this question should be the prospectus, the annual report that lists their current holdings, and the evaluations that you might see in the *WSJ, Fortune, Morningstar,* or whatever periodical you like to read for reference.

Bond funds come in a great many different flavors. Some are highly volatile, and some are highly predictable. Some produce high taxable current income, and some produce little current income.

On the question of objective, *Morningstar* has a very helpful feature.

For each fund that they evaluate they also identify two or three other funds that they think are most similar to the one in question. By using that feature you might start with one fund that suits you and then find another that is better in some regards. Or you might find one fund that you like that has a load, but another very similar fund that has no load.

2. THE MANAGEMENT AND THE STRATEGY

This is tough; obviously when you give them your money, you are only buying their management skill. But how can we evaluate the managers? If you watch the various financial news shows on television, you will hear about different managers and sometimes see an interview with one of them. That is helpful if you happen to catch the person who manages a fund you are interested in.

Another way to evaluate them is to look at the past performance. If a manager has been with one fund for ten years, certainly the past ten years performance of that fund says something about that manager. However, if the fund has a new manager, the past performance may not mean anything for purposes of current investment plans. Two helpful sources are the *Morningstar* reports and the *Value Line Mutual Funds Reports*. Both of those will attempt to evaluate the current management and investment strategies. That gives you at least two opinions, and they may be the best information available. If you read *Barron's* or the *WSJ* or *Investors' Business Daily,* or some other financial publications, they will frequently carry in-depth interviews with fund managers, or analyses of specific funds that may hit the area you want to see. Some of the publications or ratings also show how long the current management of a fund has been there. The fact is that evaluation of a fund manager can be very useful if you have any good information, but frequently that information is not easily available. Some people would advise you not to buy a fund if you don't have adequate information about the management. That will have to be your call, because information about a fund's manager is frequently sketchy at best.

3. FUND SIZE (IN CURRENT ASSETS)

It is not clear whether size means much. Some people think that if a fund is too small, it cannot properly diversify. On the other hand, if a fund is too large, it might become just a proxy for the market, or the managers might not be able to properly track all of their investments. The idea is that a management practice that was highly effective for $80 million and thirty stocks might be less effective when managing $800 million and two hundred stocks. If a fund was highly successful because of one person's brilliant analysis and insights, she might be stretched too thin when the fund grows to a much larger size. It is arguable how these factors play out in real life. Many investors over the past four years have started to shy away from the great Magellan Fund because of its size. Magellan has, however, been spectacularly successful over that time frame.

A Mutual Fund Can Grow Out of Hand

4. RISK

The risk level of a fund is always highly debatable. Funds and their managers are subject to all of the same risks that we have looked at throughout the book. Most of the publications that we have mentioned say something about the risk level of different funds, and they don't always agree. There is a reasonable argument that the funds will manage the risks better than we do individually. For example, consider a high-yield bond fund. That means a fund that probably is 75 percent invested in junk bonds and pays a pretty strong current annual yield. If you buy just one of those junk bonds, you will need a lot of experience and research to see and evaluate the risks. And can you judge the likelihood that the bond rating may be changed sometime soon? Probably not. But the fund manager and all of her elves have databases and experience and they do that for a living. They will almost certainly do a better job than we in selecting junk bonds to buy. Beyond that, you or I may buy one or two junk bonds. If one of them defaults, we have a large problem. The mutual fund may buy one hundred junk bonds; if one of them defaults, that is less of a problem. This is the classic example of diversifying among an asset class to spread the risk. Just because a fund buys a lot of securities where each individually has risky characteristics does not mean that the fund is too risky.

The sector funds may also inherit risk that comes with their territories. Suppose you buy just one electric utility company stock. If prevailing long-term bond interest rates rise very much, utility stock values will fall. You can mitigate that risk by diversifying your investments. But if the fund manager has an objective that says 80 percent invested in electric utilities, he cannot diversify away from that risk.

You might therefore choose to avoid that fund. You might not. Even when you foresee a risk of rising interest rates, there is the chance that you are wrong, and the utilities funds may give you a useful balance and diversification to guard against your own bad judgment.

A well-chosen mutual fund might also give you a reasonably easy entree into an area of the markets that you were hesitant to enter on your own. Small cap stocks generally bring along higher risks than blue chip companies. The small company's management may have trouble dealing with growth, or it might be easy for a competitor to come into their markets and compete effectively. At the very least, it is more difficult to get good up-to-date information on small caps. That might be the ideal area to use a mutual fund. A fund that specializes in small cap stocks will spread the risk through diversification and also have better sources of information than we have.

It would be nice if we could all agree on a neat measurement of risk. The problem of reporting a good, solid, agreed-upon number for risk seems to be too difficult. Many fund analysts or writers settle for using something called beta, that's the Greek letter, ß. Why a Greek letter? They want to put an air of mystery and scientific pretension around it. Beta is a number that may be calculated and assigned to a stock or a mutual fund as an indicator of volatility. The calculation depends on some statistical parameters that measure how much the security price moves up and down relative to how much the market is moving up or down. Don't worry about the calculation; that is the work of gnomes. Instead you may want to focus on two questions: how should I interpret beta, and is it truly indicative of anything?

For the question of interpretation, the key is that beta = 1 is an average. Beta greater than one indicates more volatility, and beta less than one indicates less volatility. If beta falls between 0.9 and 1.1, this is close to normal market volatility, but when it is greater than 1.3 or so, this starts to look like high volatility for a mutual fund. Below 0.7 looks like pretty low volatility for a mutual fund. As for the second question, "does it really mean anuthing?", that is the stuff of doctoral dissertations. For our purposes, it is enough to consider your peace of mind and comfort level with your mutual funds. The funds with higher values of beta are going to cause you more anguish and more elation as they run up and down. The funds with lower values for beta are going to be your steady riders; they should not go up and down quite as much as the overall market. The ones with beta nearly equal to one are going to bounce around about as much as the market bounces around.

Take special note, however, that beta equal to 1 does not necessarily mean safety, or even low volatility. It means that in the past this mutual fund (or stock) has been about as volatile as the rest of the market. If the entire stock market goes into a dive, the beta equal to 1 funds will probably dive right along.

This may or may not be of any value to the investor. After all, a basketball bounces up and down more than a cannon ball, but that does not mean that the basketball is more dangerous. A mosquito inside the house causes more anguish than a dragon outside. The essential factor for you to know is that there is a calculation that produces a number called beta, and many people use that as a substitute for actually figuring out what the real risks are.

For specific reference, the *Fortune* magazine mutual fund ratings omit a discussion of risk; the *Barron's Market Week* listings ignore risk; the *Barron's Mutual Funds Quarterly* has no indicators of risk; the Waterhouse Securities *Information and Comparison Guide* simply lists beta for each mutual fund, with a brief comment up front about what beta means; the *Charles Schwab Performance Guide* does the same; the *Wall Street Journal* does not show a risk or ß for each fund, but it does give a letter grade from A to E based on the total return relative to the fund's objectives peer group, which is related to the risk level. The more detailed reports and analyses on mutual funds that you can find from *Morningstar* or the *Value Line* show beta and also give some discussion of the funds risk factors, and rank the funds according to factors that include risk among others.

Consumers' Reports uses a different approach that is interesting. They indicate risk by measuring the fund's performance relative to the return on Treasury bills. That is reasonable because Treasury bills are arguably the lowest-risk investment one can make in financial markets. If a fund sometimes does worse than Treasury bills, that would be the very essence of risk. You don't have to agree with them, but the approach is worthy of consideration. It says: pick a standard, whatever standard you think is useful for your decision making, and measure the performance of the fund relative to that standard over a period of years.

So the lessons in this are that risk is measured differently by different folks. There is no single best or simple way to pin it down. The bottom line is that you cannot expect to find a clear and simple statement of the risk levels in different funds. You can find a lot of words and the ß number dancing around the subject of risk. There is also a very real and legitimate question as to whether beta has any validity in guiding investors to avoiding risk, but at any rate it comes closer than any other measurement to being accepted in the investment community.

5. FEES

They are in the prospectus, and they are thoroughly discussed and compared in most of the publications we use. If you can't understand the fees description in the prospectus, don't buy the fund. It is not always appropriate to buy the funds with the lowest fees (see Magellan, for example), but it is always a mistake to buy a fund if you don't know about the fees. Refer back to chapter 9 for more explanation of fees.

Even as I write this, the U.S. Congress is considering a bill that would allow the mutual funds industry greater freedom in how or when or if they disclose information to the investing public. No matter how that process works out, you should insist on complete and clear reporting. If the Congress passes some dumb law, that does not mean that they will accept the responsibility for your investing results, or personally help you stay out of trouble. Remember Rule #1: If you don't understand it, don't buy it!

6. EARNINGS REPORTS

Read the earnings reports. You should at least see what kinds of assets the fund currently owns, and what has changed in the past six months. I am very much influenced by the clarity and the presentation of the reports. I think they reflect on the intelligence and the priorities of the management. As I stated earlier, the *Hulbert Guide* uses the clarity and information of the reports as one factor in their overall evaluation of funds. One nuisance factor in funds' reports is the timing of the information. Some funds take up to a six-month delay between the end of a fiscal year and publication of their annual report. When you read a report, check to see if it is up-to-date information.

7. PAST PERFORMANCE

This is the easiest data to find. Many newspapers and magazines and most of the funds broadcast huge volumes of data about past performance. They always say that "past performance is not a guarantee of future results," but we know what the message is—they are actually trying to sell us past performance. But what is the value in past performance data? It clearly says something about the management who was there during the past performance. But is that the current management?

Past Performance Is Past Performance

You should look at past performance data carefully. Examine the values for one year, five years, or ten to see if this fund is consistently among the leaders of its peer group. It would be asking too much to require that a fund consistently stay first or second in its peer group, but you could reasonably say you want a fund that was first or second last year, and in the upper half for the past five and ten years. Appraise the fund among its peer group. If you can't identify the peer group, spend some time studying the newspapers and magazines; especially study the *Morningstar* reports in your library, which will show you peer group analysis. If your fund is a small-cap growth stock fund, it is in a relatively high-risk area and should give pretty good returns. If it doesn't, the risk may be higher than you want to accept for those rewards. Don't compare that stock against just a municipal bond fund that is in a far lower risk group and carries tax advantages, too.

And even though past performance is no guarantee of anything, there is some reason to expect that the fund that was strong last year should do well this year, though it is helpful if you can separate the degree of success due to good management from the success just due to being in a strong bull market. For example, there have been some years when just about any fund that specialized in computer technology should have done very well. If the entire sector was strong in 1995, that may not mean that the one fund you are looking at was especially good.

To illustrate that point, suppose the Fast Buggy Fund earned 24 percent total return in a year. Its peers are the auto industry funds. On average those funds earned 15 percent during that year and the auto industry stocks alone averaged 12 percent total return (price gain plus dividends). Then Fast Buggy looks pretty good. If the same manager was going to stay on this year, and if I wanted to have money invested in that sector, I might want to own Fast Buggy. On the other side, maybe the Slick Silicon Fund made 28 percent last year, but its peer group (high-tech and computer parts) averaged 49 percent return and its stock sector averaged 35 percent total return. That makes us think that the management of Slick Silicon was a drag on profits instead of boosting them. A relative analysis of total return indicates that we hold onto Fast Buggy, but we would be better off with a different high-tech fund instead of Slick Silicon. For both of them it is clear that a large part of their results is due to being in the right sector. If you don't have faith in their respective market sectors doing well again, maybe you don't want either fund this year.

8. TAX CONSIDERATIONS

Depending on your current income level and your overall investment strategy, it might be important to consider tax advantages with different types of funds. If you think this is important to you, or if you are unsure about tax considerations, talk to a tax advisor or financial planner. Some funds produce little or no current income for the shareholders. If they take in profits, they have to disperse them to shareholders, but the funds' management can often manage so that they have very little income or capital gains to report from year to year. If the fund holds stocks that are growth oriented, they will probably produce relatively little income from dividends. You can buy various funds that would give income exempt from federal, state, or local taxes, or sometimes all three. For example, if a fund only deals with municipal bonds from your home (tax-reporting) state, and if it does not generate any capital gains, that income would be exempt from both federal and state taxes.

Even if you do not receive any income from the fund, you may have taxes to pay. If the fund generates taxable income and you have it all turned around and reinvested in fund shares, there is still a tax claim on the income that was available to you.

If you are buying funds through your 401(k) or IRA or other tax-sheltered retirement plan, it does not make sense to buy tax-sheltered investments. Those funds produce lower relative returns just because they are tax-sheltered; other investors pay more to receive tax sheltered income. But within your tax-exempt IRA or 401(k), the tax advantage of a fund gives no added value to you. If you want to use income-producing funds within your IRA or 401(k), go for the higher yield, not a duplicative tax shelter.

For example, suppose two funds called AAAAX and BBBBX both have current net asset value per share of $10.00. Let's say that Tom could buy 1,000 shares of each for his IRA or for a separate income-producing taxable account. Tom has the top 39 percent marginal tax rate. The AAAAX fund gives 7.5 percent taxable total return, and the BBBBX pays 5.2 percent tax-free total return. We can look at the net profit from each fund either in the IRA or not in the IRA:

Investment	Return	Tax	Net return
AAAAX in the IRA	$750	0	$750
BBBBX in the IRA	$520	0	$520
AAAAX in the taxable account	$750	$292.50	$457.50
BBBBX in the taxable account	$520	0	$520

So in the IRA, AAAAX is better, but out of the IRA, BBBBX is better.[72]

9. INCOME NEEDS

Some people need to get current income from their investments and some do not. You decide for yourself which is more important to you.

---

[72] There is a tacit assumption here about Tom's future tax rates, but this is not the time to get into all of that. This analysis has to be altered if Tom thinks that after his retirement, his tax rate will be higher than it is now.

If you do get current income, it may be taxable, but you have some control over that. Some funds are designed to produce current income, others no current income, or others a mix of current income and other capital growth.

If you want tax-exempt current income, you probably want to use municipal bond funds. If you use U.S. Treasury bond funds, they will be only partially tax-exempt. Junk-bond funds may be ideal for generating high current income, but the chances for capital appreciation would be unpredictable.

Each fund is going to give a balance of profits from capital gains, and profits from yield paid out by the fund. You have to pick and choose to make that balance suit your needs. Here are some generalizations of how the balance might go for various types of funds (+ means more strength in this area, and – means less; a blank means no generalization can be easily made):

Type of fund	Capital gain	Yield
small cap fund	+	–
large cap fund	+	
municipal bonds fund		+
junk bonds fund	+/–	+
growth and income fund	+	+
income fund	–	+
international fund	+	

There are large variations within classes. If you want to own a fund to help produce income, don't just look at the classification, but also look at the record of dividends paid over the past year or two. For example, utilities funds can be managed with an emphasis on producing current yield or emphasis on producing asset value growth.

Even if you are primarily interested in current income, look at the other measurements of the fund's performance. It is possible for a manager to generate higher current yield by, in effect, robbing the fund's assets. In that case the current yield might be followed up by a nasty surprise in the value of the investment if you need to sell it one day, or the yield might be unsustainable.

10. CURRENT HOLDINGS

In *Morningstar,* the *Value Line Mutual Funds Survey*, or the funds' own self-generated reports, you can find a list of their largest holdings. That list, wherever you get it from, will probably be current as of several months before you read it. Most funds will give you the current ten or twelve largest investments if you call their toll-free 800 customer-service numbers. Look those over to get a feel for what the fund really does with your money.

Stars

If you are going to do anything with mutual funds, you will have to hear about stars. One star to five stars, the stuff that builds advertising campaigns.

The *Morningstar Mutual Funds Reports* include a rating of one star (worst) to five stars (best) for each fund. The stars ratings are assigned relative to one-year, three-year, and five-year risk-adjusted returns. If you read their publication, you can find a good explanation of how they do it. For our purposes, it is sufficient to note that when you see stars, it is not a good time to turn out the lights and snooze. The stars are very widely advertised and there is some danger that investors might think of them as a final and complete grade of the fund's value. Even the *Morningstar* editors take some pains to warn their readers that it is not that easy. By all means look at the stars ratings, but do not quit there. Stars should tell you something, but they will not do your thinking for you.

Evaluation Form

The first few times that you try to evaluate a mutual fund, it might be helpful to use a copy of the form provided on the following page. It might help to ensure that you don't just forget some important points. You have my permission to make as many copies as you like of the next page, which has the form for evaluating funds. Indeed, you have my blessing to modify the form if you have some good ideas—and please, send me those modifications for the next edition.

MUTUAL FUND EVALUATION FORM

Name of the Fund: _____

Name of the Investment Company: _____

Their toll-free customer number: 1-800- _____

Objective: _____

- Is this consistent with their current top ten holdings ? ❑ yes ❑ no
- Does this fit my diversification needs? ❑ yes ❑ no

Manager's Name: _____

- How long has he or she been there? _____
- Does the performance over that time frame look good? ❑ yes ❑ no

Size: • dollar value of total assets = _____

Risk: • What do I see as the risks in their investment style _____
- does it fit my needs? ❑ yes ❑ no
- What is their beta? ß = _____

Fees: • Front load = _____ • redemption fee = _____
- 12-b1 fee = _____ • ongoing expense level = _____
- Did I understand the fees presented in the prospectus? ❑ yes ❑ no

Reports: • I have read the prospectus ❑ yes ❑ no
- and the latest annual report ❑ yes ❑ no
- I understood them ❑ yes ❑ no .

Past performance:

- Total return for past year = _____
- for past five years = _____
- Is that okay relative to the market in general? ❑ yes ❑ no
- Or relative to their peer group? ❑ yes ❑ no

Taxes: Will this fund generate taxable income? ❑ yes ❑ no

Income: Will this fund generate any current income? ❑ yes ❑ no

Current holdings: I have looked at them ❑ yes ❑ no

Recommended Further Reading

The Hirsch book, now out of print, has some debatable conclusions which may not be useful to all investors, but the ideas are instructive.

Hirsch, Michael. *Multifund Investing*. Dow-Jones & Co., 1987 (out of print).

Laderman, Jeffrey. *Business Week's Guide to Mutual Funds*. New York: McGraw-Hill, updated annually.

Barron's Mutual Funds Quarterly

Forbes Annual Survey of Mutual Funds

U.S. News & World Report Annual Investor's Guide

Morningstar Mutual Funds Report

Morningstar Closed-End Funds Report

Value Line Mutual Funds Report

CHAPTER 11

Investing or Gambling— What's the Difference?

Small Investors need to know:

• Is this investing or gambling?

• What's the difference?

• Who are the investors, traders, and gamblers?

• What about a fast buck in options or futures?

• What is liquidity all about?

• What does it do for us?

• Why doesn't everyone invest the same way?

Experienced people who take a long view of the markets offer similar advice; nobody said it better than Charles Dow: The people who try to get rich quick usually lose badly, and the people who try to earn a consistent reasonable return on their money sometimes end up by getting rich.

Investing, Trading, or Gambling?

Those who are following Dow's advice, trying to make a reasonable steady return on their money over a longer time frame, are investors. Others, who commonly buy into financial positions expecting to turn the deal around within weeks or months, are called traders. And those who not only have the short time frame, but also expect to make big profits within the short time, are gamblers.

The Small Investor Is Not Too Sure about This

Investors buy stocks expecting that over the long run prices will go up, and if the company is well managed, their profits will mount. They hope to buy stock with gradually rising prices and dividends that will pay back more each year, or they may buy a five-year U.S. savings bond, paying 5.5 percent yield, content with the prospect of actually holding the bond for the full five years.

When I was cautiously and nervously getting started at actively managing our money, one of the first decisions I made was that we would start with some safe and sound investments that I would plan to hold for a long time. My personal investment strategy led me to using stocks and mutual funds. Early on I discovered that many of the mutual funds would give you their earnings reports with a list of the current portfolio; also, some of the investment advisors who write or do public speaking will tell you about their current investments. So I was able to get a pretty strong consensus opinion for buying electric utilities, as well as samples of the current holdings of a few successful big-money managers. I started out with Potomac Electric, Allegheny Power Systems, Carolina Power and Light, and Bellsouth. They all fit into several pieces of my investment strategy, which include invest-

ment prejudice in favor of (1) good dividends, (2) companies that operate in the Southeast U.S., (3) large capitalization companies, and (4)
companies with strong histories. In the first year, each of those companies gave us over 10 percent total return with very low apparent risk.
Just as with every other investment, the reward and the risk are partly
due to their business operations and management, and partly due to
market psychology. The favorable factors were a generally rising stock
market; dramatically falling interest rates over most of 1991–93; and
lastly, something of a flight-to-safety mentality in the stock markets at
various times during those years. All of those factors helped my utility
stocks for two years. Two of them have changed. But at any rate, those
four stocks represented a long-term investor's hopes and good luck. (I
have since sold all four and repurchased Potomac Electric.)

The investor is like the driver who knows where she is going, plans
accordingly, and works the plan. She does not expect to make the trip
faster than everyone else. The trader, on the other hand, is more like a
taxi driver, who is never locked into a long-term trip but expects to
turn a profit on a bunch of short trips.

Traders look for quick results and will often buy stocks to keep for
only a few months, perhaps as long as a year. They have to do their
research and analysis, but are hoping to find something that others
have missed. If a trader thinks that she can buy a stock today at $25
and expect to sell it within six months at $40 or more, she must see
something that the rest of the analysts don't see. If everyone saw the
same prospects, the price would have been bid up closer to $40
already. She may see some evidence that the company will be bought
out at a premium over market price. It may be that the trader thinks
that she, or her sources, know more about new product development
within the company. The trader's nightmare is that there may be a
good reason why no one else is buying the stock that he has just
jumped into. The strategy of the trader is apparently workable for
some, but it obviously carries greater risk and requires specialized
knowledge and experience that most of us don't share. I generally
recommend long-term investing, but I have tried a bit of trading as
part of my diversification scheme. I not only mix investments, I mix
methods. Two of the trading ideas that appear reasonable to me are
momentum-driven and adviser-driven.

The momentum idea is based on the old Wall Street truism that a trend will continue until it changes. Stock technical analysts like to look at "volume momentum," the belief that increased volume lends momentum, and hence credibility, to trends in prices.[73] That idea got me into Westinghouse at 16¾. and out two months later at 19⅜. That looks good in percentage terms; the actual dollar amount was small because I considered it as a bit of a gamble. But, a short-time holding is not always bad. Every investor will have reason to rethink a position occasionally, but it shouldn't be a way of life.

In the summer and fall of 1991 I had been watching Westinghouse go through an unhappy slide in both stock price and profits. The stock finally got down to around $15 a share with 1991 earnings looking like $1.60 and the dividend paying $1.40 per year. It looked very interesting for a genuine blue chip. A cut in the dividend was widely forecast, but one day in late December the price started bouncing around and moving upward; was this the beginning of a trend? I thought the worst was over and the downside risk was minimal—the price then was about 1 ½ times book value, and they had been pounded by bad news for a year. The stock had sold in the high thirties just a year and a half earlier. Revenues per share were still 90 percent of their all-time high, and they were making money. That was not too bad in December of 1991. I bought WX at 16 ¾ on December 27.

Over the next few weeks, the stock went up to near $21, and I was feeling pretty clever. However in the meantime, as is the case with all of my investments, I was tracking news reports about Westinghouse the company. The news was all bad. Early in March the price had dropped below $20, and I was spending too much energy worrying about it, so I sold at 19⅜ on March 11. A decent profit, after commissions, of 9 percent in ten weeks. Does that make me a trader? Or a gambler? I think that makes me a conservative small investor with a three- to five-year horizon who watches the store and dumps something if it becomes uncomfortable.

---

[73] If IBM has a normal daily volume of 1.5 million shares, and over a week or so goes up three points on daily volume around 1 million, that is not a very strong move; however, if it goes up three points on a daily volume of about 3 million shares over a week, then that is a significant move.

Treat your investing like a military or business project. You have to have a well-thought-out objective. Be willing to take the necessary risks to achieve the objective. However, if the situation changes, or you get important new information, you should be ready to change your plans. That's a reasonable course of action for small investors. Plan in relation to your horizon. Plan to profit from dividends and long-term company growth. At the same time, keep an eye on your investments and be prepared to sell if you are no longer comfortable with a particular investment.

The Small Investor Keeps an Eye Out

The advisor-driven part of my "trading" action is based on another part of my diversification scheme. I diversify where I look for advice and how to make decisions. I can do some good analysis and have confidence in my own judgment, but I always feel that there are other respectable opinions. There are two sources that I have confidence in. This is not just based on results, but rather that what they say and publish appears to have solid reasoning and research behind it. My two candidates for prime advisors are the *Value Line* and Martin Zweig. They both offer fundamental facts and figures,[74] but their buy/sell recommendations are primarily short-term oriented. They are also not shy about changing a recommendation on short notice. Their opinions were factors in my decisions to buy four stocks. Those were National Presto, FAB Industries, Bassett Furniture, and Schering-Plough.

Good news, bad news. OK? All good companies, no doubt about that. The question is whether their stock was good for this small trader. So here's how that worked.

Presto was on a tear when I got it. Up from 40 to 60 in the past year. Balance sheet, sales, earnings, everything looked real strong, so I bought in at an all-time high of 60. What a thrill! It zoomed up to 65, 70, 75, 80, 82, 83, then dropped to 82, 80. At the time I was carefully practicing my personal rule of never giving back all of a good gain. Even though I thought (still do), that the company was great, I set a stop loss at 72 to protect my gains. What a stroke of genius! Presto slumped 80, 76, 72, 66, 60, 55. So I was out at 72, with a real good gain over about five months. This is a trader's dream, everything coming up roses. It's like golf, you see; if you ever do anything right, you may be hooked.

Schering-Plough. Right! Good old Plough! Unquestionably a great and strong company, but is it a good investment for me? (You?) Same picture as Presto going in. Almost the same analysis. I bought in at 65, at an all-time high, in fact even the same day that I bought National Presto. I made two mistakes: (1) I did not set a protective stop sell limit; and (2) I watched it nose dive for six months, because I was in love with it. Can you see it? 65, 63, 60, 58, 55, 52, 49, and I'm still holding it! Well we got lucky, climbed back 50, 51, 52, and I bought more. I bought enough more to bring my average cost to $60 per share. Lots of fun: 52, 55, 58, 60, and I'm even! But this time I set a stop sell limit order at 55 to protect something. Bang, three days later it hits the limit and I'm out at 55. Net loss, with brokerage fees, about 10 percent in ten months. Now I still believe that Plough is a good solid building block for many long-term small investors, but I handled it like a trader, so you can see how that works.

---

[74] The *Value Line* is perhaps the best source of basic hard data. Although Zweig uses the company data, his analysis is strongly influenced by market timing and technical considerations.

FAB and Bassett? I bought both of them after strong runs, FAB at an all-time high. Bought FAB in April of '92 at 30⅝; sold in December of '93 at 34½; collected a little dividends. Bought Bassett in July of '92 at 40¾, and sold it in February of '94 at $31½. But there was a split, so I had 25 percent more shares than I bought. That looks like a small gain in share values, and they produced some small dividend payments.

Anyone who expects to try being a trader had better have the sell discipline very carefully worked out. Look where I would have been if I had sold Plough at 60 on the way down and bought it again at the same point where I did buy, 52.

what actually happened	what might have been
bought 60 shares at 65	bought 60 at 65
bought 40 shares at 52	sold 60 at 60
sold 100 shares at 55	bought 100 at 52
	sold 100 at 55
brokerage fees total $165	brokerage fees $220
net loss $645	net loss $220

...plus, in the second scenario, I would have felt safer to hold it for another year, which would have been a better move.

If you can't resist the urge to try a little trading, please consider the flip side of your hopes: if you think the market is missing some positive factor that you see, it is possible that the others are seeing some risk that you have missed. In other words, you may outsmart the crowd on occasion, but you will not outsmart them consistently. Can somebody make a profit that way? Yes.

Apparently there are a few guys and girls out there who can manage that kind of action. The basic theory is that they may have to take a lot of little losses in trying different stocks, but they win by hitting a few big gains. You can try that: Every time you buy a speculative stock, set a stop loss limit order 10 percent below the purchase price. Then counting brokerage fees, you would never lose more than maybe 13 percent or 14 percent on any stock. Look at two ways that might work out.

First, if you just had $10,000 to speculate with, you might buy one stock and take a 12 percent loss, buy another and take a 13 percent loss, buy another, you hit your winner and take a 50 percent gain. If that entire cycle took one year, the net for the year would be a gain of $1,484. That's 15 percent on a year. That's good work. But did you have the stomach to stick it out? After the first trade you were down $1200; after the second you were down almost $2300. Did you have the nerve to put your remaining money into another speculative stock? And do you want the headaches of working that kind of business when you could have bought a nice safe utility or mutual fund and had a fair chance at a 10 percent return?

There's another way to look at the trader's action. Instead of buying just one stock at a time, you might have $30,000 to use equally in three stocks: three $10,000 purchases. Say they give the same kind of (percentage) results as above, so the gains/losses are -$1200, -$1300, and +$5,000. This is a net gain of $2,500, or up 8 percent on your $30,000. Is it worth the headache and risk? That depends on how you react to the thrill of the action.

What all the pros and gurus say is to cut your losses, and let your winners run. They are telling us to get out if a stock has been behaving badly, but stick with it if it is behaving well. Ha! Easy for them to say; tough to do in practice. If you did your homework and had good reasons to buy a stock at $21, it's difficult to reverse your judgment and sell it when it drops to 18. On the other hand, if it went up to 30 during the next three months, you feel that you earned your profits, and you may want to grab them. That is the really tough call: when you are looking at 40 percent profit, do you cut and run, or let it have some more time to work? Remember Rule #7.

I've heard advice both ways. Some respected managers have advised people to take a fast 20 percent gain anytime they have a chance, because tomorrow is another day. But if you want stocks that double in six months, you'll never have them if you always bail out after 20 percent. This is a place for planning and discipline.

When you buy the stock, and periodically thereafter, look at the company, the stock price, and the market, and make the tough decisions: Do you hope to get 25 percent out of this stock, or hope to get a price of $37? Will you sell at $32, or keep a stop loss limit price set 15 percent below the stock?

In 1992 I bought IBM at $85 ¼ and watched the price go up to $100 pretty fast. I wanted to hold it, but I didn't want to give up all the gain, so I set a stop loss order at $92. Pretty quick, it fell right through 92, on the way down to 40. I got out with an 8 percent gain in a few months. If I hadn't set the limit price, I might have held it all the way down.

That was a tough decision. I know IBM and I know their business. I was confident that the stock was a good long-term holding (but at what price?). See Rules #5 and 7. If you don't want to practice the selling and protective discipline, you better not even consider trading for short-term gains. My experience has been that my protective sell-limit prices have saved me a good bit of money, even though every time I worry about selling too soon and I feel badly about abandoning a position. I have made my mistakes in buying and I have made my mistakes in holding, but usually, when I have sold a stock, it turned out to be the right move. Who knows how long that will last? But I think I am learning something.

The Small Investor Bails Out of IBM

Some people make money in the fast action, trading mode, but this requires a different set of skills and a different kind of work. A trader may typically buy stocks based on technical analysis of turning points in the market or in the price of a particular stock. A trader may also sell stocks or switch mutual funds based on a sense of market momentum swinging from one sector to another. The basic hope of the trader is that good profits can be made on short-term trends. That's true, *if you can measure and forecast the short-term trends.* That's where we probably drop out. It requires ready access to changing information, and steady, experienced evaluation of the information. It's too much work and too much analysis for the average small investor. It's better left to professionals. You may read and hear widely differing opinions among professionals about whether anyone can do this for consistent profits, but it's certainly no business for amateurs.

One last, forlorn group is the gamblers. The gamblers may rely on luck, hot tips, or advice from someone who has no investment at risk, or analysis from someone who has no credentials for doing the analysis. The gamblers may be people who think they can beat the crowd all of the time, or think they can find huge gains that almost everyone else is overlooking. The gamblers I have known seldom look twice at an investment unless they are thinking about a 50 percent run-up within a few months; so they tend to ignore the steady eroding effects of repeated 2 or 3 percent costs for brokerage fees.

I have two friends who are to some extent gamblers. One is a married man about my age who uses a large brokerage firm. I also know his broker, who is an honest, capable man, but the two of them made some mistakes. When my pal (let's call him Frank) got started playing the stock market, the broker was hot into biotechnology stocks, just like a lot of people. Frank had reasoned that he deserved to, and could, make 30–40 percent a year on his investments. They overloaded on drug companies and biotechnology towards the end of 1991. Each time that I talked to Frank about it, he was convinced that something or other was going to come back to where he bought it and he could get out even. Frank is holding a bunch of losers. Incidentally, Frank has another account where he doesn't use a broker's advice. He does better and works much more cautiously in that one. In that way, he is smart. He keeps the gambling account separated from the other investments where he has particular long-term needs in mind.

The other friend, Jack, is more analytical. A twenty-seven-year-old bachelor with a very good job and a solid career, he wants to have some fun and excitement in the markets. He looks to double his money in a few months, or he won't touch a stock. He studies his plunges, but he plunges! Penny stocks, very small capitalization companies, biotechnology firms that are five years away from ever having a product: That is his terrain. Who should criticize? Jack knows what he is doing. He is using venture capital that he can afford to lose. If he loses every penny of it, he will still have a good job and great career prospects. When he is 40, he'll probably change because he's a smart guy, but right now he is a very aggressive gambler.

Liquidity

How much cash can you raise in seventy-two hours if you need it? If you have a home worth $150,000 with $65,000 left on the mortgage, and bank accounts holding $18,000, and cars worth $30,000, and jewelry that cost $5,000, and furniture that cost $9,000, plus some stocks and bonds with a current market value of $62,000, *then* how much cash can you raise in seventy-two hours? To make it easy, say this is Monday morning. I'll guess that in seventy-two hours you might raise $30,000 on the house (depending on your relationship with your local bank), $18,000 from the bank accounts, $20,000 from the cars, $500 from the jewelry, and $500 on the furniture, plus maybe $55,000 on the investments (depending on your broker). That is assuming that you can swallow those heavy losses on assets.

One of the primary components of safety in anything you own is liquidity. Liquidity means the ability to convert assets into cash quickly and easily, or the ability to be able to use an asset to settle your debts quickly. Different kinds of assets carry different measures of liquidity. Cash is perfectly liquid, because Uncle Sam says, "Legal tender for all debts." Someday in the future, if U.S. currency fails to be an acceptable medium of exchange, we'll have to find another measure of liquidity; but if that ever happens, we'll all have worse problems than paying our bills.

Other assets have different measures of liquidity. For example, the gold in your dental crowns may be valuable, but it's not a very liquid asset.

Let's look at a few:

Asset type	Liquidity
Cash	Perfectly liquid
Savings account	Almost perfectly liquid, except on holidays and provided you don't want to withdraw $200,000 on very short notice
U.S. savings bonds	Almost perfect, except on holidays
Stocks on NYSE	Usually highly liquid; may fail in times of market panics; may have to wait five to seven days for cash
Mutual fund shares	Usually highly liquid; same warning as stocks
Your home	Not very liquid; varies with the local real estate market
Jewelry	Liquidity depends on how much you're willing to cut the price

One of the most critical features of any investment or financial market is the liquidity it presents. Liquidity actually helps all investors feel confident of what they have from day to day.

How does that work? Suppose you own 80 shares of General Motors and, for whatever reason, decide to sell them. In an active, liquid market, such as the New York Stock Exchange, it's easy. Maybe this morning you checked in the paper and found that GM closed at 54½ the night before. You can be fairly certain of a gross sale amount very close to 80 X $54 ½ = $4,360. So maybe at about 10:00 A.M. you call your broker and ask for a current price. She tells you, "54 ⅞ bid, 55 asked." You say, "Sell 80 at the market," and probably within 30 seconds she will tell you they can confirm the sale of 80 GM at a price of 54 ⅞ for a total value of $4,390. The brokerage fee is $110, and they will transfer $4,280 into your cash account (in five days). Nice day's work, since you bought it at $30 in the fall of 1991.

But what if the market wasn't liquid? Suppose you put in your call to the broker at 10:00 A.M. and ask for a price on GM. How would you feel if she said, "We don't have a price, there have been no sales since yesterday"? If you go ahead and tell her to sell the 80 shares at whatever price she can get, she might say, "O.K., I'll get back to you later." Then about the middle of the afternoon she calls back and tells you, "We can confirm the sale of your 80 shares of GM. We sold 60 shares at 54, and the last 20 at 52. That's a gross sale of $4,280, with a brokerage fee of $350." You get $3,930. The brokerage fee had to go up, because their job became much more difficult, and their volume went way down.

So in a less liquid market, you would (or at least, could) lose in several ways: possibly lower prices when you need to sell, uncertainty about how or when the deal might go through, and much higher fees for the salesperson.

Options and Futures: If You Had to Ask

The futures and options guys actually help us all out by putting up big money that is bet on movements in prices of many stocks or commodities or indices. They are also ready to step in and close positions after relatively small price moves. The effect is that markets, stocks, and commodities become more liquid than they might be otherwise.[75] They also provide a kind of insurance policy for people who already own the stocks or commodities. That insurance goes under the term *hedging.*[76]

Hedging is a legitimate and important financial practice...*for the professionals* who have large positions at risk. Remember one of the advantages you have over the manager of the Magellan Fund: you can dump all of your stocks, or invest all of your cash in a controlled predictable way within a few minutes. He cannot. He has a legitimate need for hedging. He has the experience and research tools to use it profitably. We do not.

---

[75] There is a problem side to this, too. In times of extreme market stress or fast changes, the futures and options markets can destabilize the market pricing mechanisms. Some of the markets put in artificial curbs on trading at those times to stop large-scale arbitrage.

[76] If you want to know about hedging, ask your broker, or find a book on options trading; the subject has no place in this book.

In November 1984 a young man named Chris Christensen went to work for the brokerage firm Prudential Bache. That was his first experience in the securities industry. Within two years he had earned a half-million dollars in commissions and won the Pru-Bache Rookie of the Year Award. Chris was either very good at working the stock market, or managed to convince someone that he was. That half-million in commissions may represent something close to fifty million dollars in customer orders. During the same two years he lost all of it in the options markets. Over the next four years he went from Prudential Bache to E.F. Hutton to Dean Witter, and back to Bache, picking up substantial bonuses and new commissions each time he moved. By the middle of 1990 he had collected well over a million dollars in commissions and signing bonuses…and lost all of it in the options markets.[77]

It's not just the derelict and naive who get burned. Chris Christensen had been trained by one of the premier brokerage firms in the country. He was considered a prize recruit by two other large firms. He had access to Wall Street's best market analysis. He had the edge of seeing what was happening to his own customers. If it can happen to people like him, and it does, every day, it can happen to any of us.

The options markets are zero-sum markets, almost. That means for every dime won, a dime is lost. It is gambling no matter how you describe it. If a small investor was as good as average among options and futures traders, the long-run result would be to break even in those markets, with steady small losses in brokerage fees. But the small investor is not as good as average among those people. Among speculators who made one to twenty trades in commodities futures in the first half of 1992, fewer than one-third came out ahead.[78] The success rate went up consistently among those with more trading activity, but never exceeded 50 percent. Futures trading is dominated by professionals who have time and experience and research on their side. They get hourly updates on their information and are ready to open or close a position on a moment's notice. The small investor, meanwhile, is at his regular job or on vacation, and may lose a lot of money before he even knows what's going on.

---

[77] *Barron's*, July 6, 1992.

[78] *Barron's*, September 7, 1992; research reported by Elliot Bercovitz, Lind-Waldock.

There is also a reasonable suspicion that the game is occasionally rigged by inside information or big-money players manipulating prices. The same kind of stuff that went on in New York in 1928, 1929, and 1930. Stories about that kind of thing still show up in the press once in a while. Both the U.S. Attorney's office and the Commodity Futures Trading Commission have brought charges and had guilty admissions from traders, including even a former vice chairman of one of the commodities markets.[79]

There are good reasons why the stock or bond markets are fairer and easier than options or futures. One of the best is that if you buy the stock or bond of a NYSE company, it's possible for everybody to win. The person you bought from may have made a profit, and there are thousands of employees and managers of the firm working as hard as they can to make the firm successful. Part of their productivity will come to you in the form of either cash dividends or increased value of the firm. There is a reasonable chance that you will gain while you hold the stock, sell it at a profit, and the next person may again gain in the same way. This is profiting from the fruits of labor and capitalism. That's a respectable way for anyone to use their money.

Among all the folks in the country who would like to be rich, there must be millions who have considered the lure of trying to make big money in a quick profit on Wall Street. Out of those millions, there appear to be a few dozen or maybe even a few hundred who can make a consistent good living at it. Go figure—what are your odds of success at that game?

Recommended Further Reading

The markets are not discriminatory, except on one count—you do have to bring money. But anybody with money is welcome into the fray. It should not be surprising then that the participants come in many shapes, sizes, and psyches. By all means read *The Mind of the Market*. It will help you recognize some of the other types and know how to deal with them. More than that: In this business, as in all others, it pays to know yourself. Smith's book will make you think about how your personal approach to investing will be different from other people's. Rothchild's book is the only other title that I have felt compelled to mention more than once in the end-of-chapter references. It is probably as close to real trouble as you can get by reading about it.

Rothchild, John. *A Fool and His Money: The Odyssey of an Average Investor.* New York: Viking Penguin, 1989.

Smith, Charles W. *The Mind of the Market: A Study of Stock Market Philosophies, Their Uses, and Their Implications.* Lanham, MD: Rowman & Littlefield, 1981.

Train, John. *The Midas Touch: The Strategies That Have Made Warren Buffett America's Pre-Eminent Investor.* New York: HarperCollins, 1988.

——— *The New Money Masters.* New York: Harper Business, 1994.

GLOSSARY

THE TERMS ARE DEFINED here in the sense that they are used in this book. This means that astute readers will note some occasional differences from more common usage.

12b-1 expense: A mutual fund's expense charge that is intended to compensate the investment company for their sales expenses.

401(k): Name given to a type of investment or savings account wherein workers may save part of their pay and invest it without current taxes on the pay or investment returns.

adviser: A person who helps with financial planning, usually a broker, investment adviser, financial planner, or insurance adviser; usually a professional in that field.

allocation: The process or results of dividing investment assets among different available choices such as stocks, bonds, mutual funds, or bank deposits.

American Stock Exchange: The second largest stock exchange in the United States.

AMEX: *American Stock Exchange.*

analysis: The process of gathering information, studying it through various tools and points of view, and drawing appropriate conclusions.

analyst: A financial professional who is employed to evaluate the potential risk, gains, or losses from financial investments.

annual rate: If an investment returned a certain percent loss or gain (p%) in a certain number (N) of days, the annual rate of return $= {}^{365}/_{\text{N}} \times \text{p}\%$.

arbitration: The process of allowing a neutral party to settle a dispute, usually instead of using the courts.

asset: Something of financial value.

average: In mathematics, the sum of a set of numbers divided by the number of values included. In the financial markets, it usually refers to a weighted average of stock or bond prices used as an indicator of overall market performance as in, for example, the Dow-Jones Industrial Average.

back load: A mutual fund expense charge that is imposed at the time of redemption of shares as a percentage of the value redeemed.

Barron's: A weekly newspaper published by the Dow-Jones publishing company that specializes in financial news and advice.

bear market: Any financial market during a period that prices are generally falling.

bears: Investors or analysts who predict falling prices for one or more types of assets, and/or sell some of their investments.

beta (ß): A number that is used to reflect the level of volatility of an investment; it is almost always determined and used relative to the volatility of some appropriate market index. $ß = 1$ for investments that fluctuate up or down as much as the relevant market index values; $ß > 1$ means the investment is more volatile; and $ß < 1$ means it is less volatile. Some investors or analysts use ß as a measurement of the historic risk level in the investment.

bills: Treasury bonds that are issued with a term no longer than one year.

blue chip: A stock that is issued by a large and secure company, or a group of investments that concentrate in such stocks.

bond: An investment in the form of a loan, or the security (promise to repay) that represents the investment.

book value: (1) The value of a business asset as it is carried on the company's financial records; (2) one view of the value of a company seen as the total assets minus the liabilities of the firm; frequently divided by the number of shares of stock and referenced as the book value per share.

bourse: A stock exchange

broker: A person who acts as a paid agent between buyers and sellers for securities sales, and is registered to conduct such business.

brokerage: The business or practice of buying and selling financial instruments for the public, for a fee. Mainly used for the firms that do so.

bull market: Any financial market during a period that prices are generally rising.

bulls: Investors or analysts who predict rising prices for one or more types of assets, and/or buy investments.

buy and hold: The investment practice of buying stocks, bonds, or funds with the intention of holding them for a long time.

call provision: A provision in a bond that allows the bond issuer to pay off the bond before its maturity date.

capitalization: The total value of money committed to something. See also *market capitalization*.

CD: *Certificate of deposit.*

certificate of deposit: An investment with a bank that promises to pay a fixed rate of return over a fixed time period; a bond purchased from a bank.

churning: The practice wherein a broker produces a large number of trades for a customer's account with the intention of collecting excessive commissions.

closed-end fund: A mutual fund that does not promise to issue or redeem new shares at any time. The investment company sells a number of shares to begin business and then those shares are traded like stock. The price of a closed-end fund's share is determined by whatever willing buyers and sellers agree to in the markets.

CNBC: A cable news channel primarily dedicated to financial news.

commission: The sales fee paid to a person, usually a broker, who manages a trade for a customer.

common stock: The shares of ownership of a publicly traded company.

compound gains: The results of growth and profit over several periods of returns when each period's profit is reinvested to gain additional profits in the next period. Also called compound growth.

compound growth: See *compound gains.*

compound rate of return: The annualized rate of return on an investment that would have given a certain profit if it had been in effect over the same time period. For example, if an investment returned nothing in its first year and 2 percent in its second year, then the compound rate of return would be close to 1 percent.

contrarian: An investor who invests differently than most other investors.

conversion: Exchanging a bond or preferred stock for common stock according to the conversion rules written into the bond or preferred stock when it was issued.

convertible: A provision in a bond or preferred stock that allows it to be converted to another security form, usually common stock, after some specified date or circumstances.

corporate bond: A bond issued by a private business.

correction: A short-term change in the trend of a market. So, a correction in a bull market would be a short-term decline.

coupon yield: The original interest payment rate written into a bond when it is created.

crash: A sudden large fall in values in a financial market.

Curb: A historical term for the *American Stock Exchange,* still commonly used in casual reference.

current yield: The percentage annual rate of return from an investment calculated by using the current actual returns as the basis for computing a full year's return. The current yield of a bond is the annual interest divided by its current price.

debenture: A loan that is not secured by any assets of the borrower, meaning that repayment depends on the ability and the integrity of the borrower.

decisiveness: The ability to make decisions and carry through to completion whatever actions may be indicated by the decision.

default: Failure to pay the interest or principal due on a bond.

discount broker: A broker, or brokerage firm, that usually charges relatively lower commission fees and provides less customer service to the investor.

diversification: The process, or the results, of allocating investment capital among different investments that might be expected to behave differently in various economic situations.

dividend: Money paid to the owners of common stock out of the profits of a publicly traded company

DJIA: The Dow-Jones Industrial Average. See *average.*

dollar cost averaging: A practice, or discipline, of investing a regular, fixed, predetermined amount in some security or mutual fund on a periodic basis.

duration: A number that can be calculated for a bond, which indicates how volatile the bond would be in reacting to market interest rate changes; lower duration means less volatility and presumably greater safety for the bond.

earnings: The profits earned by a company after taxes, interest on debt, depreciation, and dividends to preferred share holders. The amount that represents profits to the common stock shareholders.

earnings per share: Total earnings of a corporation divided by the number of outstanding shares of common stock.

EDGAR: A database with extensive data on companies and their financial reports that is available free to users of the Internet.

EPS: Earnings per share

equity: A share of ownership in a company, usually represented by the stock.

face amount: The original principal amount for a bond when it is created.

face value: The total *face amount* of a bond or group of bonds.

family of funds: A group of funds that are managed by the same investment company.

financial data: The information that describes all of the assets and liabilities, revenues and expenses, and changes in those quantities for a company. Every publicly traded company is required to make its financial data available to the public (can be found easily on *EDGAR*). Also called financial reports.

financial reports: See *financial data.*

flexibility: An investor's ability to buy and sell different kinds of investments and to move money among different kinds of investments.

front load: A mutual fund charge that is imposed at the time of purchase of shares, as a percentage of the value invested.

full-service broker: A brokerage firm that offers research, advising, and other financial services in addition to buying and selling in the financial markets.

futures contract: A contract whereby a party promises to deliver for sale a specific amount of a particular good at a specified price on a future date.

greater fool: An investor who buys stock when it has already been over-priced in the markets.

growth company: A company with increasing sales and profits—and proba-bly increasing stock value.

growth fund: A mutual fund that generally concentrates its assets in stocks of *growth companies.*

growth stock: The stock of a company that is considered to be a *growth company.*

growth theory: A theory of stock selection that focuses on estimated future earnings and growth to forecast the future value of stocks.

guru: One who claims to know more than the rest of us.

hedging: Investing in certain securities, options, futures, with a view to bal-ancing the risks in other investments.

index: A calculated number that represents the price levels and price changes for a group of securities, for example, the Dow-Jones Industrial Average, the Dow-Jones Utilities Average, the S&P 500 Average; each index is usually a weighted *average*, but the weighting methods differ between indices.

Individual Retirement Account: An account that an individual sets up with a bank or another financial company for saving part of their current income tax-free; the account is used for support upon retirement.

interest: The annual return that is paid for a loan as a price for the use of the loaned money.

intermediate term: Time period for bond holdings of two to six years, or for stock holdings of three months to a year; this is subject to widely varying interpretations by different investors or advisors.

Internet: A worldwide computer connection facility, access to which requires a computer, a modem, and an account with some service provider such as America On-Line or Compuserve.

invest: To use one's money to (hopefully) earn more money by lending it or buying securities that may produce future income or growth in market value. Essentially, to give money to another party in hopes of getting it back later with a profit.

investment club: A group of private investors who agree to pool their invest-ment capital and share the work and risk of investing through group analysis and discussion.

investment company: A company that owns and operates a mutual fund.

investment grade: Describes a bond or group of bonds that are rated BBB or Baa or higher by the ratings agencies.

investor: A person who puts money at risk in financial markets in hopes of making profits.

IRA: *Individual Retirement Account.*

junk bonds: Bonds that are rated below BBB or Baa by the major investment ratings companies; these are considered to be less safe than investment-grade bonds for expected repayment of yield and principal.

liability: A claim against the assets of a firm; for example, a bond sold by a firm represents a claim against the assets for both interest payments and final repayment, and this is a liability of the firm.

limit order: An order to a broker to buy or sell a security at the best price they can get above (for a sale) or below (for a purchase) some price specified by the investor.

liquidity: The ability to recover the cash value from an investment or other asset.

load: A fee charged to mutual fund shareholders as a percentage of their shares' value, either at the time of purchase or redemption of the shares.

Macintosh: A personal computer built by Apple Computer Corporation.

mania: A period of great excitement or public rush to buy stocks that causes prices to rise rapidly.

market capitalization: The total market value of all the stock of a company. This changes as the stock price changes.

market order: An order to a broker to buy or sell a security at the best price they can get in current market conditions.

market price: The price that is currently being accepted by both buyer and seller in the open markets; for a stock or bond this is recognized as the sale price for the last sale of the security.

market rate: The interest rate that the bond markets impose on a bond, or group of bonds, to determine their current *market price.*

market sector: A group of companies that have some common characteristics in their businesses or stocks, such as the auto sector or the small capitalization companies.

market value: *Market price.*

markets: Organizations, places, or groups that are established for the purpose of buying and selling financial instruments.

maturity: The time at which a bond matures and must be repaid.

momentum: Refers to trends in stock prices or volume of sales of the stock.

money market fund: A mutual fund that specializes in short-term bonds, or very short-term loans among financial institutions.

Morningstar: A firm that does extensive research on mutual funds, publishes their own periodical review of funds, and sells their research to other firms.

municipal bond: A bond issued by a state or local government or agency backed by a state or local government.

mutual fund: A fund collected from the investing public by an investment company, for the purpose of investing in stocks, bonds, other funds, or anything else that the investment company declares in the fund's prospectus.

NASD: *National Association of Securities Dealers.*

NASDAQ: The NASD automated quotation system, a computer network that provides brokers with information management services for trading stocks of over 2,000 companies.

National Association of Securities Dealers: A self-regulating professional association of securities dealers.

NAV: *Net asset value.*

net asset value: The net asset value per share of a mutual fund is computed as the total of assets owned by the fund minus the total liabilities of the fund, divided by the number of shares outstanding.

New York Stock Exchange: A stock exchange in New York City that provides registration and trading services for stocks of most of the largest American companies.

niche fund: A mutual fund that invests in only a small sector of assets—perhaps Brazilian bonds, European automobile companies, or suchlike.

no-load: Used to describe a mutual fund that does not charge an initial sales commission.

notes: Treasury bonds that have original term to maturity of two to ten years.

NYSE: *New York Stock Exchange.*

objective: The description (in the prospectus) of the things that a mutual fund may invest in.

option: A contract that promises that the originator of the contract will buy (or sell) a specified number of a security at a specified price within some time frame. The second party to the contract has an option, but not an obligation, to take the other side of the future transaction, as well as to let the contract expire with no action taken.

original issue discount: Term used to describe a bond that is originally sold at a price below its face value.

OTC: *Over the counter.*

over the counter: Term used to describe either markets away from regulated stock exchanges or the stocks that are traded in those markets.

panic: A period during which investors rush to sell all of their financial assets and cause a rapid fall in prices.

par value: The par value of a bond equals the *face value.*

P/E: *Price/earnings ratio.*

personal investment strategy: An individual investor's plan to allocate and manage investments to suit his or her personal needs and risk acceptance.

POP: The *public offering price* of a mutual fund.

portfolio: The collection of investments owned by an investor or a mutual fund or other organization.

preferred stock: A class of stock that has provisions for a specified dividend rate and seniority over a company's common stock in case of a distribution of the company's assets. The preferred stock may commonly have various other provisions attached that distinguish its value from the common stock, such as voting rights or convertibility.

presplit basis: A stock price, for shares after a split, that equates to the equivalent value of the original shares before the split. So, if a stock's price before the split was $20, and shares split 2 for 1, the new share price is $10. Then, if the new price goes up to $12, this would equate to the presplit share price of $24. If the original shares had been at $18 at some time before the split, then this would equate to the new shares being $9, *on a presplit basis.*

prevailing rates: The interest rates that the markets impose on a bond or group of bonds to determine their current prices.

price/earnings ratio: The ratio obtained by dividing the price of a stock share by its associated earnings per share. This is useful only if the earnings per share are positive, i.e., the company has some profits to distribute.

principal: The dollar value of an investment.

prospectus: A description of a mutual fund that is provided to prospective shareholders.

public offering price: The price per share of a mutual fund when an investor buys it; it is equal to the net asset value for no-load funds, and slightly higher for front-load funds.

publicly traded: A stock that is registered and approved by the SEC or a state securities agency for sale to the public through financial markets.

redemption: Selling mutual fund shares back to the investment company.

registered investment adviser: A person who has passed an examination on investment law and ethics and has paid the SEC and any state where advice will be offered to register as an investment adviser.

research: Analysis or study that is carried to a higher level by repetition, sophisticated methods, dedication, or the professionalism of the worker.

retirement account: A savings account that is intended to provide income after a person retires.

risk: The possibility of losing money in an investment or, more broadly, any danger or obstacle that an investor may face.

risk-free investment: A lie, a bad joke, a figment; there is no risk-free investment.

risk-oriented investment: Investment practice that recognizes and analyzes opportunities and risks to suit one's personal investment strategy.

Russell 2000: A group of stocks, or their associated price index, that includes 2000 *small capitalization stocks*; this is a representative index for the behavior of stock values for all small cap stocks.

sales load: Commission on sale of mutual fund shares, also called *front load*.

S & P: *Standard & Poor.*

S & P 500: A group of stocks, or their associated price index, that includes 500 *large capitalization stocks*; this is a representative index for the behavior of stock values for all large cap stocks.

savings bond: U.S. Treasury bond identified as series E, EE, or HH, with a ten-year term and certain tax advantages.

screens: Methods used to find stocks or bonds that satisfy specific conditions, frequently used with computers and databases to select a few qualifying securities from among a large group.

SEC: The United States *Securities and Exchange Commission.*

secondary market: The market that deals with buying and selling bonds, or any securities, after their original issue.

sector: *Market sector.*

Securities and Exchange Commission: The U.S. federal agency that regulates the registration and sale of securities.

security: Principally a stock or bond, but sometimes other types of financial instruments; anything that indicates ownership, or right to benefits of ownership or rights to payment.

seniority: Provision attached to a bond that its interest and principal will be paid before some other obligations of the company.

share: A part of the ownership of a company, represented by the common stock; sometimes share, stock share, and stock are used synonymously.

socially responsible funds: A class of mutual funds that write their objectives to be in some way in the public interest.

split: The practice whereby a company chooses to increase its total number of shares by issuing new shares in proportion to those already out. Each stockholder gets the same proportional increase in shares held, accompanied by a proportional decrease in the stock price, so the total value is unchanged.

spread: The difference between the offered and asked prices for a stock or bond.

Standard & Poor: A securities analysis and research firm that publishes important reports and opinions on the value of stocks and bonds.

stock exchange: A business or association that is established to help people buy and sell stocks.

stock market: An organization or place that exists to support the purchase and sale of securities by public investors.

stop order: An order to a broker to sell a stock at market value if the price ever drops to some value specified by the investor; a stop order becomes a *market order* after the trigger price is realized in the market.

strategy: An investment plan to allocate funds among diverse investments over a period of time.

subordinate: Provision attached to a bond, or other obligation of a company, that its interest and principal payments will occur after some other debt is paid.

technical analysis: The practice of predicting prospective price changes of a security, or group of securities, by analyzing prior price changes and looking for patterns and relationships in graphs of price history.

term: The time to repayment of a bond from its original issue.

trade: The act of buying or selling a security; sometimes used to denote a short-term investment.

trader: One who buys and sells securities, sometimes used to connote an emphasis on short-term investing.

trading: (1) Buying and selling financial instruments or securities; (2) frequent or short-term buying and selling.

transaction: Any purchase or sale of securities.

Treasury bond: Bond issued by the U.S. Treasury Department.

Value Line: A financial analysis and research firm that publishes reports and opinions on the value of stocks and mutual funds, including one titled *Value Line,* which includes analyses of companies and their stocks and securities along with recommendations for what stocks to buy or sell.

value theory: A theory of stock selection that focuses on current earnings, products, management, and financial reports to determine the value of a company and its stock.

volatility: The tendency of prices to increase or decrease in some specified time period; usually measured through the calculation of a quantity called *beta* (ß) relative to some specified market index.

volume: The number of shares traded within some specified time period.

Wall Street Journal: A daily newspaper published by the Dow-Jones publishing company, specializing in business news.

Wilshire 5000: A group of companies, or their associated price index, that represents the majority of all firms traded in regulated American public stock markets.

WINTEL: Term used for personal computers that rely on Microsoft Windows and Intel processors or compatible products.

WSJ: Wall Street Journal.

yield: The rate of interest payments on a bond, which may refer to either current yield, yield to maturity, or coupon yield.

yield ratio: The ratio of the annual dividend paid for a stock to its price.

yield to maturity: The compounded interest rate that would produce the current value of a bond considering both interest payments and final repayment of principal.

zero coupon bonds: Bonds that, instead of paying interest at regular intervals, save up everything and pay it all at once at the maturity.

I might learn as much from you as you have from me. I encourage readers to write with their questions, suggestions, complaints, or stories. The world of investing is infinitely varied and each of you has a unique point of view to express. I will give personal responses to some of the letters, although I cannot promise to answer all. All letters received will become the property of the author and will be considered for reference material, without any identification of the source, in future publications. Letters to the author may be mailed to

Jim Gard
Suite 1B-101
1821 Hillandale Road
Durham, NC 27705

INDEX

A

Advest Group, Inc., 25
AIM Constellation Fund, 220
American Heritage Fund, 20
American Stock Exchange, 28, 138
America On-Line, 100
Arbitration, 25–26
Asset allocation, 89–93, 217, 224–33
AT&T, 174–75
Automated Customer Account Transfer
    System, 85

B

Back-end load, 197, 206
Banks
    investment services through, 71–72
    keeping money in, 45, 46, 47
Barron's, 63, 95, 183–84
Barron's Mutual Funds Quarterly, 15, 71, 193, 220,
    240
Bassett, 254, 255
Bear markets
    definition of, 30
    examples of, 30, 33–35
Beta, 239
Biogen Inc., 33
Bonds
    buy and hold, 114, 120, 130
    call provision, 113, 119
    characteristics of, 109
    convertibles, 115–17, 221
    corporate, 115, 124
    coupon rate (yield), 110
    current yield, 111, 122–25
    definition of, 106–8
    duration, 230
    examples of, 26–27
    face value, 110
    interest rates vs resale value, 53–54, 127–29
    investment grade, 119
    junk, 46, 47, 113, 119
    language of, 109–10
    liquidity of, 32
    maturity, 110
    municipal, 65, 114–15
    mutual funds for, 129, 223, 235
    par value, 111
    price, 111, 126–27
    ratings, 112–13
    resale value, 110–11
    risks of, 46, 120–27
    tax-exempt, 65
    types of, 113–19
    U.S. Treasury, 69, 114, 124
    valuing, 122–25
    work level of buying, 46
    yield to maturity, 122–25
    zero coupon, 117–19, 126, 202
Books, 101–2
Bottom fishing, 36
Bourses, 28
Brokerage fees, 28, 63–64, 76, 167–68
Brokerage seminars, 102
Buffett, Warren, 152
Bull markets
    definition of, 29
    examples of, 29–30, 33
Business Week, 96, 221
Buy signals, 163

C

Calloway Golf, 181–83
Call provisions, 113, 119
Cap. See Market capitalization
Capital gain, 7
Century Shares, 77
Certificates of deposit (CDs), 14
CGM Capital Development Fund, 70
Charles Schwab, 75, 77, 78, 224–25, 240
Checkpoint Systems, 159–60
Christensen, Chris, 262
Chrysler Corporation, 9, 51, 156
Churning, 26, 167–68
Cigna Corporation, 25
Closed-end funds, 201–2
CNBC, 102, 214
CNN, 102
Coca-Cola, 151–53, 156–57
Commodity Futures Trading Commission, 263
Company size, 62–63
Compound growth, 37–39
Computer software, 98–101

Consumer Reports, 217, 240
Contrarian strategies, 225
Convertibles, 115–17, 221
Corporate bonds, 115, 124
Corrections, 35–36
Coupon rate (yield), 110
Crashes, 34–37, 168–72
CREE Research, 144–45, 156, 160, 178
C-Span, 102
Current yield, 111, 122

D

Dean Witter, 75, 101
Diversification
    definition of, 56–59
    expenses of, 63–64
    of information sources, 63, 253–54
    through investment clubs, 139–40
    through mutual funds, 70, 191–92, 216
    in practice, 59
    ways of, 59–64
Dividend reinvestment plan (DRIP), 13, 154
Dividends
    definition of, 7
    earnings and, 148–54
    from mutual funds, 209
    reinvesting, 13, 154–55
DJIA. See Dow-Jones Industrial Average
Dollar cost averaging, 164–65
Dow, Charles, 88, 249
Dow-Jones Industrial Average (DJIA)
    beating, 185
    changes in, 29–30, 33–36, 53, 170, 171
    companies in, 28, 52, 133
    definition of, 28–29
    history of, 134–37
Dow-Jones Service, 100
Dow Theory Forecasts, 97
Dreyfus, 198, 200, 201
DRIP. See Dividend reinvestment plan
Drug companies, 33
Duration, 230

E

E. D. Jones, 77
EDGAR, 101, 213
Elderly
    comfortable levels of risk for, 19
    special attention for, 82
Emerson Electric, 149
Equivalent compound rate of return, 37–39
Evergreen, 77–78

F

FAB, 254, 255
Face value, 110
Fidelity Investments, 75, 78, 198, 218
50-Off Stores, 184
Financial Accounting Standards Board, 52
Florida Federal Savings and Loan, 26–27, 49
Forbes, 96
Ford, 54, 142–43, 172
Foreign markets, 28
Fortune, 96, 239
401(k) plans, 64–65, 244
Franklin, 77
Front-end load, 197, 205, 206, 219
Futures, 261–63

G

Gabelli, Mario, 15, 17
Gabelli Equity Fund, 15
General Electric Corporation, 9, 54, 149
General Motors, 54, 159–60
General Telephone Company (GTE), 12, 20
Graham, Benjamin, 155
Grant's Interest Rate Observer, 97, 98
Greater Fool, The, 31

H

Hedging, 261
Hewlett-Packard, 49–50, 177
"Hot" tips, 17–19
Hovnanian Enterprises, 20
Hulbert Financial Digest, 97, 205

I

IBD. See Investor's Business Daily
IBM, 10, 19, 20, 24, 29, 32, 54, 173, 176–77, 257
Information sources
    diversification across, 63, 253–54
    gurus, 183–85
Inside information, 26–27, 263
Insurance, 91
Interest rates
    bond values and, 53–54, 127–29
    inversion, 129
    market, 111–12
    predicting, 130
    prevailing, 111–12
Internet, 100
Investment advisors, 79–82
Investment clubs, 139–40
Investment companies, 71–72. See also Mutual
    funds

Investment newsletters, 96–98
Investor's Business Daily (IBD), 95, 213
Investor's Digest, 97
IRAs, 64–65, 78, 85, 244
IRS. See Tax considerations

J

Jackson, Tom, 11
Junk bonds, 46, 47, 113, 119

K

Kiplinger's Personal Finance, 199

L

Limited partnerships, 230–31
Limit orders, 176
Lipper Analytical Service, 71, 193
Liquidity, 17, 32–33, 259–61
Loads, 197–98, 219–20
Lynch, Peter, 10, 183

M

Magazines, 95–96
Magellan Fund, 10, 24, 192, 220, 237
Manias, 168–72
Market capitalization, 157, 159–60
Market orders, 174–75
Market psychology, 11, 53
Markets
    averages, 28–29, 185
    diversification across, 60
    stocks, 27–28
Market sectors, 31, 157–60, 238
Maturity, 110
McClellan Market Report, 97
Merrill Lynch, 75, 77, 78, 101
Microsoft, 24
Money Club, The, 214
Money managers, 15–16, 37, 79, 81
Moody's ratings, 112–13, 119, 126–27
Morningstar, 98, 100, 235–36, 240, 242, 246
Morrison Knudsen Corporation, 20
Municipal bonds, 114–15
Mutual Fund Forecaster, 199
Mutual funds. See also Investment companies
    advantages of, 69–70
    asset allocation funds, 224–25
    balanced, 220
    blue-chip funds, 196
    bond funds, 129, 223, 235
    buying, 203–4, 205
    capital gains, 245
    changes in the industry, 210–13

    closed-end, 201–2
    convertibles, 221
    current holdings, 234, 246
    definition of, 70, 188–89
    disadvantages of, 70–71
    diversification through, 191–92, 216
    dividends, 209
    earnings, 234, 241
    efficiency of, 190–91
    emerging markets funds, 221
    evaluating, 234–47
    examples of, 207–9
    expenses, 205–7
    families, 198
    fee structure, 197–98, 205–7, 219–20, 234,
        240–41
    functioning of, 189–90
    global funds, 222
    gold funds, 221
    grading, 82–83
    growth funds, 196, 221
    income funds, 197, 221
    large-cap funds, 221–22
    liquidity of, 260
    loads, 197–98, 205–7, 219–20
    management, 192–94, 234, 236
    net asset value, 202–3
    no-load, 219–20
    number of, 44
    objectives of, 234, 235–36
    past performance of, 20, 192–94, 216, 234,
        241–43
    prospectuses, 194–96, 205, 223
    public offering price, 202–3
    redeeming, 204, 205, 209–10
    risk levels of, 46, 198–99, 234, 237–40
    size of, 234, 236–37
    small-cap funds, 196, 222, 238, 245
    socially responsible, 199–201
    special niche, 212–13, 221, 238
    stars, 246
    through stockbrokers, 77–79, 205
    stock funds, 194–97
    tax considerations, 243–44
    types of, 194–97, 217–25
    work level of buying, 46
    yields, 245
Mutual Funds Factbook, 213
Mutual Funds Forecaster, 218

N

NASD (National Association of Securities
    Dealers), 85
NASDAQ (National Association of Securities